Copyright ©2025 by James Corbett

10 9 8 7 6 5 4 3 2 1

The author asserts the moral right
to be defined as the author of this work.

ISBN 979-8-9916552-0-0 (First Paperback Edition)

ISBN 979-8-9916552-1-7 (First Hardback Edition)

Editions Shukutou
Published by Diversified Graphic LLC
Atlanta, Georgia

All rights reserved. No part of this publication may be reproduced, stored in a retrieval system or transmitted, in any form or by any means, electronic, mechanical, photocopying, recording or otherwise, without the prior permission of the publisher.

The photograph on page 191 is dedicated
to the public domain under CreativeCommons 0:
https://commons.wikimedia.org/wiki/File:WTC-7_-_IMG10.jpg

Publisher's Cataloging-in-Publication Data
Names: Corbett, James, 1979-.
Title: Reportage : essays on the new world order / James Corbett.
Description: Atlanta, GA : Editions Shukutou ; Diversified Graphic LLC, 2025. | Summary: Twenty essays examining the global decision-making power, history, culture and mindset of elite institutions, individuals and interests.
Identifiers: LCCN 2024925256 | ISBN 9798991655200 (pbk.) | ISBN 9798991655217 (hardback) | ISBN 9798991655231 (ebook) | ISBN 9798991655248 (audiobook)
Subjects: LCSH: Globalization. | Geopolitics. | International relations. | Propaganda. | LCGFT: Essays. | BISAC: POLITICAL SCIENCE / Geopolitics. | POLITICAL SCIENCE / Propaganda. | SOCIAL SCIENCE / Media Studies.
Classification: LCC JZ1318.C67 2025 | DDC 327--dc23
LC record available at https://lccn.loc.gov/2024925256

REPORTAGE
Essays on the New World Order

REPORTAGE
Essays on the
New World Order

JAMES CORBETT

Editions Shukutou

MMXXV

To my children,
and their children,
and their children's children:
j'ai fait mon possible.

Contents

Foreword iii
by Whitney Webb

Author's Preface vii

A Note on Notes xiii

Reportage: Adventures in the New Media 1

The 9/11 Terror Trade 13

Up/Down Politics 23

They Don't Want Your Genes in the Pool 61

The Ptech Story 89

Selling Your Soul for a Matrix Steak 103

How to *Really* Defeat Globalism 113

Biotech Billionaires and GMO Doomsday 139

How to Enjoy Your Servitude 179

The Three Types 190

The Strange Life of Maurice Strong 193

The Real Meaning of "Independence" 211

The 9/11 Whistleblowers 221

Why We Must Oppose Bilderberg 233

A Brief Introduction to Spontaneous Order 249

Who Controls the Environmental Movement? 261

Escaping The Grand Chessboard 273

And Now For Something Completely Different... . . . 307

A Letter to the Future 315

Why I Write 323

Index 335

Foreword

by Whitney Webb

TODAY'S MEDIA CLIMATE has undergone major shifts over the past two decades. Yet, despite those massive changes, the media remains a central battlefield in the war for hearts and minds. In this war, well-meaning people have been routinely targeted with the goal of leading them to adopt viewpoints and support policies that benefit their rulers, "The Powers That Be," over their own interests. This is often accomplished with the help of well-crafted crises that prompt the public to embrace fear, to leave their critical thinking far behind and to do what they are told by "trusted" voices in media.

As the media climate has developed in recent years, we have witnessed the destruction of mainstream media's credibility and the rise of independent, or alternative, media. But as the independent media have come to dominate in the wake of mainstream media's (largely self-induced) death spiral, the same social engineers behind mainstream media's manipulations have found a home behind certain figures in "independent" media who are willing to play that same role, albeit in different robes. As a result, the media landscape has become increasingly difficult to navigate thanks to this new "mainstream alternative media," as some have called it. However, a few veterans of truly

---

Whitney Webb is Contributing Editor of *Unlimited Hangout* and the author of *One Nation Under Blackmail*.

independent media continue to light the way.

For close to 20 years, James Corbett has been among the most consistent, well-sourced and credible voices in independent media, educating generations of truth-seekers—not only on the facts of our collective predicament but on how to be better critical and rational thinkers and on solutions that could hopefully aid us in our efforts to fight for a better world. Parts of James' intellectual journey, from the time he began The Corbett Report to the present, are chronicled through this collection of essays, revealing how a truly honest and well-meaning person with a powerful intellect has grappled with the biggest issues and crises of the past two decades and the lessons learned.

Given James' long-standing presence in the independent media space, he has covered practically every topic of note and stands largely alone in being able to speak on most (if not all) of the facets that comprise the global march toward a new, technocratic world order. He has also always had the fortitude to tackle head-on "controversial" topics like 9/11 Truth, which—though it may be more "socially acceptable" to discuss now—was once a sure way to attract vitriol. James' talents, combined with an iron-clad dedication to the truth, even when it is difficult to deal with, has helped so many of us—myself included—see through our rulers' lies and question more. Indeed, the first time I ever came across a Corbett Report podcast, over a decade ago, I was so impressed with his objective analysis of the news, with his sourcing and with his strong moral compass that, when it came time for me to start writing a few years later, I knew it was James' approach that I wanted to emulate.

One of James' greatest strengths is a deep knowledge of history, particularly the largely hidden history that never seems to quite make it into school history books. James' knowledge base in this regard allows him to give powerful and often essential context to current events, revealing that what seems like a "new" occurrence is often steeped in old plans and old ambitions that explain so much about our world today. Yet, while many with such a talent for history can often get stuck in the past (pun intended), James is also notable for looking ahead and reminding us that the future, despite the elites' centuries of planning, is unwritten and that we alone have the power to change it. To do so, we must stop looking for political saviours and toward manufactured heroes and instead realize that we must reclaim our own power if we are to chart our own future and reject the future that The Powers That Be have designed for us.

Whether you are a long-time follower of The Corbett Report or were more recently introduced to James' work, I invite you to learn from the words and the research of one of independent media's greatest voices and greatest teachers. I personally have learned more about the world and our current predicament from James than from anyone else. If you are like me and seek to arm yourself with the facts of what we are facing and then use that knowledge to chart a new course for the next generation, there is no better resource than the mind and the work of James Corbett.

Author's Preface

THE BOOK you are holding in your hands was fifteen years in the writing. I hesitate to put that sentence to paper because I realize it almost certainly gives the wrong impression.

To be clear: No, I have not been stuck at my writing desk for the past fifteen years, agonizing over each word in this book every single day. Rather, I put pen to paper on the first essay of this collection fifteen years ago, worked on the other essays intermittently—writing and rewriting and re-rewriting as time allowed—and put the finishing stroke on the last jot (or was it the last title?) just days ago.

As you can imagine, a lot has taken place since I began writing this collection in 2009, both in my own personal life and, of course, in the wider world of politics and society that is the primary concern of this volume.

For my own part, I got married, had two children, purchased a single-family house, and, somewhere along the way, turned my humble podcasting side gig into a full-time career.

Meanwhile, the world outside has likewise undergone a total transformation. From the economic fallout of a global financial crisis to the geopolitical fallout of conflicts around the world, from the unveiling of the globalists to the rise of the populists, from the post-9/11 Homeland Security paradigm to the post-scamdemic biosecurity paradigm, the world of 2024 is remarkably different from the world of 2009.

And yet, at the same time, our predicament today is remarkably similar to the one we found ourselves in at the time I started the book. Free humanity is still battling the same gang of greedy globalists, egocentric eugenicists, and power-mad plutocrats that we were confronting back then. They may be further along in their unfolding agenda of technocratic control, but our struggle against them is largely the same.

To some extent, then, this book is a meditation on the paradox of the passage of time: *plus ça change, plus c'est la même chose.*

Naturally, I've learned many things over the past decade and a half, come to many realizations, grown in my understanding, and changed my views on all manner of subjects. Back in 2009, for instance, I was a statist who was apt to suggest writing your Member of Parliament or voting for a third-party candidate as solutions to our plight. Today, I'm a voluntaryist who believes that the way to improve our world is not by casting a vote for yet another would-be political ruler but by investing our time, energy, attention, and resources in building our own independent communities from the bottom up.

This book, then, not only documents the hidden history of the deep state and reveals the covert agenda of those seeking to steer global events. It not only suggests courses of action for those of us seeking to reclaim control of our own lives. It also provides insight into the development of my own thinking on these subjects over the course of fifteen years of research.

The essays in this collection have not been arranged in the order they were composed, however. Instead, they have been arranged so that topics flow logically from one to the next and so that insights gleaned in one piece might help the reader contextualize the information imparted in a subsequent one. In this fashion, I hope the book, if read front to back, fosters an iterative understanding of its main subject matter: the New World Order.

So, what is the New World Order? You will not find a simple definition of that term in these pages. Rather, the essays showcase many (but certainly not all) of the aspects of this multifaceted idea.

Having said that, it is certainly not necessary to read this book from front to back or in any particular order. Each essay was written separately and so can be consumed singly and appreciated on its own. If a certain title appeals to you, flip to that page and start reading. The rest of the essays will still be right here, even if it takes you fifteen years to read them all.

Of course, seeing a book like this through its prolonged birth pangs all the way to delivery would not have been possible without the support of many, many midwives. To name them all would be impossible; but, at the risk of offending anyone I don't cite, I would be remiss if I did not single out some of my friends, colleagues, and family members for special recognition.

First, I would like to extend my sincere thanks to Aritha van Herk and to all the students in her creative writing workshop at the University of Calgary in the late 1990s. Before stepping into that classroom, I thought I knew how to write. Fortunately, van Herk and the incredible group of talented writers and readers in the workshop proved me wrong. Their careful critique taught me (I hope) how to make my writing engaging, even inspiring. But if you find my prose ponderous, you can credit that class for it not being much, much worse.

I would also like to thank all of my colleagues in the independent media, but especially James Evan Pilato of MediaMonarchy.com—the only person with whom I can imagine doing New World Next Week for the past fifteen years and counting—and Broc West—the only person who I can imagine as my video editor for the past ten years and counting. Thank you both for your insights, your hard work, your humour—and for keeping me sane in insane times.

They say that behind every good writer is a good editor. I don't dare opine on the quality of my writing, but I can absolutely opine on the quality of this book's editing. Susan, from the sunny climes of the Southern States, is a diligent, meticulous editor whose second set of eyes have been pouring over my words for the last several years. She has not only suggested *le mot juste* at *le bon moment* to make a sentence sparkle but has many a time helped me see how my perfectly clear and completely understandable thoughts may not be so understandable to a third party. Thank you, Susan, for your tireless efforts and for helping make these essays as excellent (that's *her* word, not mine!) as they can possibly be.

I'd like to extend my sincere and heartfelt gratitude to The Corbett Report members who have made this work possible. Please know that your moral support, your monetary contributions, your feedback in the comments section of the website, and your assistance in spreading the word about this information are all deeply appreciated.

Next, a huge thank you to my parents. I realize now that my mother and father did not simply provide me with a loving and supportive home, though they certainly did that. More importantly, they gave me a fine example of how to provide the same kind of home to my own family. It is my sincere wish that I can pass that gift on to my children.

Finally, I cannot imagine where I'd be without the patience and encouragement of my darling wife. And I would not want to imagine what my life would be like without the wonder and joy that my beautiful boy and my adorable daughter bring to it.

This book is for my children, and for all our children. Although the particulars may be different, our task is the same one that has faced every generation since the dawn of humanity: to raise our children in truth, in wisdom, and in love. As long as we continue to do so, I have faith that the future will be bright.

James Corbett
July 2024
The Sunny Climes of Western Japan

A Note on Notes

ARE YOU the average reader who notices those little superscript numbers after a sentence, knows they take you to the endnotes, and skips right over them? You know, the type of person who'll occasionally look up a note if some tidbit in the text sounds particularly interesting, but who otherwise just ignores them?

Great! Then you can stop right here and skip ahead to the essays. This "Note on Notes" isn't for you.

But since you're still reading, let me just say: "Welcome to my book, fellow research nerd!"

If you're anything like me, you'll browse through all the endnotes first to determine if this is a work of serious research or not. Then, having decided it is, you'll start each essay with one finger holding open that page and another finger on the endnote section, so you can quickly flip back and forth. You'll probably even highlight the interesting endnotes as a reminder to check out those sources later.

And, if that is you, then flip away! I've tried to make it as easy as possible for you to find my sources.

As you'll soon discover, in this book I've opted for endnotes over footnotes. Personally, I find footnotes crowd the page too much and make it too distracting for the regular reader. And, although I sometimes appreciate it when an author expands on an idea and provides additional information in the note, I have opted to put all the relevant information about a subject in the text itself. The endnotes in this book serve only as a straightforward citation of sources.[1]

The endnotes do not conform precisely to a particular writing style guide. Instead, I have striven to provide exactly as much information as is necessary for you to independently search for the source yourself. For books, this includes the publisher and year of publication; for websites, the name of the website as it appears on the website itself and the date of publication (if available); for videos, the exact title of the video and the name of the uploader. Misspellings and grammatical mistakes in titles have been preserved for the sake of accuracy.

This being the internet age, many of the citations lead back to online publications. As an inveterate researcher yourself, you're no doubt aware that an online citation brings with it two distinct challenges.

First, there is the problem of impermanence: links tend to break over time, meaning that over the course of several years most of the online posts cited in this volume will no longer be accessible at their original address.

And second, there is the problem of readability: long URLs are unwieldy and as such are useless to all but the most meticulous of readers.[2]

In an effort to feed two birds with one scone, then, I have tried wherever possible to cite archive.today website capture links. For those who are unfamiliar with archive.today, it's a web archiving site that saves screenshots of web pages. Those website captures are preserved at the same archive link even if the original page gets changed or removed. Not only does this solve[3] the problem of impermanence, it also helps with the problem of readability, as archive links are considerably shorter and easier to read (and reproduce) than regular URLs.

Unfortunately, not all content is capturable by archive. today. PDFs, for example, cannot be archived by this service. Likewise, videos are not archivable. In these cases, link shorteners have been employed; specifically, youtu.be links in the case of YouTube videos and bit.ly links in the case of PDFs or Wayback Machine links. I recognize that link shorteners are privacy nightmares at best and giant leaps into the online abyss at worst, so if you don't feel comfortable using those links, I fully understand and respect that decision. Luckily, all the information needed to track down the references is available in the endnote itself, so there should be no need to use the link provided.

Having said all that, enjoy the book![4]

NOTES

1. The endnotes in this particular non-essay being the only exceptions.

2. I, for one, find it laughable when an author faithfully reproduces some *http://www.completely-unreadable.com/citationfullof-m34ningl3ssg4rbage?=that_is_only_parsable_by_a_machine* in his endnotes, knowing full well that even if some incredibly careful researcher with too much time on her hands were to go to the trouble of typing all of that into her browser, she would still likely end up (because of the aforementioned problem of impermanence) with a "404 Page Not Found" error message.

3. Of course, I am well aware that there is no guarantee that archive. today will always exist. Like everything else on the internet, it can (and presumably will) cease to exist at some point, and no piece of "archived" information should be taken as a gurarantee that that information will always be there. Having said that, it's the best option available at the moment, and if and when the archive goes down, you will still have all of the data (website name, article title, author, date of publication, etc.) necessary to find the source yourself.

4. And the endnotes.

Reportage:
Adventures in the New Media

"As an ook comth of a litel spir." [1]

CONSIDERING it was written in Middle English more than 600 years ago, you'd be forgiven for not recognizing this line from Geoffrey Chaucer's epic poem *Troilus and Criseyde*. But you probably do recognize its modern English variant: "Mighty oaks from little acorns grow."

I, for one, can attest to the truth of this mighty metaphor.

In my case, the acorn took the unlikely form of a studio apartment in a ratty, rundown, roach-infested two-storey building in the outer reaches of a sleepy town nestled in Japan's equivalent of "flyover country." And that humble acorn would become not only my home sweet home in the fall of 2006, but the birthplace of my own mighty oak.

You see, being a 26-year-old teacher at an English conversation school in western Japan at the time, I knew two things. Firstly, I knew that—given my entry-level salary and the student loan debt from my fun but economically ill-advised time earning a master's degree in Anglo-Irish Literature at Trinity College Dublin—I didn't have oodles of money to be shelling out on a swank penthouse apartment in the heart of Tokyo's trendy Omotesando. And secondly, I knew that it was time for me to bite the bullet and get a place of my own, sans roommates, for the first time in my life.

And so it was that I found myself moving into my, shall we say, "spartan" abode in September 2006, ready for whatever adventures single living would bring . . . or so I thought.

Indeed, as I soon discovered, I was mentally prepared for living on instant ramen. And for waking up at two in the morning when my upstairs neighbour sprang to life, clomping back and forth across his creaky floorboards for no adequately explained reason. And even for the sight of a cockroach scurrying for cover when I came home at the end of the day and flipped on the light.

But, as it turns out, I was not prepared for the most unexpected lifestyle change of all: the internet. The apartment I rented was cheap in every respect, but, amazingly, it came with a free internet connection. So, not one to look a gift horse in the mouth, I plugged the LAN cable sticking out of my apartment wall into my beat-up old laptop and hopped online.

And, unbeknownst to me, that little acorn I had planted began to sprout.

Now, don't get me wrong. This was 2006. Of course I'd been online before. In fact, I'd been online for a decade at that point, a veteran of the days of yore when you plugged your 14.4 kbps modem into the phone jack and braced yourself for the ungodly racket of electronic screeching that heralded your arrival in that then-uncharted territory known as "cyberspace."

But in 2006 it had been years since I'd had an internet connection in my apartment—four years, to be precise. And I soon discovered that a lot had happened on the world wide web in my absence.

Podcasts had happened, for one thing. With the internet at my fingertips, I finally had the time to explore the nascent world of podcasting and began subscribing to news and current events podcasts, Japanese learning podcasts, jazz podcasts, literary podcasts, and whatever else tickled my fancy. (Anyone else remember the original Planet Japan podcast with Amy and Doug?)

Streaming video had happened, for another. The long-promised vision of online, on-demand access to video content was finally becoming a reality, enabled by brand-new streaming video platforms like Google Video and some upstart website called "YouTube."

To put yourself in that 2006 state of mind, imagine cycling down to the prefectural library for your weekly browse of the scant English book section and coming across the mirror-covered Christmas edition of TIME magazine announcing that You ("Yes, You!") were TIME's 2006 Person of the Year. Imagine reading TIME lead technology writer Lev Grossman's decidedly purple prose lauding "Web 2.0" platforms like YouTube and MySpace "for seizing the reins of the global media, for founding and framing the new digital democracy, for working for nothing and beating the pros at their own game." [2]

And then imagine cycling back to your cramped studio apartment for an evening of instant ramen and noisy neighbours and watching history documentaries on YouTube.

Well, I don't have to imagine it. I lived it.

But then a funny thing happened. The YouTube algorithm, evidently recognizing that I liked to peruse politically charged content, started recommending videos about 9/11 Truth.

In retrospect, it's easy enough to understand what was happening: the fifth anniversary of 9/11 had just transpired, prompting a record number of activists to descend on New York. They made their voices heard not just on the streets of the Big Apple but even on the airwaves of the establishment media. Unthinkably in today's political climate, C-SPAN actually broadcast the proceedings of the American Scholars Symposium on "Theories About September 11th," an event held in Los Angeles in June 2006 that featured talks by some of the leading 9/11 Truth advocates in academia at the time.[3]

Back in 2006, however, I knew nothing about the rising tide of 9/11 Truth, much less about how such a movement, energized by the Web 2.0 revolution being hailed by TIME magazine, was on the verge of kickstarting a revolution in public consciousness that we're still living through today. Sure, I knew that conspiracies existed, but 9/11? A conspiracy? That was a bridge too far. It was absurd. It was disrespectful.

Still, I would click on some inane video about "flying orbs" destroying the Twin Towers or whatever claptrap was trending on YouTube that day just for a quick, derisive laugh. *What fools believe in this nonsense?* I'd wonder.

At some point, however, one of the videos wasn't as eye-rollingly ridiculous as I was expecting. Even though it made some outlandish claim—perhaps something about the CIA meeting with Bin Laden in Dubai in the summer of 2001 or some equally off-the-wall story—it contained just enough verifiable information to look up the information for myself. And, sure enough, there was a report in *Le Monde* on October 31, 2001, that cited a "professional partner of the administrative director" of the American Hospital Dubai who said Bin Laden had travelled to the United Arab Emirates for kidney dialysis in July of 2001 and there met with a representative of America's Central Intelligence Agency[4]—a report immediately denied by the hospital itself, naturally.[5]

Or perhaps it was a video about a clandestine US military plan in the 1960s to commit terror attacks in the US and blame them on Fidel Castro as a justification for launching an invasion of Cuba. This claim, too, struck me as utterly outrageous ... until I followed it back to its source. This time, I ended up in the digital database of the National Security Archive, where I found a PDF file containing a scan of the original Operation Northwoods documents.[6] Far from allaying my fears, the document instead confirmed that this preposterous-sounding plan for a US military "false flag" terror campaign in the US was not only true but had actually been signed off on by Lyman Lemnitzer, the Chairman of the Joint Chiefs of Staff, and forwarded to the Secretary of Defense, Robert McNamara, for review in March of 1962.

I wish I could remember precisely which video or series of videos got me chasing these "wild rumours" down the internet rabbit hole. I would happily give that video credit if I could remember what it was, and I would gladly explain what particular piece of surprising information prompted me to keep digging. All I know is that I spent the fall of 2006 learning more about the world than I had learned in my previous 26 years combined.

So, what did I discover when diving down those YouTube rabbit holes?

I discovered the documentaries of Alex Jones, from *9/11: The Road to Tyranny*[7] to *Terrorstorm*[8] to *Dark Secrets: Inside Bohemian Grove*.[9] I watched the original news footage reporting that multiple bombs had been discovered at the Alfred P. Murrah Federal Building on the day of the Oklahoma City bombing.[10] I heard Peter Power—the audibly shaken managing director of crisis management firm Visor Consultants—tell ITV News on the day of the 7/7 London terror bombings that, at the time of the attacks, he was "actually running an exercise [...] based on simultaneous bombs going off precisely at the railway stations that [the bombings] happened."[11] And I saw the actual hidden camera footage of the "Cremation of Care" mock human sacrifice that takes place before the assembled crowd of politicians, financiers, and captains of industry at Bohemian Grove in the heart of the California redwoods each year.[12]

I discovered the work of Adam Curtis, from *The Century of the Self*[13] to *The Power of Nightmares*[14] to *Pandora's Box*.[15] I absorbed information on Edward Bernays, the American nephew of Sigmund Freud and the father of modern-day public relations. I learned that the creation of what we know as "Al Qaeda" was a convenient legal fiction cooked up by prosecutors in a Manhattan courtroom in January, 2001. I marvelled at the failed Soviet experiment in technocratic utopianism at Magnitogorsk.

I discovered *The Money Masters*[16] and *The Creature from Jekyll Island*.[17] I used these works to fill in the gaps in my knowledge of the money creation process in general and the history of the Federal Reserve—America's central bank—in particular.

Given the sheer volume of new material—a veritable Niagara Falls—I was drinking in during that disorienting autumn, is it any wonder I failed to notice that the little acorn sprout in the corner of my room was being watered too, and was fast growing into a sapling?

Yes, all of this new-to-me evidence of how the world really works, downloaded (quite literally) in the hours between my days at work and my nights out with friends, served to turn my world on its head within the span of a few short months. In the fall of 2006, I was James Corbett, English teacher and aspiring author. But by the spring of 2007, I was James Corbett, English teacher and aspiring podcaster.

Although that transition may not sound big, I assure you it was. As someone who had never considered becoming any sort of "journalist" (let alone a podcaster) and had even actively foresworn the possibility when asked what I was going to do with my English degree, it was a profound shift.

Subsequently, I spent the spring of 2007 looking into designing and hosting a website, buying recording equipment, practicing my "radio" voice (or is that a "podcaster" voice?), and trying to think of the most neutral-sounding name I could find for a news and politics podcast. And then, on June 1, 2007, I treated the world to the first episode of my brand-new podcast, The Corbett Report.

This is where I should say that "the rest is history." Except that, as I write these words in 2024, "the rest" is still very much the present. Seventeen amazing years, tens of millions of downloads and a (deleted) 600,000-subscriber YouTube channel later, a lot has changed with regard to the work I'm doing and the way I'm doing it. But, at base, The Corbett Report is still the same thing it always was: the record of one man's attempt to uncover long-suppressed truths and to relay those truths via a new media paradigm.

Perhaps the best way to chart the tenor of those seventeen years is to cite Richard Stengel, the managing editor of TIME from 2006 to 2013. In the now-infamous issue declaring "You" the TIME Person of the Year in 2006, Stengel justified that decision by touting the radical democratization of information that the online media revolution would no doubt bring about.

> There are lots of people in my line of work who believe that this phenomenon is dangerous because it undermines the traditional authority of media institutions like TIME. Some have called it an "amateur hour." And it often is. But America was founded by amateurs. The framers were professional lawyers and military men and bankers, but they were amateur politicians, and that's the way they thought it should be. Thomas Paine was in effect the first blogger, and Ben Franklin was essentially loading his persona into the MySpace of the 18th century, *Poor Richard's Almanack*. The new media age of Web 2.0 is threatening only if you believe that an excess of democracy is the road to anarchy. I don't.[18]

And here's what Stengel—who, after leaving TIME, went on to serve in the Obama State Department and eventually authored *Information Wars: How we Lost the Battle Against Disinformation and What to Do About It*—had to say about that same subject in 2023:

> Instead of the few creating for the many, the many now create for one another. The idea was and still is a radical one. If I got anything wrong, it was in not anticipating the downside of this new information calculus, the rise of hate speech and disinformation, and how a democratized system could be used against the very idea of democracy. I still think that the benefits outweigh the costs—and that the future of the media still depends on, well, You.[19]

And you know what? He's not wrong. I mean—don't misunderstand me—*he is wrong* about the "hate speech and disinformation threatening democracy" part. But he's not wrong when he writes that the future of the media still depends on you.

Indeed, Stengel is a case study in the phenomenon of once-upon-a-time gatekeepers of the old media establishment beginning to realize that they can't tell people what to believe and how to think as easily and effectively as they once did. Their desperate attempt to invent a whole new vocabulary—misinformation, disinformation, "malinformation"—to justify online censorship only underscores the point: they have lost control over the hearts and minds of the public.

Yes, the new media revolution has already happened. Like it or not, the toothpaste is out of the tube now and there's no putting it back. One person with a microphone and a genuine desire to spread knowledge—even a lowly English teacher in a roach-infested apartment in western Japan—can make a difference in this world.

Take it from me. I should know.

Now, if you'll excuse me, I'm off to water my ook tree.

NOTES

1. Chaucer, Geoffrey. *Troilus and Criseyde*. Edited by R. A. Shoaf. (East Lansing, MI: Colleagues Press, 1989.) Page 95.

2. Grossman, Lev. "You (Yes, You) Are TIME's Person of the Year." TIME. December 25, 2006. archive.is/UtBmh

3. "September 11th Terrorist Attacks." C-SPAN. June 25, 2006. bit.ly/3RpJqct

4. "Juillet 2001: Ben Laden rencontre la CIA à Dubaï." Le Monde. October 31, 2001. archive.is/Wz8a1

5. "Ben Laden aurait eu cet été un contact avec la CIA à Dubaï." Le Monde. November 1, 2001. archive.is/Kerjq

6. "Memorandum for the Secretary of Defense. Subject: Justification for US Military Intervention in Cuba (TS)." National Security Archive. March 13, 1962. bit.ly/3RFf72S

7. Jones, Alex, director. *9/11: The Road to Tyranny*. 2002.

8. Jones, Alex, director. *Terrorstorm*. 2006.

9. Jones, Alex, director. *Dark Secrets: Inside Bohemian Grove*. 2000.

10. "News Footage Of Multiple Bombs In Oklahoma City Bombing." Internet Archive, uploaded by AllAmericanRevolution, January 23, 2024. bit.ly/3yeh9jf

11. "Peter Power 7/7 Terror Rehearsal." Internet Archive, uploaded by altCensored.com, March 19, 2023. bit.ly/4bdJlRV

12. "Bohemian Club Cremation of Care Ritual.mp4." Internet Archive, uploaded by altCensored.com, January 18, 2024. bit.ly/3WxG7Et

13. Curtis, Adam, director. *The Century of the Self*. BBC, 2002.

14. Curtis, Adam, director. *The Power of Nightmares*. BBC, 2004.

15. Curtis, Adam, director. *Pandora's Box*. BBC, 1992.

16. Still, William T., director. *The Money Masters: How International Bankers Gained Control of America*. 1996.

17. Griffin, G. Edward. *The Creature from Jekyll Island: A Second Look at the Federal Reserve*. Fourth edition. (Westlake Village, CA: American Media, 2002.)

18. Stengel, Richard. "Now It's Your Turn." TIME. December 25, 2006. archive.is/t6ZvW

19. Stengel, Richard. "TIME's Choice of 'You' for Person of the Year in 2006 Was Mocked—But Now Seems Prescient." TIME. February 28, 2023. archive.is/0xZaL

The 9/11 Terror Trade

ON SEPTEMBER 12, 2001, before the dust had even settled on Ground Zero, the US Securities and Exchange Commission opened an investigation into a chilling proposition: an unknown group of equities traders with advance knowledge of the 9/11 plot had made millions betting against the companies involved in the attacks.

As Antonio Mora of ABC News explained on September 20, 2001:

> What many Wall Street analysts believe is that the terrorists made bets that a number of stocks would see their prices fall. They did so by buying what are called "puts." If you bet right, the rewards can be huge. The risks are also huge—unless of course you know something bad is going to happen to the company you're betting against.
>
> One example: United Airlines. The Thursday before the attack more than two thousand contracts betting that the stock would go down were purchased. Ninety times more in one day than in three weeks. When the markets reopened, United's stock dropped, the price of the contracts soared and someone may have made a lot of money, fast.[1]

Although the put options on AMR Corp. and UAL Corp.—the parent companies of American Airlines and

United Airlines, respectively—are usually cited in reference to the 9/11 informed trading, they represent only a fraction of the suspicious trades leading up to the attack. Between August 20th and September 10th, abnormally large spikes in puts appeared in trades involving dozens of different companies whose stocks plunged after the attack, including Boeing, Merrill Lynch, J.P. Morgan, Citigroup, Bank of America, Morgan Stanley, Munich Re, and the AXA Group.

Traders weren't just betting against the companies whose stocks dove after 9/11, however. There was also a sixfold increase in call options on the stock of defence contractor Raytheon on the day before 9/11. These calls allowed the traders to buy Raytheon stock at $25. Within a week of the attack, as the US military began deploying the Raytheon-supplied Tomahawk missiles it would eventually use in the invasion of Afghanistan, the company's share price had shot up 37% to over $34.[2]

The SEC wasn't the only regulator interested in this particular 9/11 money trail. Authorities around the globe—from Belgium to France to Germany to Switzerland to Japan—opened their own investigations into potential insider trading before the attacks. It wasn't long before this global financial manhunt started yielding clues on the trail of the terror traders.

On September 17th Italian Foreign Minister Antonio Martino, addressing the Italian stock market regulator's own investigation into potential 9/11 trading, said: "I think that there are terrorist states and organizations behind speculation on the international markets."[3]

By September 24th the Belgian Finance Minister, Didier Reynders, was confident enough to publicly announce Belgium's "strong suspicions that British markets may have been used for transactions."[4]

The president of Germany's central bank, Ernst Welteke, was the most adamant: "What we found makes us sure that people connected to the terrorists must have been trying to profit from this tragedy."[5]

These foreign leaders were not alone in their conviction that insider trading had taken place. University of Chicago finance professor George Constantinides, Columbia University law professor John Coffee, Duke University law professor James Cox, and other academics, as well as acclaimed options traders like Jon Najarian, all expressed their belief that some investors had traded on advance knowledge of the attacks.[6]

The scale of the SEC investigation was unprecedented. It examined over 9.5 million securities transactions, including stocks and options in 103 different companies trading in seven markets, 32 exchange-traded funds, and several stock indices. It drew on the assistance of the legal and compliance staff of the 20 largest trading firms and the regulatory authorities in ten foreign governments. And it was coordinated with the Federal Bureau of Investigation, the Department of Justice, and the Department of the Treasury.

The result of this probe?

> We have not developed any evidence suggesting that those who had advance knowledge of the September 11 attacks traded on the basis of that information.[7]

Although that conclusion makes it sound like the investigation did not find evidence of insider trading, a closer reading reveals a sleight of hand; the investigators are not saying that there was no insider trading, only that there is no evidence that "those who had advance knowledge of the September 11 attacks" participated in such trading.

This begs the question: who had advance knowledge of the attacks, and how did the SEC determine their identity?

The *9/11 Commission Report* begs the question even more blatantly in its treatment of the anomalous put option activity on the UAL stock on September 6th: 95 percent of the puts were placed by "a single U.S.-based institutional investor with no conceivable ties to al Qaeda." Again, it is taken as a foregone conclusion that a lack of ties to "al Qaeda" means there could not have been advance knowledge of the attack, even if informed trading on the event demonstrably took place.

To be sure, insider trading almost certainly did transpire in the weeks before 9/11. Although some have pointed to the Commission Report's "no conceivable ties to al Qaeda" line as proof that the theory of investor foreknowledge has been successfully debunked, the intervening years have seen the release of not one, not two, but three separate scientific papers establishing the statistical likelihood that advance knowledge was the reason for the anomalous trading leading up to the attacks.

In "Unusual Option Market Activity and the Terrorist Attacks of September 11, 2001," University of Chicago professor Allen Poteshman concluded: "Examination of the option trading leading up to September 11 reveals that there was an unusually high level of put buying. This finding is consistent with informed investors having traded options in advance of the attacks."[8]

In "Detecting Abnormal Trading Activities in Option Markets," researchers at the University of Zurich used econometric methods to confirm unusual put option activity on the stocks of key airlines, banks, and reinsurers in the weeks prior to 9/11.[9]

And in "Was There Abnormal Trading in the S&P 500 Index Options Prior to the September 11 Attacks?" a team of researchers concluded that abnormal activity in the S&P 500 index options market around the time of the attack "is consistent with insiders anticipating the 9-11 attacks."[10]

That leaves us with two key questions: who was profiting from these trades, and why was no one ever indicted for participating in them?

In attempting to answer these questions, 9/11 researcher and author Kevin Ryan uncovered an important clue in a 2003 FBI briefing document that was declassified in 2009. In "Evidence for Informed Trading on the Attacks of September 11" he examines this document, which describes the results of the Bureau's investigations into two of the pre-9/11 trades that it had identified as suspicious.[11] One of those trades was the purchase of 56,000 shares of Stratesec in the days prior to 9/11. Stratesec, which provided security systems to airports (including Dulles Airport) as well as to the World Trade Center and United Airlines, saw its share price almost double when the markets reopened on September 17th, 2001.[12]

The Stratesec trade traced back to a married couple whose names are redacted from the memo but who are easily identifiable from the unredacted information: Mr. and Mrs. Wirt D. Walker III. Wirt is a distant relative of the Bush family and a business partner of Marvin Bush, brother of George W.[13] According to the briefing document, Wirt and his wife, Sally, were never even interviewed, because the FBI's investigation of them had "revealed no ties to terrorism or other negative information."

In addition to begging the question of the perpetrators' identity yet again, this characterization is provably false. As Ryan notes:

> Wirt Walker was connected to people who had connections to al Qaeda. For example, Stratesec director James Abrahamson was the business partner of Mansoor Ijaz, who claimed on several occasions to be able to contact Osama bin Laden. Additionally, Walker hired a number of Stratesec employees away from a subsidiary of The Carlyle Group called BDM International, which ran secret (black) projects for government agencies. The Carlyle Group was partly financed by members of the bin Laden family.[14]

More importantly, and not coincidentally, Walker has multiple connections to the Central Intelligence Agency.

> Mr. Walker ran a number of suspicious companies that went bankrupt, including Stratesec, some of which were underwritten by a company run by a first cousin of former CIA director (and President) George H. W. Bush. Additionally, Walker was the child of a CIA employee and his first job was at an investment firm run by former US intelligence guru, James "Russ" Forgan, where he worked with another former CIA director, William Casey.[15]

Were these connections the reason the FBI thought better of questioning Walker about his highly profitable purchase of 56,000 Stratesec shares right before 9/11?

The CIA also figures prominently in another line of investigation. As Erin Arvidlund noted in her examination of the 9/11 trading story for *Barron's* in October 2001:

One large UAL put order was sent to the bustling CBOE floor in the days prior to September 11 by a customer of Deutsche Bank. The primary trading post for UAL expected to handle the whole 2,500-contract order. Instead, the customer split that into chunks of 500 contracts each, directing each order to various exchanges around the country simultaneously, according to people familiar with the trade.[16]

Arvidlund reports that the unusual order was brokered by Deutsche Bank Alex. Brown, a firm that until 1998 was chaired by A. B. "Buzzy" Krongard, who was a former consultant to CIA Director James Woolsey. At the time of 9/11, Krongard was himself the CIA's executive director, making him third in command at the agency.

According to researcher Michael Ruppert, Krongard's job at the brokerage "was to oversee 'private client relations.' In this capacity he had direct hands-on relations with some of the wealthiest people in the world in a kind of specialized banking operation that has been identified by the U.S. Senate and other investigators as being closely connected to the laundering of drug money."[17]

Perhaps the most frank admission of insider trading is notable for three things: it was recorded on video, it has never been investigated by any agency or law enforcement official, and it was made by former CIA agent and frequent foreign policy commentator Robert Baer—the real-life inspiration for the character portrayed by George Clooney in *Syriana*.[18] Talking to citizen journalists after a speaking event in Los Angeles in 2008, Baer was recorded on video making a startling assertion about 9/11 insider trading: "I know the guy who went into his broker in San Diego and said 'cash me out, it's going down tomorrow.'" Questioned about his claim, Baer added: "His brother worked at the White House."[19]

This truly remarkable statement bears further scrutiny. If Baer is to be believed, a former CIA agent has firsthand knowledge that a White House insider had foreknowledge of the attacks, and to this day not only has Baer never revealed the identity of this person, but so far no one from the "respectable" mainstream media or from any government investigative body has ever followed up with him about his statement.

So how is it possible that the SEC overlooked, ignored, or simply chose not to pursue such tantalizing leads in its investigation? The only possible answer, of course, is that the investigation was deliberately steered away from any information suggesting that non-al Qaeda actors had foreknowledge of the event.

Unfortunately, we will likely never see documentary evidence of government, corporate, or investor complicity coming from any regulatory body or investigative agency. When one researcher requested access under the Freedom of Information Act to the documentary evidence that the 9/11 Commission used to conclude there had been no insider trading, he received a response asserting that "the potentially responsive records have been destroyed."[20]

Even investigators at the Chicago Board of Exchange (CBOE) itself were shut down in their attempt to conduct an independent investigation of the 9/11 terror trades. "Documents were destroyed," one frustrated CBOE researcher told the *Economic Policy Journal* in 2006.[21]

Instead, we are left with sources who refuse to be identified saying that CBOE records of pre-9/11 options trading have been destroyed and second-hand accounts of brokers who had heard talk, pre-9/11, of an event that was "going down."

In a roundabout way, perhaps the 9/11 Commission reveals more than it lets on when it tries to dismiss key insider trades with the pithy observation that the traders had "no conceivable ties to al Qaeda." If those with foreknowledge of the attacks *weren't* connected to al Qaeda, what does that say about the identity of the real 9/11 perpetrators?

NOTES

1. "9/11 Wall Street Blames Put Option Inside Trading On Terrorists." YouTube, uploaded by 911InvestigationVids. August 19, 2012. youtu.be/QUHZcUwHrJ8

2. "Bank of America among 38 stocks in SEC's attack probe." Bloomberg News. October 3, 2001. archive.fo/h2uDw

3. "Bin Laden 'share gains' probe." BBC News. 18 September 2001. archive.fo/G2NWN

4. Bogdanowicz, Tom and Brooks Jackson. "Probes into 'suspicious' trading." CNN. September 24, 2001. archive.fo/eSZUl

5. Drozdiak, William. "Bankers seek source of pre-attack trading." Houston Chronicle. September 23, 2001. archive.is/0mVzU

6. Poteshman, Alan. "Unusual Option Market Activity and the Terrorist Attacks of September 11, 2001." Journal of Business, vol. 79 no. 4, 2006. Page 1704.

7. Jones, Nate. "Document Friday: 'Terrorist-Insider-Trading?' The SEC's Pre-September 11, 2001 Trading Review." Unredacted: The National Security Archive Blog. April 30, 2010. archive.is/SxrFV

8. See endnote 6.

9. Chesney, Marc, et al. "Detecting Abnormal Trading Activities in Option Markets: Supplemental Appendix." Swiss Finance Institute Research Paper No. 11-38. January 22, 2015. archive.is/MfH8F

10. Wong, Wing-Keung, et al. "Was there Abnormal Trading in the S&P 500 Index Options Prior to the September 11 Attacks?" Multinational Finance Journal, vol. 15, no. 3/4. 2011.

11. Ryan, Kevin. "Evidence for Informed Trading on the Attacks of September 11." Foreign Policy Journal. November 18, 2010. archive.fo/QpWZh

12. "Memorandum for the Record (MFR) of the Interview of FBI Briefing on Trading of the Federal Bureau of Investigation Conducted by Team 4." National Archives Catalog. August 15, 2003. Page 5. archive.is/TV09j

13. Burns, Margie. "Bush-Linked Company Handled Security for the WTC, Dulles and United." Common Dreams. February 4, 2003. archive.fo/2IAfk

14. See endnote 11.

15. See endnote 11.

16. Arvedlund, Erin E. "Follow the Money." Barron's. October 8, 2001. archive.is/kUkry

17. Ruppert, Michael C. "Suppressed Details of Criminal Insider Trading Lead Directly into the CIA's Highest Ranks: CIA Executive Director 'Buzzy' Krongard Managed Firm That Handled 'Put' Options on UAL." From The Wilderness Publications. October 9, 2001. archive.fo/BqFlV

18. Siegel, Robert. "Ex-CIA Agent Robert Baer, Inspiration for 'Syriana.'" NPR. December 6, 2005. archive.fo/cYtKT

19. "WeAreChangeLA 'debriefs' CIA Case Officer Robert Baer about apparent Mossad and White House 9/11 foreknowledge." 9/11 Blogger. October 20, 2008. archive.is/BnxBT

20. "Re: Freedom of Information Act (FOIA), 5 U.S.C. § 552 Request No. 09-07659-FOIA." United States Securities and Exchange Commission, Office of Freedom of Information & Privacy Act Operations. December 23, 2009. corbettreport.com/images/callahanfoia.gif

21. "Options Investigation and 9-11." Economic Policy Journal. July 21, 2006. archive.fo/YKTwY

Up/Down Politics

THE PARABLE OF THE ANTS

ONCE UPON A TIME there was a colony of ants living on a loop of string. The string was so thin that the ants could move in only two directions, forward and backward. With little else to do on their narrow trail, the ants spent most of their time arguing about which direction to head in their daily travels. When these spats broke out, the ants took sides.

One group of ants, who called themselves "forwardists," contended that to move forward was to make progress. And since progress was, in the forwardists' estimation, the key to happiness, they believed all the ants should move forward all the time.

Another group, known as "backwardists," disagreed. They chastised their forwardist friends for confusing progress with happiness. True happiness, the backwardists preached, lies in knowing where you came from, not in dreaming of where you had never been.

For a while the forwardists and the backwardists lived and worked together happily enough, despite their differences. One day, though, a fast-moving backwardist inadvertently ran into an inattentive forwardist coming the other way, knocking him off the string. Recriminations followed. Angry forwardists and spiteful backwardists started to separate and form competing camps. Ants who had never had a strong opinion on the matter—the ones who moved forward on some days and backward on others—were forced to pick sides. As a result, children were separated from their parents, spouses divorced, siblings split up, friendships dissolved.

At first, there was nothing more than an imaginary dividing line between the two encampments. Soon enough the ants, industrious and ornery as only ants can be, erected a barbed wire fence between them. Then, as battle lines hardened, they replaced the fence with a brick wall. Before long, guards were stationed on either side of the wall to make sure no one breached it. The ant opponents stopped speaking to each other, except to hurl the occasional taunt or insult across the divide.

Within a generation, no one even remembered what the wall meant anymore or what the whole argument was about. The philosophies became muddled. So muddled, in fact, that some forwardists began walking backward and some backwardists walked forward.

Despite the confusion, the ants remained determined to pass their traditions down through the generations. Forwardists told their children scary stories about the monstrous backwards ants who ate forwardists' children for breakfast, and the backwardist children were likewise taught that forwardists were ravenous beasts who preyed on all but their own kind.

The fearmongering intensified until, inevitably, skirmishes broke out along the dividing wall. The skirmishes became battles. The battles, wars.

One side would beat back the other. The losers would regroup and mount their own offensive, forcing their aggressors to retreat. And so it went, back and forth, with no clear victor.

The constant conflict began to take its toll on the ants. Finally, exhausted, forwardists and backwardists called for a truce. Both sides agreed to go their separate ways, never to reunite. Early one morning, the sides struck camp and began their great journey, heading in opposite directions.

The forwardists, wary of their backwardist foes, peeked over their shoulders as they marched off, making sure their old enemies really were leaving them forever. The backwardists, knowing full well that forwardists could never be trusted to keep their word, also glanced behind them to be certain their rivals were disappearing into the distance. Each side was satisfied that the other was indeed slipping farther and farther away.

Naturally, the ants in each group were relieved to be rid of their nemeses at long last. They all figured they would find virgin territory on the string in which they could settle peacefully.

But then, a most remarkable thing happened.

Off in the distance, each ant leader saw something approaching. As the two leaders drew nearer, they discerned not a single form ahead of them, but many forms. A long line of moving forms, marching single file. They looked tiny. They looked black.

At last, the objects were close enough for the leaders to recognize individual shapes. Ants. And not just any ants, but the very ants they had sworn to never see again.

Suddenly, all the ants in each long line realized, to their horror, that the unthinkable had occurred. Forwardists and backwardists, who had set out in opposite directions and had travelled without changing course, were now heading toward each other. What they believed to be a permanent split from the other camp of ants had in fact been the reverse. Halfway around the string, the old enemies were converging.

POLITICS AND THE SECOND DIMENSION

To us humans, it's easy to see what happened to the ants. Not realizing that the string they lived on was one big loop, they had walked in a circle. From their one-dimensional perspective, they were travelling in a "straight" line in "different" directions. From our three-dimensional perspective, however, we can see that their straight line was not straight at all, but curved. And although they were moving "apart" in one dimension, they were actually "reuniting" in a second dimension. Their different paths brought them to the same spot, the way two ships setting sail from the same place, one headed east, the other west, meet on the other side of the globe.

The point of the parable, then, is this: what seems baffling from a one-dimensional point of view makes perfect sense from a multi-dimensional perspective.

So, does an allegory about ants have anything to do with us humans? Are there issues in our society that seem perplexing from a limited, ant-like point of view but make perfect sense from a broader perspective?

Well, let's think about politics. We are told that politics exists on a line known as "the" political spectrum, as if there's no other way to conceive of our political system. This spectrum consists of a left wing, a right wing, and varying points in between, including a centre. It is said to be the basis for Western political democracies. From America to Australia, Canada to France, the UK to Germany, New Zealand to the Netherlands, political parties have staked their claim to one segment or another on this straight line. Indeed, how could they avoid doing so? For the line, we are assured, is the entire political universe.

Along this line there are left-wing parties and right-wing parties, left-wing politicians and right-wing politicians, left-wing pundits and right-wing pundits, left-wing voters and right-wing voters. Occasionally there are even centrist parties, politicians, pundits, and voters. But any political subject that does not fit somewhere on this line is literally unimaginable.

As a result, every few years, when election time comes around, we are presented with a choice: do we want to elect someone on the left, on the right, or in the centre? Often our choice is motivated by anger at whoever was in power last.

Say you're a worker who's struggling to make ends meet while the government hands out billions to Wall Street fat cats. Or you've been successful in your job and have made some decent money, only to find the tax collector demanding more of your earnings. Or you're concerned about your civil rights, your privacy rights, your constitutional rights, all of which are being shredded by politicians who are turning your country into a police state.

Election day arrives. Feeling empowered, you show up at the polling station and pull the lever to throw the rascals out. Your fellow citizens, similarly fed up with the status quo, do the same. The political pendulum swings from left to right or right to left. Then, by the next election, when the public is once again angry at the government they put into power, the process repeats itself, and the pendulum swings back the other way.

Somehow, nothing ever really seems to change. Big businesses keep getting bigger and small businesses continue disappearing. The rich get richer. The poor take out adjustable-rate mortgages pushed on them by unscrupulous bankers and end up homeless after the bubble pops.

It appears we have hit upon a paradox. We are told that this straight line, this left-right spectrum, comprises the totality of the political universe, yet no matter whether we choose from the left, the right, or the centre of that spectrum, we always end up with more or less the same problems. It's baffling.

Which brings us back to our similarly baffled ants. They, too, lived in a one-dimensional universe. They, too, believed they could move in only two directions. They, too, went their separate ways but ended up at the same spot. They were mistaken because they couldn't see the curve in the string. Oblivious to their movement in the second dimension, they didn't understand they had been walking in a circle.

Have we, like the ants, been unwittingly living on a loop of string? Are we holding a one-dimensional view of a multi-dimensional problem? Could it be that there is more to our political universe than this seemingly straight line?

If we are on a loop of string, after all, and if we are all headed in the same political direction, it may be difficult to perceive our circumstances. Like the ants, our perspective is not broad enough to notice the curve in the string, and we may be walking in circles without realizing it.

So, is there a second political dimension? And if there is, what does it look like?

Let's find out.

We'll call the political direction in which the Western "democracies" are currently heading the "up" dimension of politics. For now, we'll identify the "up" wing of the political grid as all of those tendencies in society that head in only one direction despite the pendulum swings in government from right to left to right to left, ad infinitum.

Just what tendencies are we talking about?

- The size and power of the government only ever expands, never contracts.

- The slice of the economic pie devoured by big multinational corporations only ever grows, never shrinks.

- Successive governments always wrest more power from the people and never cede back the power taken by previous administrations.

- Unelected, non-democratic, supranational bodies like the United Nations, the World Trade Organization, the World Bank, the International Monetary Fund, and the World Health Organization only ever gain power over member states, never relinquish it.

- Wars only ever move from one battlefield to another, never end and never result in lasting peace.

Other aspects of the unchanging "upward" direction of our current political system could no doubt be found, but that list should suffice for now.

If there is also a "down" dimension to politics—a "down" wing—then it should be easy enough to determine what it would advocate; all we have to do is reverse direction by negating the "upward" tendencies and instead:

- Reduce the size and power of government.

- Support small and locally owned business.

- Repeal laws and regulations that restrict individual rights and liberties.

- Withdraw from international treaties and organizations that subsume national autonomy.
- End wars of aggression.

Surprisingly, the "down" wing's platform looks like the very agenda most people believe they're choosing when they go to the voting booth to cast their ballot in each election. No one wants to hand over control of their lives to Big Brother (or at least they say they don't). No one wants their country to engage in the mass slaughter of innocent people (or at least they say they don't). No one wants the mom-and-pop store on the corner to go out of business (why would they?). And yet all these results are exactly what we get time and again, no matter which party is in power.

If we are indeed living on a political loop, it seems the left and right are both never-endingly spiraling "upward," always away from the "downward" direction we say we're seeking.

At this point we are faced with a series of questions. If the majority of people want "downist" policies and practices, why do we end up with "uppist" government after "uppist" government, and why have we never recognized this reality? Is there a coordinated "uppist" movement? If so, who is behind it and how does it operate?

MEET THE UPPISTS

So, is there a coordinated uppist movement? As we shall see, there certainly is.

How, then, does that movement operate? And who is behind it?

We would be hard-pressed to find a better description

of how the uppist movement controls the left-right political spectrum than the one found in *Tragedy and Hope: A History of the World in Our Time*, the 1,300-plus-page magnum opus of celebrated historian Carroll Quigley:

> The argument that the two parties should represent opposed ideals and policies, one, perhaps, of the Right and the other of the Left, is a foolish idea acceptable only to doctrinaire and academic thinkers. Instead, the two parties should be almost identical, so that the American people can "throw the rascals out" at any election without leading to any profound or extensive shifts in policy.[1]

And we would be hard-pressed to find a better description of who is controlling this phoney left/right political charade than this passage from the very same book:

> There does exist, and has existed for a generation, an international Anglophile network which operates, to some extent, in the way the Radical right believes the Communists act. In fact, this network, which we may identify as the Round Table Groups, has no aversion to cooperating with Communists, or any other group, and frequently does so. I know of the operations of this network because I have studied it for twenty years and we were permitted for two years, in the early 1960's [sic], to examine its papers and secret records. I have no aversion to it or to most of its aims and have, for much of my life, been close to it and its instruments. I have objected, both in the past and recently, to a few of its policies (notably to its belief that England was an Atlantic rather than a European Power and must be allied, or even federated, with the United States and must remain isolated from Europe), but in general my

chief difference of opinion is that it wishes to remain unknown, and I believe its role in history is significant enough to be known.[2]

In other words, there is a clandestine network of influential figures (the "Round Table Groups" referred to by Quigley) who cooperate with both the left and the right sides of the traditional political spectrum to carry out their own self-serving agenda. In this way, they rig the system so that voters can never effect fundamental change. And, as Quigley laments, they wish to remain unknown despite their significant role in shaping world events.

Hmmm. This sounds exactly like the coordinated uppist movement we were just speculating about, doesn't it?

Here, it should be noted that Quigley was not some "crackpot conspiracy theorist," but a respected, Ivy League-degreed professor of history at Georgetown University's School of Foreign Service and a leading scholar on the evolution of civilizations. Bill Clinton name-checked Quigley in his 1992 Democratic presidential nomination acceptance speech:

> As a teenager, I heard John Kennedy's summons to citizenship. And then, as a student at Georgetown, I heard that call clarified by a professor named Carroll Quigley [...].[3]

Let's take a moment to consider what this means. A president was inspired by a professor who penned a book describing how the political system was being covertly manipulated by a secret society—a network of influential men who acted "in the way the Radical right believes the Communists act."

Should we be alarmed at the Quigley-Clinton connection? Or is this just a coincidence of no consequence?

To find out, we have to examine the network Quigley referred to as the "Round Table Groups." This web of "semi-secret discussion and lobbying groups," as he characterized it, was established with money left by mining magnate Cecil Rhodes in his Rhodes Trust. From their home base in England, the groups formed a series of interlocking organizations around the globe, including the Royal Institute of International Affairs in the United Kingdom and the Council on Foreign Relations in the United States. Headed by such early-twentieth-century luminaries as Lord Milner and Lionel Curtis, these Round Table organizations, Quigley notes, "grew up along the already existing financial cooperation running from the Morgan Bank in New York to a group of financiers in London led by Lazard Brothers."[4]

And what were the actual aims of this network? Quigley helpfully explains that, too:

> [T]he powers of financial capitalism had another far-reaching aim, nothing less than to create a world system of financial control in private hands able to dominate the political system of each country and the economy of the world as a whole. This system was to be controlled in a feudalist fashion by the central banks of the world acting in concert, by secret agreements arrived at in frequent private meetings and conferences. The apex of the system was to be the Bank for International Settlements in Basle, Switzerland, a private bank owned by and controlled by the world's central banks which were themselves private corporations.[5]

Sound outlandish? Well, let's fact-check some of these claims.

Secret meeting of private bankers controlled by the Bank for International Settlements (BIS)? Check.

One such meeting was exposed by the Australian media in February, 2010. Organized by the BIS, the meeting took place in Sydney under complete secrecy and high-level security.[6] It included representatives of the US Federal Reserve, the European Central Bank, the Bank of Japan, and other central banks. After the meeting was exposed and the BIS was forced to release records of what was discussed, it was revealed that Governor Yves Mersch of the Central Bank of Luxembourg had given a lengthy speech on the need for a supranational authority to regulate a global system of pseudo-currency behind the scenes of the international monetary order.[7]

Plans to form a world system of financial control? Check.

The very day after attending the 2008 meeting of the ultra-secretive Bilderberg Group,[8] Timothy Geithner, then president of the Federal Reserve Bank of New York and soon-to-be US Secretary of the Treasury, wrote an op-ed in the *Financial Times* calling for a "unified framework" of international financial controls by the very central banks that had so miserably failed to prevent the crisis in the first place.[9]

The fact that Geithner had literally just attended the Bilderberg meeting before penning this piece is no small matter, considering that his fellow heavyweight attendees ranged from the chairman of the Federal Reserve to the head of the European Central Bank to the president of the World Bank. Other notables at the meeting included high-level investment bankers at Lazard Frères (see the Quigley reference to Lazard above), heads of state, royals, and over a hundred other powerful personages in the business and financial realms and in political posts throughout Europe and North America . . . including Barack Obama and his Secretary of State Hillary Clinton (see the essay "Why We Must Oppose Bilderberg" elsewhere in this book).

Indeed, if we were in search of some sort of coordinated uppist movement, we would find no better place to start our sleuthing than the Bilderberg conference.

Never heard the name "Bilderberg"? That's by design.

Although the former publisher and CEO of *The Washington Post* was a regular attendee at the group's annual gathering, the paper refused to even acknowledge Bilderberg's existence during those decades.[10] And despite the fact that reporters from *The Economist* hobnob with a virtual *Who's Who* of world leaders and giants of industry at the site of the Bilderberg conclave each year, you'll find nary a mention of it in the pages of their publication.[11] And even though such prominent TV news anchors as long-time Canadian national news anchor Peter Mansbridge[12] and long-time CBS News and PBS stalwart Charlie Rose[13] have attended Bilderberg meetings over the years, they have never reported on (or even acknowledged the existence of) the conference.

Why are these newshounds and press kingpins shying away from what would undoubtedly be the story of the century—namely, the inside scoop on an annual secret meeting of the most powerful and prestigious people in the Western world?

There are two schools of thought on that conundrum. In one are the Bilderbergers themselves, who ask us to believe that the press respects the right of the so-called ruling elite to meet and discuss world events frankly, without fear of negative publicity. In the other are outside observers, who attribute the news blackout to the fact that privileged "journalists" and media moguls are themselves part of the uppist power structure and thus have nothing to gain—and perhaps everything to lose—by reporting on its true inner workings.

I'll let you decide for yourself which answer passes the smell test.

But all this raises the question of why we should care what the Bilderbergers say in secret. Does it really matter what the Queen of the Netherlands, the head of Daimler-Chrysler, the Secretary-General of NATO, the US Secretary of Defense, the president of the World Bank, and several dozen other captains of industry, finance, and government gab about when they get together for an off-the-record, deep state discussion?

Yes, sad to say, it does.

Let's answer the next question, then: what do they talk about?

Fortunately for us, we don't need to speculate. Through the years, numerous insiders and even some intrepid investigative reporters have shed light on the precise topics covered at Bilderberg gatherings. Unfortunately for us, what has been exposed reveals the highly coordinated uppist agenda that we suspected (and that Carroll Quigley demonstrated) has been taking place behind the curtain: ever-greater centralization of control over everything and everyone on the planet by the self-appointed ruling class. This process of centralization goes by many names—"globalization," "one-world government," and the "New World Order"—but its goal is always the same: putting as much power as possible in the hands of a privileged few.

One example: In 2003, the BBC released an audio documentary on the Bilderberg Group that featured interviews with attendees of that year's annual meeting.[14] The report also revealed that the Bilderbergers' own archives contain proof that, ever since the group's founding in 1954, members had been planning the formation of a monetary union for the European continent. These documents have since been released and are now openly available on the internet.[15]

The role of these secretive uppists in the creation of that monetary union was further confirmed in March 2009, when the former commissioner of the European Union, Étienne Davignon, admitted to the eu*observer* that the Bilderberg Group (which he was chairing at the time) had in fact paved the way for the creation of the unified European currency, the euro.[16]

Lest there be any lingering doubt about where the impetus for the establishment of the European Union came from, it should be noted that the EU was officially born just two years after the Bilderbergers' call for European integration at the group's 1955 conference.

By now, it should be no surprise that Bilderbergers were integral to the creation of the EU itself. Bilderberg co-founder Józef Retinger was himself an important member of the European Movement, which helped lay the institutional groundwork for the EU. Retinger also helped recruit Paul van Zeeland, the co-founder of the European League for Economic Cooperation, to join the influential Bilderberg Steering Committee, which helps select attendees and plan the agenda for the annual meeting (again, see "Why We Must Oppose Bilderberg" elsewhere in this book). Another important Bilderberger, Paul-Henri Spaak,[17] was the eponymous head of the Spaak Committee, an intergovernmental panel of European foreign ministers that paved the way for the signing of the

Treaty of Rome.[18] That treaty established the European Economic Committee, the forerunner of the EU, and Spaak's name features prominently as one of the treaty's signatories.

The architects of the Treaty of Rome were wise enough to refrain for many years from labelling the establishment of the European Union as the power grab that it was. Finally, by the turn of the millennium, the Bilderbergers and their fellow uppists were confident enough in the effectiveness of their decades-long pro-EU propaganda campaign that they drafted a constitution for the European Union as a whole. A continent-wide discussion on the ratification of the constitution ensued. The proposed constitution included all the legal powers needed for the EU to operate as a supranational regional government, complete with an unelected president, a standing army, a flag, and an anthem.

As it turned out, the uppists had badly misjudged Europeans' feelings about the European project. Opponents of the proposed constitution from both the "left" and the "right" of the so-called political spectrum united to defeat the proposal in an alliance that seems perplexing only to those who do not see the "up" and "down" in the politics of globalization. In 2005, the proposed constitution was derailed by the French[19] and the Dutch,[20] whose governments had actually allowed voters to choose whether or not they wanted to cede their sovereignty to this unelected, unaccountable, supranational government of well-connected power players (uppists through and through). After the citizens of these two countries rejected it in national referenda, the continental constitution was scrapped.

Or was it?

Having learnt a valuable lesson, the proponents of the EU constitution were careful not to repeat their mistake. In a stealthy move, they rebranded the document as a treaty and promptly set about getting it ratified. Though identical in substance to the defeated constitution, the Treaty of Lisbon was permitted, simply because it was now classified as a "treaty," to bypass the referendum process in every country in the Union save one: Ireland.

The Irish constitution gives citizens the right to vote on any treaty that would modify it. So, in a 2008 referendum on the matter, close to a million Irish voters rejected the uppists' dream of an EU constitution.[21]

Technically, a single member nation's dissent should have ended the ratification process then and there. What happened next, however, perfectly exposes the uppists' worldview and their vision of how the political game should be played. No sooner had the Irish trounced the uppists' constitutional power grab than British Foreign Secretary David Miliband insisted that the UK would "keep the ratification process going"[22] and European Commission President José Barroso declared his belief that "the treaty is alive and we should now try to find a solution."[23]

It seems the uppists had already decided they weren't going to let pesky Ireland's stubborn independent streak get in the way of their goal. Instead, they turned to that time-honoured tactic of bullies everywhere when they don't get their way: "Nuh-uh. Doesn't count. We want a do-over!"

And so, in October 2009 the Irish people were once again asked to vote on the very same treaty they had rejected just sixteen months earlier. Like sleight-of-hand magicians pretending to pull a rabbit out of a hat, slick

European bureaucrats offered all manner of verbal assurances in a bid to appease voters, though they didn't change so much as a single word of the document. The Irish were made to vote on the treaty again—and presumably again and again and again—until they "got it right." And after a hotly contested campaign in which the EU Elections Commission and the Irish government both broke their own laws,[24] the worn-out Irish populace was browbeaten (with the aid of a highly suspect vote-counting process[25]) into finally ratifying the treaty. The Bilderbergers, Eurocrats, and other assorted uppists could rejoice. They had achieved their aim of continental hegemony.

MEET THE DOWNISTS

EXTENDING THE ANALOGY, if "uppists" are those who—like the Bilderbergers, the Round Table members, the Eurocrats, and all the other elitists—impose conformity, censorship, centralized power, and top-down control, then "downists" are those who struggle against these impositions and strive for their opposites: freedom of thought, freedom of speech, decentralization of power and control, etc.

Taking that to be an accurate definition of downism, we are forced to conclude that the vast majority of humans are, in fact, downists. Assuming you, dear reader, are not part of the global jet-setting power broker caste—the 6,000 or so people that Kissinger underling David Rothkopf self-aggrandizingly calls the "superclass"[26]—then chances are you, too, are one of those downists.

Of course, as is the case with any such label, some people don't fit neatly into the downist category. There are those, for example, who work in the spaces between the uppists and the downists: the low-level bureaucrats and functionaries without whom the vast uppist control structures would not be able to function. They include the middle managers who make sure that the corporate machine continues to churn out an endless supply of cogs and widgets; the soldiers who fight and die for the interests of the military contractors and geopolitical string-pullers; the political functionaries who maintain the balance of power in favour of the ruling class. Although they suffer under the uppist system of control as much as anyone else (perhaps more than anyone else), they do receive benefits from that system in a trickle-down fashion, with bonuses, promotions, and the promise of an eventual move to the "upper" (make that "uppist") class. With these incentives and other forms of manipulation, a few thousand superclass uppists can persuade millions of erstwhile downists to assist them in bringing about their system of control.

Other downists may genuinely believe in the principles, ideals, and aims of the uppists: bigger governments, expanded wars of aggression, and the consolidation of money and power in the hands of an exclusive few. These are the downists who have unwittingly fallen for the clever spin that the uppists have put on their plans.

According to these spinmeisters, the purpose of government is to defend the poor and downtrodden, not to act as a trough for the banking and corporate bigwigs that keep the politicians in their back pocket (and print the currency to boot). They further claim that the entire regulatory system, the judiciary, and all the other apparatus of the uppist state exist to ensure that everyone plays by the rules, not to act as a truncheon used to beat back any would-be downist competition that threatens their uppist monopoly. In the uppists' twisted version of reality, wars are always fought to institute "democracy" and "freedom" and "peace," not to line the pockets of uppist-owned defense contractors or uppist-created banks, which amass huge profits from covertly financing both sides of every major conflict.

All the while, the uppist-controlled "education" system spends exorbitant amounts of time and money training children from a very young age to believe that the United Nations, the central banks, and other quasi-governmental, non-democratic institutions in fact represent the will of the people—and are most assuredly not a place for billionaires to meet with other billionaires to launch pet projects and schemes that will turn them into trillionaires. Given the immense efforts and funds the uppists have poured into persuading us that we should put more and more power into their hands, it is unsurprising that many well-meaning downists have taken the bait.

Indeed, considering the all-out psychic assault from the uppist-controlled, uppist-funded corporate media, elementary and secondary schools, academia, tax-free foundations, think tanks, and other institutions seeking to put across an uppist-advancing agenda, it's little wonder that so many people who would benefit from downism end up ignorantly supporting uppism. These gullible folks can be easily whipped up by uppist rhetoric into a type of religious fervour that dismisses any objection to the uppist belief system with the thought-stopping *ad hominem* sneer, "Oh, you're just a crazy conspiracy theorist."

Finally, and perhaps most important to the discussion at hand, many downists can be duped into passively allowing or even actively advancing the uppist takeover of society when uppists employ the oldest trick in the book: divide and conquer. The means by which this ruse is accomplished has already been explained—and by the establishment's own mouthpiece, Carroll Quigley, no less. Let's read it again:

> The argument that the two parties should represent opposed ideals and policies, one, perhaps, of the Right and the other of the Left, is a foolish idea acceptable only to doctrinaire and academic thinkers. Instead, the two parties should be almost identical, so that the American people can "throw the rascals out" at any election without leading to any profound or extensive shifts in policy.[27]

By limiting the chief concerns of politics to a handful of issues that can be staked out by one or the other of the two (controlled) sides of the argument, uppists can lead an entire society toward a certain goal in the exact same way that we move from one point to another: first by taking a step with the right foot, then the left, then the right, and so on. This tactic for gaining political consent is easy enough for alert downists to see—and to see through. But when the uppists deploy all forms of psychological manipulation, from tribal colours (red vs. blue) to misleading visualizations (right vs. left) to false dichotomies (welfare state vs. warfare state), unsuspecting downists on both sides of the political aisle are lured into supporting one or another aspect of the same uppist agenda, even when that agenda works against all downists' best interests.

It may seem hard to believe that uppists have been getting away with this scam for centuries (if not millennia) with nary a peep from the downists they have distracted, deceived, divided, and deprived. But now that technology has given us access to all manner of once-hidden information, the uppists are finding their secrets harder to hide, much to their dismay. As a result, we're becoming aware of our true position in this uppist-dominated system. More and more of us are beginning to unhook ourselves from the matrix of control that ties us to the corporatist, bankster-driven, globalist politicians who promise change but continue to deliver the same old, same old.

And although the uppists are gradually adapting to this shifting climate and are learning to disguise their agenda in populist rhetoric, the very popularity of those politicians professing their opposition to the globalist system is a sign that the public is finally waking up to the lies we have been told.

In short, we the people are realizing that it is the uppists, not each other, who are our true political enemy. And the uppists realize that we realize it!

THE BATTLE IS ENGAGED

WE COULD OVERTURN the system overnight if enough of us were aware of our true position as downists living in an uppist system. But in this battle for control, the uppists have retained their power over most downists by cleaving to two maxims: "All's fair in love and war" and "If you can't beat 'em, join 'em."

We can see both maxims very much in effect during this period of global political awakening.

Take "All's fair in love and war." This motto reminds us that actions that would generally be frowned upon in our day-to-day interactions are considered acceptable when used against our enemies during times of war. Thus, sending a battalion of soldiers on what amounts to an involuntary suicide mission is—in the eyes of the military planners—justifiable if it helps to defeat the enemy.

How else to understand the uppists' popping of the housing bubble in 2007, a bubble that they themselves had spent much of the previous decade expanding? Superficially, it would appear that, by setting the stage for the subprime mortgage meltdown, the uppists had committed a self-defeating act of self-destruction. But we know that the architects of the uppist financial order would never purposely self-immolate. We must conclude, then, that the near collapse of the world economic system was, in fact, the uppists' boldest move yet in an all-out attack on their true enemy: the downists.

To understand this point, we must first make a crucial distinction between currency and wealth. Currency is merely an instrument of exchange. Wealth, however, is power. From the up/down perspective, we can see that the banksters' aim is not to accumulate currency but rather to gain the power afforded by controlling the currency. If there is an opportunity to sacrifice some currency for actual power and control, you can bet your bottom dollar the uppist banksters will jump at it.

For the uppists to achieve their goal of increased power, the economic collapse had to be severe and keenly felt by a wide swath of the public. It had to involve the spectacular downfall of some peripheral members of the uppist power structure (think Lehman Brothers and Bear Stearns). Even more critically, the crisis had to justify concocting a series of mechanisms that the uppists implemented to maintain control of the system itself. These mechanisms included the staggering $29-trillion-dollar "bailout" (conducted through the economic back door of the secretive US Federal Reserve)[28] and the "permanent crisis mechanism" (devised by the European Union's central bankers to deal with the problem they themselves had manufactured).[29]

Thus, the real purpose of the economic meltdown of 2007 is not to be found in the story of the housing bubble itself (fascinating as it is), but in the way that crisis was used to forward the uppist agenda of centralization.

Indeed, forwarding that agenda is why UK Prime Minister Gordon Brown took the opportunity to announce the creation of a "new world order" at the emergency G20 meeting convened in April 2009 to discuss the financial crisis.[30]

Forwarding that agenda is why uppist mouthpieces like *Newsweek* began running editorials praising the idea of a global central bank[31] and why the uppists' economic rag, the *Financial Times*, began openly promoting world government[32] just as the world's largest economies began their first-ever coordinated interest-rate cuts to combat a global recession.[33]

Forwarding that agenda is why the governor of the People's Bank of China called for the US dollar to be replaced as the world reserve currency by an IMF-administered global banking asset.[34]

And forwarding that agenda is why the Bank for International Settlements (the "apex of the system," per Quigley, as you'll recall) began rewriting the regulatory framework for the international banking system, including the introduction of the "bail-in" mechanism[35] that was employed to such devastating effect in Cyprus in 2013.[36]

In other words, the uppists used the very real global economic crisis of 2008 as a cynical ploy to further their plans for global government.

Yes, the uppists are at war with humanity. And since, according to their maxim, "All's fair in love and war," they see nothing wrong with wreaking havoc on the global economy so long as it advances their agenda.

Now, how about "If you can't beat 'em, join 'em?" How does this second maxim apply?

Uppists infiltrate the ranks of the downists. Instead of openly opposing the downists, they secure their greatest victories by pretending to align themselves with their adversaries. (Remember, misdirection and deception are age-old uppist tactics.) One method of infiltration is to create counterfeit movements designed to mobilize the downists and thus direct them toward counterproductive ends. In this way, the uppists can effectively use the downists' own energy against them.

For a case study in this type of infiltration, let's examine the short-lived Tea Party phenomenon that swept through American politics in the late aughts. Although largely forgotten today, the Tea Party began in 2006 as a "Boston 9/11 Truth Tea Party" protest against the uppist establishment's lies about the events of September 11, 2001.[37] The idea caught on quickly, serving as a protest model for other downist movements—the Ron Paul Revolution among them. Soon, Ron Paul supporters were holding their own tea parties to support their campaign to "End the Fed," halt foreign wars of aggression, stop presidentially sanctioned torture, and restore constitutional restrictions on the government generally. As the Ron Paul Revolution picked up steam, more and more people began to join in these protests. "End the Fed" rallies, for example, were held in 39 cities across the United States on November 22, 2008.[38]

Recognizing the potential of such a movement to serve their purposes, however, the uppists decided not to quash this uprising, but to divert it into their tried-and-true paradigm of political control: the left/right dichotomy of the so-called political spectrum. Before the uppists' entrance, mainstream Republicans and mainstream Democrats alike had been booed and jeered at Tea Party events.[39] Those crowds, being downists, put all uppists, left and right alike, in the same boat—and hoped to sink it. But in this new strain of fake downism, uppist candidates speaking to crowds at political rallies sounded as if they were anti-establishment.

In one particularly memorable instance, Texas Governor and Bilderberg attendee Rick Perry, addressing anti-tax protesters on April 15, 2009, affected a thick Southern drawl and expressed sympathy for Texans who wanted to secede from the union.[40] Gullible listeners, unfamiliar with uppists' craftiness, were overjoyed to hear this mainstream politician mouthing their talking points.

The deception continued as candidate after candidate dutifully adopted the anti-establishment message of the Tea Partiers until the complete subversion of the Tea Party came about. The uppists, aided by the establishment media they control, framed the fledgling downist movement as a purely right-wing concern and mocked it accordingly. Naturally, this myth of a right-wing bias in the Tea Party became a self-fulfilling reality. Tea Partiers obligingly overreacted to media criticism, which they perceived to be coming from "the left," by cheering on the very same establishment right-wing candidates they had started out booing. And so it was that the manipulative uppists sank the Tea Party ship by boarding it as allies and steering it directly into the clutches of the media pirates.

Donald Trump's 2016 presidential election campaign drew from the same playbook of misdirection and subversion. Millions of downists in the United States were energized by a "maverick" presidential candidate who appeared to be challenging the political pieties of the era. He criticized the US' disastrous wars of aggression in the Middle East. He floated the idea that NATO might be "obsolete." He opined that America should get along with Russia and other perceived enemies. He called out his main Republican primary challenger, Ted Cruz, for being bought and sold by Goldman Sachs (who happened to employ Cruz's wife). He stated plainly that globalism is a failed ideology and that it's time to concentrate on domestic affairs.

But then, predictably enough for those who understand how the game is played, this "downist" candidate morphed into an uppist president. Within 100 days, Trump had launched a Tomahawk missile strike in Syria[41] and had increased US participation in the massacre in Yemen.[42] He had declared NATO "no longer obsolete" after all[43] and had appointed no less than five Goldman Sachs bankers to staff his administration.[44] And, just to spell it out for anyone who missed this remarkable transformation from Candidate Downist to President Uppist, Trump assured *The Wall Street Journal* and its readers, "Hey, I'm a nationalist and a globalist. I'm both."[45]

That's right. If you can't beat 'em, join 'em. Or at least pretend to join 'em until you're elected.

The symmetry of the uppists' left/right control paradigm always requires that events on the right be mirrored on the left, and vice versa. Hence, the exact same strategy of protest and diversion that they employed in trashing the Tea Party and in transforming their latest presidential puppet, Trump, must also occur on the other side of the political spectrum. And it has.

Case in point: On September 17, 2011, protesters occupied Zuccotti Park in New York's financial district, setting off the Occupy movement that would sweep the globe in the coming months. Although the protest was first suggested by *AdBusters*, a Canadian anti-capitalist magazine and not-for-profit organization with murky foundation (i.e., uppist) funding,[46] the movement's ranks swelled with folks who were simply fed up with the bankster bailouts and business as usual in Washington, D.C.

One of the great ironies of the era is that neither the Occupiers nor the Tea Partiers seemed to realize that their movements held many common concerns. The genuine protesters in both groups were motivated by outrage at the government's handling of the 2008 banking crisis. They equally deplored the fact that the Beltway fat cats were in bed with special interests and had stopped listening to the people. And they equally demanded that their mutual adversaries, the uppists, help Main Street, not save Wall Street.

But despite their substantial similarities, the Tea Partiers and Occupiers were driven apart by the uppist-owned media, which pounded home the message that they were each other's mortal enemies. Not only were they tricked into warring against one another, but both movements were enticed into expending energies on supporting the uppist Democrats or the uppist Republicans in the 2012 election cycle.

The uppists, having realized they must put a stop to the stirrings of downism among the Tea Partiers and Occupiers, had cunningly infiltrated both camps and redirected the downists' attention away from their shared goals to matters of no real significance.

Ever since 2001, the uppists have been using 9/11 as the perfect excuse to train the apparatus of state power—

police departments, intelligence agencies, the military—not on foreign nations or on shadowy terrorist groups but on fellow Americans, the uppists' ultimate target. Yes, under the guise of "Homeland Security," many US government guns now point directly, both literally and figuratively, at US citizens. This development makes clear what had long been hinted at: uppists consider their real enemies to be neither tin-pot dictators nor turbaned terrorists but, instead, regular old beer-drinking, family-loving, jeans-wearing downists who, the uppists fear, just might have the clout and the will to dismantle the police state during this period of destabilization.

This conclusion is derived not from speculation, but from the uppists' own documents.

In April of 2006, a Texas Department of Public Safety Criminal Law Enforcement guide surfaced listing typical attributes of the common terrorist: they buy baby formula and beer, wear Levi's jeans, travel with families, and carry driver's licenses.[47] In other words, just about every adult in the United States is a potential terrorist, if you believe the uppists.

But that's not all.

In March 2009, a Virginia training manual on how to recognize "terrorists" was made public. It warns state employees that sketch pads, notebooks, maps, charts, cameras, tape recorders, and SCUBA equipment are all examples of paraphernalia that indicate potential terrorist activity.[48]

That same month, a secret Missouri Information Analysis Center report was leaked, revealing what Missouri police were being told to look out for in the rise of a dangerous new "militia movement." Among the tell-tale signs that someone belongs to this burgeoning movement, according to the document, is support of third-party political candidates.[49]

For that small but growing percentage of the population that is breaking free of the old political paradigm and becoming consciously downist, the fact that the uppist-controlled homeland security grid is being aimed squarely at them comes as no surprise. They already know that the Pentagon has called all forms of political protest "low-level terrorism"[50] and that the US Army Reserve was deployed, along with local law enforcement and the FBI, to monitor the aforementioned End the Fed rallies in November 2008.[51] At this point, only those still trapped in the left-right duopoly of political control are clueless about the uppists' intention of stamping out all dissent against their agenda of centralization and consolidation of power.

What's clear to "awake" uppists and downists alike is that they are engaged in a struggle for political supremacy. Their weapons are not guns but words, and their battle is being waged not on a physical battlefield but in a mental domain: the minds of the public.

At this moment in history, downists are facing their greatest test and finding their greatest opportunity. Technology has put all the facts about the true up/down nature of politics at their fingertips. Armed with that truth, downists should be able to prod the slumbering, uppist-supporting left/right public awake and get them to see how the uppists have been deceiving them. In this way, the masses can be induced to quit cooperating with the uppist-controlled system and to join the downist rebellion.

Meanwhile, the uppists, for their part, continue to spend billions of their paper dollars and euros and yen and pesos—and all their other uppist-controlled, central bank-issued fiat currencies—on the most massive, coordinated PR campaign ever waged against humanity. Their goal is to keep the public convinced that the only reality is the left/right paradigm created by those very uppists.

Not having the power of truth on their side, uppists must inject their own deceptive definitions of words and their own flawed interpretations of downists' motives into the political discourse in an attempt to keep their up/down secret from being exposed.

What kind of "deceptive definitions?" Well, how about the label "extremist," which uppists slap on anyone who resists their slave-like system of control? Or "racist"? Or "terrorist"? Or "conspiracy theorist"? The effect of such inflammatory language on weaker-minded individuals—who have been programmed their entire lives by uppist-controlled propaganda dispensed by the school system, by "fake news," and by corporate advertising—is to keep them in line. And, in so doing, keep them from discovering the true nature of their political reality, concealed, as it is, behind all uppist-dominated institutions.

RECLAIMING HUMANITY

WE'VE SEEN the victories that the uppists have secured by sticking to their hoary maxims "All's fair in love and war" and "If you can't beat 'em, join 'em."

How about the downists? Is there an old adage they might use to organize their opposition to the uppist agenda?

Perhaps this: "The pen is mightier than the sword." Granted, in this internet age, the "weapon" of choice may be the keyboard rather than the pen, but the sentiment remains.

As mentioned above, both uppists and downists have employed the power of the pen to their advantage. But it's safe to say that the downists are starting to win the war for hearts and minds with this tool. Scrawling their words with mighty strokes of truth, the downists have been able to effectively disarm the defenders of the uppist system. As a result, more and more people once under the spell of the uppists are becoming aware that the uppists act not in the interests of the common citizen but solely in the interests of a tiny, tight-knit network of oligarchs who operate in secret and who control almost the entirety of the world's wealth. With this awareness comes the freeing realization that key cogs in the uppist machinery of control can be removed from the system so that, at a certain critical point, the machinery itself will cease to function.

The question, as always, is whether the downists can win converts faster than the uppists can implement their controls. This is far from an idle question.

In December 2008, Zbigniew Brzezinski—the late uppist who served as National Security Advisor under President Jimmy Carter—wrote a *New York Times* op-ed detailing what he called "the global political awakening."[52] In it, he fretted that the vast majority of humanity was becoming politically active in the face of increasing (and increasingly obvious) social and economic disparities.

> For the first time in history almost all of humanity is politically activated, politically conscious and politically interactive. Global activism is generating a surge in the quest for cultural respect and economic opportunity in a world scarred by memories of colonial or imperial domination.

Essentially, Brzezinski is describing the rise of the

downist ideology, a political movement conceived to counter the very uppist oligarchy that he himself represented. Yet by cloaking his message in the language of victimhood and oppression, he sounds almost sympathetic to the downist cause.

But Brzezinski showed his true feelings in a candid November 2008 lecture:

> I once put it rather pungently—and I was flattered that the British foreign secretary repeated this—as follows. Namely, in earlier times it was easier to control a million people—literally, it was easier to control a million people—than, physically, to kill a million people. Today it is infinitely easier to kill a million people than to control a million people. It is easier to kill than to control.[53]

We learn that for an uppist like Brzezinski, the choice is stark: *what cannot be controlled must be killed*. Thus, he must frame the global political awakening not as a chance for the long-suppressed masses to throw off the yoke of uppist suppression, but as a worrying development that could result in "global chaos."

There are two things to take away from his observations. The first is that the number of converts to the downist cause is growing. The second is that those downists are up against tremendous odds. They are squaring off not only against an entrenched uppist class that has steered world events for generations, but against a system in which the same uppist class prints the money that funds the PR campaign that promotes the uppists' interests.

If, as Brzezinski chillingly observed of our era, it is indeed easier to kill a million people than to control them, how can the downists hope to defeat such an oppressive, seemingly omnipotent opponent?

The answer is as simple as it is heartening. Seismic changes are already taking place in the political arena, and they will not cease.

Sure, establishment uppists will continue to devote their careers to maintaining control of their uppist system and to keeping it intact. But they cannot halt the resistance to that system, nor can they prevent the rapid rise in the number of new resisters.

The thing Brzezinski and his ilk dread most is not violent revolution. They understand that violence by rebellious masses bolsters their position by convincing left/right dupes of the uppist system that the downists really are "extremists" or "racists" or "terrorists." No, what the uppists dread most is the awakening itself—the simple spreading of the knowledge that their system, the left/right political obfuscation we have been force-fed our entire lives, is an illusion. For they know that the long-slumbering downists, once stirred, are an unstoppable force against the uppists' fragile, fear-based system.

Like the backwardist and forwardist ants in our parable, we downists once believed we were living on a straight line. We were baffled every time we set off in a different direction only to arrive back at the same spot.

But we know better now. We see that we do not live in a single dimension, but in a multi-dimensional reality.

We see, too, that we need no longer let ourselves be divided and conquered by would-be controllers. We can remain united and unconquerable.

And, equipped with that knowledge, we downists need not attempt to vanquish the uppist system. The uppist illusion, exposed as the two-bit parlour trick it really is, will simply vanish.

NOTES

1. Quigley, Carroll. *Tragedy and Hope: A History of the World in Our Time.* (New York: Wm. Morrison, 1974). Pages 1247-1248.

2. See endnote 1. Page 950.

3. Clinton, William J. "Address Accepting the Presidential Nomination at the Democratic National Convention in New York." The American Presidency Project. July 16, 1992. archive.fo/2jbbs

4. See endnote 1. Page 951.

5. See endnote 1. Page 324.

6. Lekakis, George and Fleur Leyden. "World bankers meet in Sydney as recovery fears intensify." Herald Sun. February 6, 2010. archive.fo/Vtf5q

7. Mersch, Yves. "The framework for short-term provision of international reserve currencies to sovereign states and their central banks." BIS Review. 15/2010. archive.fo/Q8mLV

8. "Official List of Participants for the 2008 Bilderberg Meeting." public intelligence. September 27, 2009. archive.is/GFqRX

9. Geithner, Timothy. "Reducing risk in the financial system." Financial Times. June 8, 2008. archive.fo/ytaTY

10. "Katharine Graham." WikiSpooks. archive.is/QiDcr

11. "The Economist." WikiSpooks. archive.is/uObmL

12. Smith, Charlie. "Premier Gordon Campbell attends Bilderberg 2010 meeting." straight.com. June 6, 2010. archive.is/sXq5s

13. "2012 Bilderberg Meeting Participant List." May 31, 2012. public intelligence. archive.is/nY1lb

14. "ClubClass - BBC Radio on Bilderberg.wmv." YouTube, uploaded by BlackSeedOils, May 1, 2012. youtu.be/0rZQwJJf-Kg

15. "Bilderberg Meetings 1955 Conference Report Garmisch-Partenkirchen, Germany." Public Intelligence. June 12, 2016. archive.fo/srko8

16. Rettman, Andrew. "'Jury's out' on future of Europe, EU doyen says." euobserver. March 16, 2009. archive.fo/W0R8N

17. "Secret Meeting Held in Cannes." The Washington Post. March 30, 1963. archive.fo/1a1uS

18. "Intergovernmental Committee on European Integration. The Brussels Report on the General Common Market (abridged, English translation of document commonly called the Spaak Report)." Archive of European Integration. archive.is/tTEBQ

19. Sciolino, Elaine. "French Voters Soundly Reject European Union Constitution." The New York Times. May 30, 2005. archive.fo/4MkbJ

20. "Dutch say 'devastating no' to EU constitution." The Guardian. June 2, 2005. archive.fo/cG7PZ

21. Corbett, James. "Free Humanity 3, EU 0." The Corbett Report. June 18, 2008. corbettreport.com/lisbontreaty

22. "UK to press ahead with EU Treaty." BBC News. June 13, 2008. archive.fo/axY0D

23. Peterkin, Tom. "EU referendum: Ireland votes against Lisbon Treaty." The Telegraph. June 13, 2008. archive.fo/TfWGP

24. Waterfield, Bruno. "EU intervention in Irish referendum 'unlawful.'" The Telegraph. September 29, 2009. archive.fo/n9Swb

25. Corbett, James. "Ballot Box Problems, Broken Laws Cast Doubt on Irish Lisbon Referendum Result." The Corbett Report. October 8, 2009. corbettreport.com/irishreferendum

26. Corbett, James. "The Process of Indoctrination." The Corbett Report. July 14, 2008. corbettreport.com/indoctrination

27. See endnote 1.

28. Felkerson, James. "$29,000,000,000,000: A Detailed Look at the Fed's Bailout by Funding Facility and Recipient." Levy Economics Institute of Bard College. December 2011. archive.is/PFt4Z

29. "Establishing a permanent crisis mechanism to safeguard the financial stability of the euro area." European Parliament. December 16, 2010. archive.is/ZFBOK

30. Porter, Andrew et al. "G20 summit: Gordon Brown announces 'new world order.'" The Telegraph. April 3, 2009. archive.fo/Ou4op

31. "Why We Need A Global Central Bank." Newsweek. October 24, 2008. archive.fo/2iw2Z

32. Rachman, Gideon. "And now for a world government." Financial Times. December 8, 2008. archive.fo/AzkPN

33. "Another day of global market turmoil despite rate cut action." The Guardian. October 8, 2008. archive.fo/aaQNs

34. Xiaochuan, Zhou. "Reform the international monetary system." BIS Review. March 23, 2009. archive.fo/L5ket

35. "Ellen Brown Explains the New G20 Bank Bail-in Rules." The Corbett Report. December 23, 2014. corbettreport.com/?p=13182

36. "Radio Liberty: The Cyprus Event." The Corbett Report. March 19, 2013. corbettreport.com/?p=7134

37. "Boston 9/11 Tea Party Inspires Nationwide Events." 911Truth.org. December 17, 2006. archive.fo/iPgYR

38. Brouillet, Carol. "November 22, 2008 — End the Fed Rallies Report from San Francisco." communitycurrency.org. archive.is/qxgqL

39. DeHaven, Ted. "Congressman Booed at Tea Party Protest." Cato At Liberty. April 20, 2009. archive.is/fKojh

40. McKinley, Jr., James C. "Texas Governor's Secession Talk Stirs Furor." The New York Times. April 17, 2009. archive.fo/04gjY

41. Garamone, Jim. "Trump Orders Missile Attack in Retaliation for Syrian Chemical Strikes." April 6, 2017. archive.is/CNES4

42. "Yemen: Trump Expands U.S. Military Role in Saudi War as Yemenis Brace for Famine." DemocracyNow! March 30, 2017. archive.is/uJkoM

43. Johnson, Jenna. "Trump on NATO: 'I said it was obsolete. It's no longer obsolete.'" The Washington Post. April 12, 2017. archive.is/udlu5

44. Firozi, Paulina. "Trump names another Goldman Sachs executive to senior administration role." The Hill. March 15, 2017. archive.is/cFAFx

45. Nicholas, Peter et al. "Why Donald Trump Decided to Back Off Nafta Threat." The Wall Street Journal. April 27, 2017. archive.fo/dHEMR

46. Egan, Mark and Michelle Nichols. "Who's behind the Wall Street protests?" Reuters. October 13, 2011. archive.fo/3sWIF

47. "Theft or Large Cash Purchases of [sic]." STUDYLIB. archive.is/Dwsio

48. "2009 Virginia Terrorism Threat Assessment, March 2009." WikiLeaks. archive.is/pvgPs

49. Miller, Joshua Rhett. "'Fusion Centers' Expand Criteria to Identify Militia Members." Fox News. March 23, 2009. archive.fo/jUmZY

50. "Defense Department sees protests as terrorism." East Bay Times. June 14, 2009. archive.fo/UzFz5

51. Nimmo, Kurt. "Army Dispatched in Response to End the Fed Protests." Federal Jack. March 21, 2009. archive.fo/oFdvI

52. Brzezinski, Zbigniew. "The global political awakening." The New York Times. December 16, 2008. archive.fo/lV30h

53. "Obama Adviser Brzezinski s [sic] Off the record Speech to British Elites Part 1." YouTube, uploaded by Deborah Gerczak, April 13, 2009. youtu.be/PiGTbaeUr9E

They Don't Want Your Genes in the Pool

THE ANCIENT EGYPTIANS BELIEVED their pharaohs were progeny of the sun god, Ra. The Japanese believed their Imperial Family descended from the sun goddess, Amaterasu, and the sea god, Ryuujin. The Chinese believed that their emperors ruled under the "Mandate of Heaven." And Europeans believed in the "divine right of kings," which held that each nation's sovereign was sanctioned by God Himself.

For as long as royalty has existed, there have been elaborate theological justifications for why monarchs should be worshipped as gods and for why they deserve to reign over their respective kingdoms.

Of course, it's easy to understand why the royals have tried, in culture after culture, to foster their subjects' belief in their divinely ordained supremacy. After all, if kings and queens and emperors and pharaohs are not gods, or at least chosen by God, why would anyone obey them? The difference between a regal king and a tin-pot dictator disappears if the king's divinity is denied.

Even today, in this era where monarchs are viewed by the general public as relics of the past, age-old superstitions about royal families persist. They are still referred to as "blue bloods," a vestige of the days when their pale, translucent skin was a visible marker of their sheltered, privileged existence, something that set them apart from the ruddy complexion of the peasantry who toiled all day in the sun.[1]

Also, there is still an elaborate (and strictly enforced) protocol for meeting the British monarch. Even heads of state had to take a lesson in royal etiquette before they were allowed to meet with Her Royal Majesty Queen Elizabeth II. Hence the Obamas' careful study of royal protocol before their first presidential visit to London[2] and the media's pearl-clutching over President Trump's breach of that protocol on his royal visit in 2019.[3]

But these rituals of class distinction are not merely for show. The royals have always considered themselves of superior stock—a breed apart from the poor downtrodden masses who toil in squalor beneath them. Hence the obsession with breeding, which nobility the world over has been at great pains to observe down through the centuries.

Or should that be the obsession with inbreeding? Certainly, the branches of many a royal family tree fold in as much as they branch out, which explains both the remarkable physical similarities among members of European royal families and the recessive disorders, like hemophilia, that have plagued Europe's inbred royalty for centuries.

Indeed, modern-day DNA analysis has shown that the Spanish branch of the Hapsburg family, the dynasty that ruled over vast swaths of Europe for over 500 years, was inbred out of existence.[4] After generations of cousins marrying cousins and uncles marrying nieces, the genetic variation between Hapsburg husbands and wives was no greater than that between Hapsburg brothers and sisters. The last member of the Spanish Hapsburgs, Charles II, died a congenitally sick, deformed man, physically unable to produce a child. Nor was this a strictly European problem: recent analysis of the DNA of iconic King Tut—Pharaoh Tutankhamen, who reigned over Egypt more than 3,300 years ago—shows that he, too, was the sickly, misshapen product of an incestuous brother-and-sister pairing.[5]

The royal fixation with family lines and inbreeding arose from the practice of animal breeding, which has been used for thousands of years to select for certain traits among livestock and pets. In fact, the ability to breed certain traits into or out of pets and livestock has been an art form, if not a science, ever since humans began domesticating animals. It wasn't much of a stretch for sovereigns to toy with these same types of breeding techniques to purify their own royal "stock" and domesticate their own "chattel," the commoners.

The animal breeding/human breeding analogy appears in some ancient texts. In the sixth century BC, the Greek poet Theognis of Megara lamented his countrymen's unwillingness to show the same attention to the breeding of men and women that they showed to the breeding of rams and horses:

> *With kine and horses, Kurnus! we proceed*
> *By reasonable rules, and choose a breed*
> *For profit and increase, at any price:*
> *Of a sound stock, without defect or vice.*
> *But, in the daily matches that we make,*
> *The price is everything: for money's sake,*
> *Men marry: women are in marriage given*
> *The churl or ruffian, that in wealth has thriven,*
> *May match his offspring with the proudest race:*
> *That everything is mix'd, noble and base!*
> *If then in outward manner, form, and mind,*

You find us a degraded, motley kind,
Wonder no more, my friend! the cause is plain,
And to lament the consequence is vain.[6]

As Theognis observes, the cloistered gentry of the so-called "nobility" have always regarded the product of unions between the "nobles" and the "commoners" as "degraded" and "motley." The implication is clear: there are inheritable genetic traits that differentiate the social castes. And, by this logic, marrying "below one's position" in society results in a mixture of the nobility's "good" genes with the commoners' "bad" genes.

But, it will be pointed out, that was over two thousand years ago, when the chasm between landed lords and property-less peasants was unbreachable. Today, by contrast, there is unprecedented economic and class mobility. With the notable exception of the world's extant royal families, humanity no longer divides itself into "noble" and "base" castes. We no longer talk in vague generalities about the "mixing" of traits between parents. Instead, we speak in precise, scientific terms of the functioning of genes and chromosomes and the structure of DNA and the importance of upbringing and environment in shaping who we are. We no longer believe (assuming we ever really did) that a Queen Elizabeth or a King Salman or an Emperor Naruhito has been chosen by God to rule over us.

Yes, ours is an "enlightened" era, in which leaders are democratically elected politicians, not hereditary monarchs. Upward mobility today is a function of ambition and talent, not peerage and lineage. Celebrities are our royalty. Some of the richest men and women in the world were average Janes and Joes who pulled themselves up by their bootstraps and are now ranked annually by net worth in glossy magazines.

Or so the story goes. The truth, though, is not quite in line with popular perception. As it turns out, there is a modern-day royalty whose members are not descendants of actual royal houses. Contemporary royals can be defined as an upper-crust breed of rulers who inherit positions of enormous power and privilege and who possess nearly unimaginable wealth. These "kings" and "queens," however, do not live in castles. They do not demand deference or fealty from their subjects. Their faces are not printed on our bills or stamped into our coins.

Compared with their royal counterparts of old, our modern monarchs are relatively inconspicuous. They are notable mostly for the buildings and banks and corporations and tax-free foundations that bear their family names. These lords of business and finance blend into crowds on Wall Street and Main Street. We can trace their rise to the fall of the monarchies of yesteryear.

By the late seventeenth century, as the world was transitioning away from medieval feudalism and toward current-day capitalism, the absolute power of the European monarchs was being whittled away. In England, the Glorious Revolution of 1688 and the Bill of Rights of 1689 brought an end to the doctrine of the total authority of the king—an authority that had already been formally limited by the Magna Carta in 1216. In 1694, the establishment of the Bank of England set a precedent for the private control of a nation's money supply, a template that was copied in country after country (including, of course, the United States) in the coming centuries. Before long, only a handful of banking families controlled the exchequers of the governments they "served," and the overt royalty of old was replaced with a new, covert royalty.

In the nineteenth century, the ranks of non-royal royals swelled with another type of nouveau riche: the cutthroat monopolists who built empires out of steel, oil, coal, railroads, and shipping.

And now here we are in the twenty-first century, with the would-be rulers of the world having traded royal robes for bespoke suits from Savile Row tailors, coats of arms for corporate logos, crowns for computers, scepters for cell phones. The throne rooms of yore have given way to board rooms, federal courtrooms, social club dining rooms, and corporate back rooms from which the rest of humanity is directed and controlled.

This new royalty, like the royalty of old, is obsessed with breeding. Rockefellers and Aldriches and Averills and Harrimans and Walkers make sure to marry Bushes and Foresters and Rothschilds (and then honeymoon at America's Buckingham Palace, the White House[7]). The members of these dynasties—our modern-day royalty—are every bit as interbred, elitist, and despotic as the lords and ladies of bygone days.

Unlike royalty of times past, however, this new breed of tyrant cannot rely on the canard of "divine right" to justify its positions of power. With the disappearance of medieval kingdoms, a new era began—one in which empiricism and scientific study took the place of religious lore. The sovereigns of our scientific age needed a scientific-sounding gloss to update the "divine right" doctrine while preserving the presumed authority of the few to rule the many. Luckily for this new breed of monarch, a pseudoscientific gloss was not long in coming.

In 1859, Charles Darwin published *On the Origin of Species by Means of Natural Selection, or the Preservation of Favoured Races in the Struggle for Life*. Within ten years, Darwin's cousin, Francis Galton, came out with *Hereditary Genius*, an inquiry into why it is that rich and successful people are more likely to give birth to rich and successful offspring. Galton did not have to look very far for evidence of this phenomenon: both the Galton and Darwin families—which, unsurprisingly, were intermarried—boasted several famous thinkers and writers, including Erasmus Darwin, the grandfather of both Charles and Francis.

Equally unsurprisingly, Galton fancied that heredity alone accounted for one's fortune, good or ill. In other words, the offspring of the rich and well-educated tended to also be rich and well-educated, not because they attended exclusive schools and were afforded every advantage in life, but merely because of their genes. With this predetermined conclusion in mind, Galton set about expending considerable energy trying to prove his theory correct. He founded societies, organized conferences, launched journals, and set up laboratories devoted to the study of how the Galtons and their fellow travellers in the upper echelons of society managed to become so wealthy (and why they deserved to be).

Essentially, Galton was positing that humans can be bred for intelligence or industriousness, just as a dog can be bred for aggression or a horse can be bred for racing. In 1883, he coined the term "eugenics"—from the Greek εὔ (well) and -γενής (race, stock, kin)—to describe the study of how human evolution could be directed to improve "the racial quality of future generations."

The very name "eugenics" itself betrays the underlying assumption of this self-serving ideology: namely, that there are "good" genes that must be promoted and "bad" genes that must be eliminated from the gene pool in order to "improve" the race. And, as with all such definitions, it is the definers who get to decide what constitutes "good" and "bad" genes and who naturally deem only themselves fit to propagate their genes into the future "for the good of the race."

Although eugenics' starting assumption seems fairly innocuous at first glance, the erstwhile eugenicist comes rather quickly to a number of extreme conclusions. One of these is the belief that the poor, disabled, or otherwise impaired are in fact products of bad breeding. If you're poor, that's because you come from poor stock. If you're a common thief, it's because you come from a family line of criminals. And if you're a rich businessman or a successful politician or a talented scientist, it's because of your good genes. The rich and powerful deserve to rule over the rest, this circular reasoning holds, because their hereditary lines have made them rich and powerful.

Another corollary of the "good" gene/"bad" gene hypothesis is that those groups of individuals able to dominate others—militarily, economically, or otherwise—not only have the right to exercise that power but in fact are obliged to do so in the interest of improving the species. In short: might makes right. If you're not inbred with us, you're ill-bred against us.

But to phrase this quackery in the language of modern science is to give it—and its adherents—too much credit altogether. After all, in Galton's time, nothing was known about heredity or genetics. The work of Gregor Mendel—an obscure Augustinian friar who, in the mid-nineteenth century, pioneered the scientific study of heredity with his experiments breeding pea plants—would not be recognized and publicized until the turn of the twentieth century, almost two decades after Galton came up with the term "eugenics."[8]

As for genetics, the word "gene" wasn't even coined until 1909, and the mechanism by which deoxyribonucleic acid (DNA) encodes genetic information was not understood until the mid-twentieth century. Until then, there had been only speculation about the existence of some sort of "protoplasm" that carried heritable traits from one generation to the next in a way that was not understood. Neither the properties nor the characteristics of this "protoplasm" were known. Nonetheless, that did not stop mainstream eugenicists like Arnold Gesell—a revered early-twentieth-century child psychologist who is the namesake of the Gesell Institute of Child Development at Yale—from pontificating on how "supervision and segregation" of those deemed "feebleminded" is necessary to "prevent the horrible renewal of this defective protoplasm that is contaminating the stream of village life."[9]

Indeed, for the cadre of "elite" Englishmen who first developed and propounded the ideology, and for the American ideologues who followed in their wake, eugenics was not so much a scientific theory as an article of faith. To their credit, the progenitors of this scientific dogma were devoted enough to the faith to practice what they preached. A quick look at the family trees of the early eugenicists reveals that they adhered to the same endogamous habits as the royalty of old. The inbred upper class believed they had a scientific underpinning to their penchant for marrying cousins and nieces: by breeding only among themselves, they reasoned, they could ensure their "pure" genes would not become debased by the "degenerate" genes of the commoners.

Charles Darwin, for one, was obsessed with inbreeding. And no wonder, considering that for generations the Darwins had intermarried with the Wedgwoods. Of course, Charles perpetuated that pattern, marrying his first cousin, Emma Wedgwood. Both were descended from the founder of the famed pottery dynasty, Josiah Wedgwood, who had himself married his third cousin.

Darwin later began to suspect there were possible drawbacks to inbreeding; three of his ten children, frail and sickly, died in childhood, and another three were childless despite long-lasting marriages. This misfortune was not unique to Charles and Emma. Of sixty-two descendants of Josiah Wedgwood, only twenty-four were able to have children who survived to adulthood. So concerned was Charles by this phenomenon—especially when his own botanical research demonstrated the detrimental effects of inbreeding in the plant kingdom—that he petitioned parliament to include a question about marriages to cousins on the 1871 British census (a request parliament turned down).[10]

Charles' misgivings did not stop the Darwins and Wedgwoods from continuing to marry each other or members of a select few families in British aristocratic, scientific circles—families including the Galtons and the Huxleys. Nor did the failure of this applied study in eugenics dissuade the Darwin-Wedgwood family from pursuing further research into the subject with maniacal fervor. If anything, the less-than-satisfactory results drove them to redouble their efforts, motivated as they were by the sliver of hope that their combined resources and intelligence could "crack the code" of inbreeding and offer up a race of superhumans.

Which brings us back to Francis Galton. Such was his frenzy in pursuing his investigations that, in addition to coining the term "eugenics," Galton established the first eugenics research laboratory at University College London, started a monthly journal called *The Eugenics Review*, and founded the British Eugenics Society. The member rolls of the British Eugenics Society (BES) read not only like a *Who's Who* of early-twentieth-century British scientists, but also like an extended Darwin-Wedgwood-Galton family tree. Its leaves included:

- LEONARD DARWIN - Despite having no scientific degree or training, Charles Darwin's son, Leonard, succeeded Francis Galton (his half-cousin once removed) as BES chairman from 1911 to 1928, then was its honorary president until his death in 1943. Having married twice (once to the granddaughter of his aunt), he failed to produce any offspring, but devoted himself to worrying about the breeding habits of the commoners.

- JOHN MAYNARD KEYNES - President of the BES from 1937 to 1944, Keynes is the celebrated economist who argued for a world central bank and global currency. His younger brother married a granddaughter of Charles Darwin.

- CHARLES GALTON DARWIN - A prominent member of the BES, Charles Galton Darwin believed that the inclination of the lower class to produce large families threatened the future of the human race. He was a grandson of Charles Darwin.

- JULIAN HUXLEY - President of the BES from 1959 to 1962, Huxley was a biologist who was well-known for arguing that human "stocks" needed to be controlled and managed like agricultural stocks. He gave the Galton Memorial Lecture twice, received the Darwin Medal from the Royal Society and the Darwin-Wallace Medal from the Linnean Society, and co-founded the World Wildlife Fund with fellow eugenicists Prince Philip of Britain and Prince Bernhard of the Netherlands. Huxley's half-niece married a great grandson of Charles Darwin.

Beyond this tight-knit network of interbreeders were other eugenics supporters who rose to positions of power and influence within the movement. It was these self-described "progressives," believers in the perfection of society through social engineering, who were in large part responsible for shaping the world as we know it.

Among the eugenics zealots was famed author and political thinker H. G. Wells. Best known for his science fiction tales like *War of the Worlds* and *The Time Machine*, Wells is less remembered as a political writer who contributed to the draft of the United Nations' 1948 Declaration of Human Rights.[11] Even less well-known are his works of nonfiction, such as *Anticipations of the Reaction of Mechanical and Scientific Progress Upon Human Life and Thought*, which predicted the rise of a technocratic world government he dubbed the "New Republic." In Wells's vision, this government would weed out the "inferior" races, identified as "those swarms of black, and brown, and dirty-white, and yellow people, who do not come into the needs of the new efficiency." Like any good eugenicist, he shows no compunction at all about condemning vast swathes of humanity to death for the "crime" of not blending into the "efficient" world order that he believed this "New Republic" would bring:

Well, the world is a world, not a charitable institution, and I take it they will have to go. The whole tenor and meaning of the world, as I see it, is that they have to go. So far as they fail to develop sane, vigorous, and distinctive personalities for the great world of the future, it is their portion to die out and disappear.[12]

Another famous eugenics enthusiast was Marie Stopes. In 1921, she founded an organization linked to Britain's first family planning clinic—called the Society for Constructive Birth Control and Racial Progress. One of its founding tenets affirmed that the clinic worked to furnish "security from conception to those who are racially diseased, already overburdened with children, or in any specific way unfitted for parenthood."[13] This "security" included compulsory sterilization of those deemed "unfit for parenthood."[14] Unsurprisingly, Stopes—who sent Hitler a copy of her book *Love Songs for Young Lovers* in 1939 and who composed a poem in 1942 with the lines "Catholics, Prussians, the Jews and the Russians, all are a curse, or something worse"[15]—was a lifelong fellow of the British Eugenics Society.[16] She bequeathed a large portion of her fortune to that organization when she died in 1958.[17] How fitting that this member of the modern-day eugenics-promoting "nobility" was honored in 2008 by the Royal Mail with a commemorative stamp bearing her image.[18]

Championed with evangelistic fervor by its disciples, the religion of racial purity and genetic royalty had soon transplanted itself across the Atlantic. One of its early proponents in Canada was Tommy Douglas, a politician so celebrated for his role as the "father of [Canadian] Medicare" that he was voted the greatest Canadian of all time in a national poll in 2004.[19] Back in 1933, at the age of 29, Douglas submitted a master's thesis to McMaster University on the subject of eugenics as a way to solve the country's economic problems. In it, he argued that "subnormals," "defectives," and "morons"—people with a low IQ or physical abnormalities, for example—were placing an undue burden on the rest of society. He advocated putting them "on a state farm, or in a colony where decisions could be made for them by a competent supervisor," and called for the state to certify "mental and physical fitness" to prevent the "unfit" from marrying and breeding.[20]

But as effective as these British and Canadian apostles were in spreading the doctrine of eugenics, their "achievements" pale in comparison to the schemes hatched by their American allies. In America, eugenics was not confined to the halls of academia or the journals of learned societies. On the contrary, so wide was eugenics' influence that it became the motivating force of the robber barons, the pet project of would-be social engineers, and the cause célèbre of a host of politicians and public intellectuals.

One of the prime movers in America's eugenicist circles was Charles Davenport, a Harvard-trained zoologist who had grown up in a strict, puritanical family of New England Congregationalists. Davenport's authoritarian father, obsessed with genealogy, traced the family tree all the way back to his Anglo-Saxon forebears in 1086. When the younger Davenport discovered Francis Galton's writing while working at a biological laboratory on Long Island, he found his purpose in life. As he later told the American Breeders Association, which became an important ally in his eugenicist cause: "Society must protect itself; as it claims the right to deprive the murderer of his life, so also it may annihilate the hideous serpent of hopelessly vicious protoplasm."[21]

Devoting himself to this pursuit, Davenport spent years trying to organize an American eugenics laboratory and society to rival that of his English hero Galton. Eventually he found the perfect spot for that laboratory: Cold Spring Harbor, a hamlet on the north shore of Long Island. There he set up a "Station for Experimental Evolution" and a "Eugenics Record Office" (ERO).

The ERO was to be the linchpin of Davenport's eugenics research. He envisioned it storing a comprehensive registry documenting the "pedigree" of every American—an ambitious goal, to be sure. But where would the ERO obtain the records for such a monumental repository? Davenport himself supplied the answer in his 1910 screed on *Eugenics: the Science of Human Improvement by Better Breeding*:

> They lie hidden in records of our numerous charity organizations, our 42 institutions for the feebleminded, our 115 schools and homes for the deaf and blind, our 350 hospitals for the insane, our 1,200 refuge homes, our 1,300 prisons, our 1,500 hospitals and our 2,500 almshouses. Our great insurance companies and our college gymnasiums have tens of thousands of records of the characters of human bloodlines. These records should be studied, their hereditary data sifted out and properly recorded on cards and the cards sent to a central bureau for study in order that data should be placed in their proper relations in the great strains of human protoplasm that are coursing through the country.[22]

Armed with that immense amount of data, Davenport and a corps of researchers, politicians, lawyers, doctors, Supreme Court justices, and other influential figures rallied around the eugenics flag and began a mass movement dedicated to "protecting the public" from the scourge of bad breeding. These early-twentieth-century eugenicists whipped the American public into both a panic and a fury over the notion that the world was being overwhelmed by the "defective" offspring of criminals, gamblers, alcoholics, wanton women, and, not incidentally, racial minorities and the disabled. Legislators in state after state began passing laws that allowed the government to involuntarily sterilize the women and men presumed to be most at risk of passing their "defects" on to their children. In this way, the country could rest easy in the knowledge that the gene pool would not be further "polluted" with this genetic "detritus."

In 1907, the first forced sterilization statute was passed in Indiana.[23] By 1914, twelve states had passed similar legislation.[24] In all, over thirty states would go on to pass laws permitting the government to sterilize citizens against their will, and more than 60,000 individuals deemed mentally disabled, ill, or socially disadvantaged would undergo the procedure.[25]

The Buck v. Bell case of 1927 brought the question of the constitutionality of these forced sterilizations before the US Supreme Court. The court decided that the defendant—a woman named Carrie Buck who had been forcibly committed, along with her mother, to a mental institution for having a child out of wedlock—was "feebleminded" and "promiscuous." As a result of this designation, the court ruled that the state was justified in having her sterilized. Writing the Buck v. Bell opinion was Justice Oliver Wendell Holmes, Jr., a rabid eugenicist who advocated executing "unfit" babies.[26] He concluded his opinion with the infamous declaration, "Three generations of imbeciles are enough."[27]

Of course, "feeble-mindedness" and "imbecility" are not clinical descriptions of any sort. What's more, Carrie Buck had conceived her illegitimate child not out of lasciviousness, but because she had been raped by her foster parents' nephew. Even the Virginia government now concedes, "Later evidence eventually showed that Buck and many others had no 'hereditary defects.'"[28] Nonetheless, the case still stood, and the Supreme Court upheld its opinion that governments have the right to stop their citizens from reproducing.

So, who were the financial backers of this dark, largely forgotten chapter of history? Why, the very self-appointed "royalty" who benefit from the pre-ordained conclusions of this pseudoscientific creed, of course. It turns out that Davenport's Eugenics Record Office, which was founded in 1910 by Mary Harriman[29] (of the Bush-Harriman Union Banking Corporation crime family[30]), was funded by the Rockefellers and Carnegies.[31]

Not content to promulgate their newfound eugenics religion only at home, the robber barons were driven to export it abroad. The Rockefellers, for example, helped to foster and fund a budding eugenical movement in Germany.

It is unremarkable that eugenics would find a ready reception in post-WWI Germany. After the arch-polemicist of American eugenical ideas, Madison Grant, argued for Nordic supremacy in *The Passing of the Great Race*— his 1916 opus on the dangers of racial mixing and the need for strict eugenics laws—a young corporal in the German army, Adolf Hitler, wrote a personal letter to Grant, referring to the book as his "bible."[32]

The German who accepted the eugenics baton from the Rockefellers and carried it back to his country was Gustav

Boeters, a physician traveling throughout America as a ship's doctor when he learned of compulsory sterilizations and restrictions on mixed-race marriages. Upon his return to Germany, Boeters began proselytizing for eugenics. He became known as a "sterilization apostle"[33] for his campaign to legalize (and eventually mandate) sterilization of the blind, deaf, "idiotic," and other "feebleminded" individuals.

It wasn't until the 1920s, however, with the formation of the Kaiser Wilhelm Institutes (KWI), that Germany attained a position of preeminence in international eugenics research. KWI—a constellation of associated research institutions born from the prestigious Kaiser Wilhelm Society—hosted research into physics, chemistry, biology, pathology, and other standard fields of scientific inquiry. The network of institutes also included an Institute for Anthropology, Human Heredity and Eugenics; an Institute for Psychology; and an Institute for Brain Research—all three of which would play an integral role in Germany's eugenics program. And, predictably, all three of these institutions were heavily financed by the Rockefeller Foundation.

Advised by long-time Rockefeller/Carnegie researcher Abraham Flexner, the Rockefeller Foundation began pumping money into the Kaiser Wilhelm Institutes in 1922. From 1922 to 1926, the Rockefeller Foundation provided $290,000 in fellowship grants and $120,000 in international fellowships to German researchers in "human psychobiology" and other eugenics-related disciplines.[34]

As Edwin Black documents in *War Against the Weak: Eugenics and America's Campaign to Create a Master Race*, Rockefeller Foundation funding began to ramp up in the late 1920s, almost single-handedly keeping German psychiatric research afloat during the period:

> Rockefeller officials were fascinated with the promise of psychiatry, and they began aligning themselves with German psychiatrists of all stripes. The German Psychiatry Institute was the first to receive big money. In May of 1926, Rockefeller awarded the institute $250,000 shortly after it amalgamated with the Kaiser Wilhelm Institute to become the Kaiser Wilhelm Institute for Psychiatry. The following November, Rockefeller trustees allocated the new institute an additional $75,000.[35]

One of the head researchers at the Kaiser Wilhelm Institute for Psychiatry, a man who would go on to become director of that institute, was Ernst Rüdin. A key architect of Germany's eugenics program in the Third Reich, Rüdin co-edited the official rules and commentary on the Law for the Prevention of Defective Progeny, which was passed on July 14, 1933, less than six months after Hitler was appointed interim chancellor of Germany by President Paul von Hindenburg.

The law—which, as American eugenicists gloated, "reads almost like the 'American model sterilization law'"[36]— mandated the compulsory sterilization of "defectives" in eight different categories: the feeble-minded, schizophrenics, manic depressives, sufferers of Huntington's chorea, epileptics, those with hereditary deformities, the blind, and the deaf. Alcoholics, a ninth category, were to be optionally added to the list, with a caution against inclusion of ordinary drunkards. Under the law, some 200 "Genetic Health Courts" were established to conduct secret proceedings in order to choose suitable sterilization candidates. By the end of 1933, these special courts had already tried 84,600 cases, finding 62,400 of the defendants unfit to breed and ordering their forced sterilization. Between 1933 and 1939, Nazi doctors had sterilized some 400,000 people, the majority of them German citizens living in asylums.[37]

Although the Rockefeller Foundation's director of natural science, Warren Weaver, noted in his 1933 report to the trustees that eugenics "would not be given support" under his proposed program, just one year later he was openly pondering whether we can "develop so sound and extensive a genetics that we can hope to breed, in the future, superior men?"[38] For its part, the Rockefeller Foundation was careful to funnel most of the funds it gave to the KWI through its Paris offices to avoid public scrutiny in the US. That funding continued throughout the 1930s until the outbreak of World War II.

After World War II, the extent of the Third Reich's eugenics atrocities became widely known in the US and elsewhere around the world. For the first time, "eugenics" became a dirty word. The role of organizations like the Rockefeller Foundation in funding the institutions and individuals who formulated the Third Reich's policies, however, went unreported.

Having been saved from the ire of public opinion, these wealthy, eugenics-obsessed "royalty" then sought for a way to continue the pursuit of their eugenics vision out of the glare of the public spotlight. They hit upon the perfect plan: they would not change the ideas or ideals of eugenics, but merely the name itself. This plan was formalized in 1957 by C. P. Blacker, the Honorary Secretary of the Eugenics Society, who distributed a memo on "The Eugenics Society's Future," in which he argued "that the

Society should pursue ends by less obvious means, that is by a policy of crypto-eugenics."[39] Or, as American Eugenics Society co-founder Frederick Osborn wrote even more succinctly in 1968: "Eugenic goals are most likely to be attained under a name other than eugenics."[40]

Accordingly, *Eugenics Quarterly*, a journal co-founded by Osborn for the purpose of publishing eugenics research, changed its name in 1970 to *Social Biology* and then, in 2008, to *Biodemography and Social Biography*.[41] The American Eugenics Society likewise rebranded itself in 1972 as The Society for the Study of Social Biology, and then, more recently, as The Society for Biodemography and Social Biology.[42] The British Eugenics Society followed suit, changing its name to The Galton Institute in 1989,[43] and then changing it again to The Adelphi Genetics Forum in 2021.[44] Throwing the public even further off the trail, the American Eugenics Society moved headquarters in the early 1950s from New Haven, Connecticut, directly into the New York City offices of John D. Rockefeller III's Population Council, from which it began to receive its funding.[45]

From the mid-twentieth century to today, the distasteful ideas of eugenics have been obscured by euphemisms like "population control," "molecular biology," "social demography," and a host of other cryptic terms. But whatever name they're hiding behind at the present moment, eugenicists continue to promulgate the same pseudoscientific dogma to the same ends that Galton and his cohorts promoted it over a century ago: to justify the existence of our modern-day "royalty," the special class who "deserve" to rule over us because of their "superior" genes.

The history of eugenics is as barely known as it is barbaric. It connects some of the wealthiest and most prominent figures of modern times to an atrocious ideology that promotes policies and practices both contemptible and condemnable. Those who remain unaware of the annals of eugenics cannot possibly understand how it has shaped the post-regnal era of wannabe royals, who have retained their superpower status long after the lies of "divine right" and "royal blood" perished.

Indeed, it isn't hard to understand why eugenics captivates the rich and privileged members of the modern ruling class. The canon of eugenics provides exactly what they require: a mythological foundation upon which to build their own wealth and power. Boiled down to its essentials, this myth states precisely the same thing as the old myth of the "divine right" of kings: that the rich and powerful are rich and powerful because they are inherently better than the poor and weak. But by cloaking itself in scientific-sounding arguments instead of appeals to divine authority, eugenics better suits modern, enlightenment-era sensibilities.

Granted, most of today's neo-royalty are not literally "kings" or "queens." Nor are they worshipped as gods on earth. But, just as frighteningly, many have unwittingly bought into the neo-nobility's political worldview. Rallying under the banner of "population control" and "environmentalism" and "sustainability," millions of deluded adults and school children are actually rallying for deindustrialization and depopulation—advocating for the very world that the eugenicists desire. A world where a privileged few rule the impoverished masses. A world where neo-lords subjugate neo-peasants in a neo-feudal society.

These neo-rulers may not wear jewel-encrusted crowns or wield golden scepters, but as long as we keep playing the part of useful idiots in their crypto-eugenic schemes, we may as well bow and curtsy and address them as "Your Majesty."

Here's the good news: no bloody revolution is required to overthrow the gene pool tyrants. Once we expose eugenics for the pseudoscientific claptrap that it is, we will be able to consign it (and its euphemistically named crypto-descendants) to the dustbin of history once and for all.

NOTES

1. "Why were people of noble birth said to be 'blue blooded'?" History Extra. December 1, 2014. archive.is/FUEgC

2. Sherwell, Philip. "Barack Obama's team prepare etiquette and gifts for President's meeting with Queen." The Telegraph. March 28, 2009. archive.fo/YYd77

3. Preston, Hannah. "Donald Trump Touches Queen Elizabeth, Breaks Royal Protocol During Visit to Buckingham Palace." Newsweek. June 3, 2019. archive.fo/VFZPj

4. Khan, Razib. "Inbreeding & the downfall of the Spanish Hapsburgs." Discover Magazine. April 14, 2009. archive.fo/cOOUF

5. Keating, Fiona. "King Tutankhamun: Latest Tests Prove the Boy Pharaoh was Product of Incest." International Business Times. October 19, 2014. archive.fo/Al1L0

6. Quoted in Darwin, Charles. *The Descent of Man*. 2nd edition. (London: John Murray, 1901.) Page 43.

7. Allon, Janet. "American Royalty: Lynn FORESTER De Rothschild Has A New Mission In Life." Avenue Magazine. April 1, 2016. archive.fo/1YSG9

8. "1900: Rediscovery of Mendel's Work." National Human Genome Research Institute. April 22, 2013. archive.fo/M9zYh

9. "Wisconsin river town was focus for eugenics campaign." Daily Herald. September 4, 2011. archive.fo/LkR0i

10. Moore, James. "Good Breeding: Darwin doubted his own family's 'fitness.'" Natural History. November, 2005. Pages 45-46.

11. Smith, Ali. "Celebrating HG Wells's [sic] role in the creation of the UN Declaration of Human Rights." The Guardian. November 20, 2015. archive.fo/TI9o9

12. Wells, H. G. *Anticipations of the Reaction of Mechanical and Scientific Progress upon Human Life and Thought*. (New York: Harper & Brothers, 1902.) Page 342.

13. Aylmer, Maude. *The Authorized Life of Marie C. Stopes.* (London: Williams & Norgate, Ltd., 1924.) Page 226.

14. Stopes, Marie Carmichael. *Radiant Motherhood: A Book for Those Who are Creating the Future.* (London: G. P. Putnam's Sons, Ltd., 1920.) Page 231.

15. Ghosh, Palash. "Marie Stopes: Women's Rights Activist Or Nazi Eugenicist?" International Business Times. October 18, 2012. archive.fo/ELhG2

16. "Marie Stopes." University of London. archive.fo/3WSzD

17. "Marie Stopes." NNDB. 2014. archive.fo/vw3cK

18. Bingham, John. "Royal Mail criticised for stamp honouring 'racist' Marie Stopes." The Telegraph. October 14, 2008. archive.fo/SB5fD

19. Babaluk, Neil. "History Idol: Tommy Douglas." Canada's History. March 10, 2010. archive.fo/TkfIS

20. Douglas, Rev. T. C. "The Problems of the Subnormal Family." McMaster University. March 17, 1933. bit.ly/2JB3mYf

21. Davenport, C. B. "Report of Committee on Eugenics." American Breeders Magazine. Vol. 1. 1910. Page 129.

22. Davenport, Charles B. *Eugenics: The Science of Human Improvement by Better Breeding.* DNA Learning Center. archive.fo/ngC81

23. "1907 Indiana Eugenics Law." Indiana Historical Bureau. archive.fo/UXjP

24. "Eugenics and Sterilization." University of Missouri Libraries. archive.fo/mhBd4

25. Kaelber, Lutz. "Eugenics: Compulsory Sterilization in 50 American States." University of Vermont. archive.fo/Eu9y

26. Schuler, Peter. "Law professor reveals another side to Oliver Wendell Holmes Jr. in new book on former Supreme Court Justice." The University of Chicago Chronicle, Vol. 20, No. 12 (March 15, 2001). archive.fo/xMb7o

27. "Buck v. Bell, 274 U.S. 200." Court Listener. May 2, 1927. archive.fo/p0AHs

28. "Buck v. Bell." The Historical Marker Database. August 11, 2008. archive.fo/8HXXP

29. "Eugenics Record Office." Archives at Cold Spring Harbor Laboratory. archive.fo/4MHcb

30. Aris, Ben and Duncan Campbell. "How Bush's grandfather helped Hitler's rise to power." The Guardian. September 25, 2004. archive.fo/FfYrk

31. Krisch, Joshua A. "When Racism Was a Science." The New York Times. October 13, 2014. archive.fo/uPthx

32. Ryback, Timothy W. "A Disquieting Book From Hitler's Library." The New York Times. December 7, 2011. archive.fo/HURVH

33. Weindling, Paul. Health, Race and German Politics Between National Unification and Nazism, 1870-1945. (Cambridge: Cambridge University Press, 1989.) Page 389.

34. Weindling, Paul. "The Rockefeller Foundation and German Biomedical Sciences, 1920-1940: from Educational Philanthropy to International Science Policy" in Nicolaas A. Rupke, editor. Science, Politics and the Public Good. (London: Macmillan Press, 1988.) Page 127.

35. Black, Edwin. *War Against the Weak: Eugenics and America's Campaign to Create a Master Race*. (Washington, D.C.: Dialog Press, 2012). Page 285.

36. "Eugenical Sterilization in Germany." Eugenical News, Vol. XVIII, No. 5. September-October 1933. Cold Spring Harbor Laboratory's Image Archives on the American Eugenics Movement. archive.fo/h2jbO

37. "Chapter 5 The Nazi Eugenics Program." High School Bioethics Curriculum Project. Georgetown University Kennedy Institute of Ethics. archive.fo/cjLlf

38. Weaver, Warren. "Progress report: the natural sciences." February 14, 1934. Page 43. bit.ly/45r7sut

39. Horvath, Anthony. "Crypto-Eugenics: Quotes of Eugenicists Discussing the Need for a Covert Eugenics Program." Eugenics.us. archive.fo/VT6Nq

40. Osborn, Frederick. *The Future of Human Heredity: An Introduction to Eugenics in Modern Society*. Vermont Eugenics: A Documentary History. archive.is/tsEYm

41. "Biodemography and Social Biology." Taylor & Francis Online. archive.fo/h3b99

42. "Society for Biodemography and Social Biology." Wikipedia. archive.fo/dCI8J

43. "About." The Galton Institute. archive.fo/f8uo1

44. "About us." Adelphi Genetics Forum. archive.is/wz7GK

45. "Background note." American Eugenics Society Records Mss.576.06Am3. American Philosophical Society Library. archive.is/21Nlu

The Ptech Story

THE "WAR ON TERROR" that we are currently living through was birthed on September 11, 2001. The neocons used the events of that day as their excuse to redraw the map of the Middle East, eviscerate the Bill of Rights, erect the Homeland Security police state, and aggressively expand the federal government's size and power.

More recently, however, we have witnessed the birth of a new era: the "war on cyberterror." Attempts to hack into sensitive government computer systems, new forms of ransomware infecting computers around the globe, and online threats to our critical infrastructure are being invoked to justify a rapid expansion of the cybersecurity establishment.

But there has yet to be a catalyzing event in the online sphere equivalent to September 11th. Or, in the parlance of the cyber warmongers, we have yet to see a "cyber 9/11."

Or so we have been led to believe. In actual fact, the most incredible cyberterror attack of all time has already taken place. What's more, it took place on 9/11, the very same day that the "war on terror" was declared. This cyber hit involved government-designated terrorists and a software company with direct access to some of the most sensitive computer systems in the United States. And the story of how it happened is all the more remarkable because almost no one has ever heard it.

Why not? Because the burgeoning cybersecurity establishment must suppress the story.

Why? Because it demonstrates that the very federal agencies that are clamouring for more power on the pretext of the cyberterror hysteria are the exact same entities that were actively complicit in the biggest breach of cybersecurity in history. And, according to the FBI agents whose investigation into the story was suppressed, this cybersecurity "failure" is what allowed 9/11 to occur and the "war on terror" to begin.

This is a story of international terror and terrorist financiers. It stretches from America to Saudi Arabia. It involves businessmen, politicians, and terror networks. And it begins in the most unlikely of places: the offices of an obscure enterprise architecture software firm headquartered in a sleepy Boston suburb.

"Enterprise architecture software" refers to a computer program that visualizes all of an organization's data, including its transactions, interactions, systems, processes, and personnel. The all-encompassing nature of this software effectively gives its user a bird's-eye view of an enterprise, allowing for real-time mapping, visualization, and analysis of a business or agency. One way this type of software can be used is to create extremely detailed and accurate projections of how changes in a business' processes would affect its bottom line. What would happen if two departments were merged, for example, or if a business were to outsource some of its production?

As this software began to mature in the 1990s, however, it went from a merely useful tool to something truly revolutionary. Sophisticated enterprise architecture software could, for instance, analyze all of the transactions taking place across a financial institution in real time and examine that data for possible money laundering operations or rogue traders. Such software could even have potentially detected and identified the insider trading leading up to 9/11 (see "The 9/11 Terror Trade" elsewhere in this book). Combined with rudimentary AI capabilities, this program would not only be able to identify illegal transactions but could stop those transactions as they are happening. If the software were sophisticated enough, it might even be able to warn the company about illegal activity before it takes place.

The utility of enterprise architecture software for organizations of all stripes should be obvious enough. It isn't surprising, then, that numerous government agencies and powerful corporations were hungry for this type of computer program in the 1990s. What is surprising, though, is that so many of them—the Defense Advanced Research Projects Agency (DARPA), the Federal Bureau of Investigation (FBI), the Secret Service, the White House, the Navy, the Air Force, the Federal Aviation Administration (FAA), the North Atlantic Treaty Organization (NATO), IBM, Booz Allen Hamilton, Price Waterhouse Coopers, and a host of other US government agencies, financial institutions, and multinational corporations—turned not to one of the tech giants but to a small, New England-based software firm called "Ptech" to supply this sensitive software.

Ptech, Inc. was founded in Quincy, Massachusetts, in 1994. Within its first two years, it had already secured a contract with DARPA to help transfer commercial software methodologies to the defense sector.[1] Then, in 1997, it gained security clearance to bid on sensitive contracts with the Department of Defense and other government agencies.[2]

By 2001, Ptech had built up a stable of clients that would make any third-party software vendor green with envy. From the inner sanctum of the White House to the headquarters of the FBI, from the basement of the FAA to the boardroom of IBM, some of the most highly secured organizations in the world, running on some of the most protected servers housing the most sensitive data, welcomed Ptech into their midst.

As a provider of enterprise architecture software, Ptech was, in effect, given the keys to the cyber kingdom of the entire US government. Its entry into this cyber sanctum enabled the firm to build detailed pictures of its clients' organizations, including their weaknesses and vulnerabilities. Ptech's analyses showed how these problems could be exploited by those with ill intent, ostensibly to help their customers defend against such attacks. Yet hidden behind its dazzling success was a worrying fact: many of Ptech's top investors and employees had backgrounds that should have raised red flags with its clients.

The firm was launched with $20 million of startup money, $5 million of which was provided by Sarmany Ltd., an investment company owned and controlled by Yassin al-Qadi.[3] Al-Qadi is a wealthy, well-connected Saudi businessman who likes to brag about his acquaintance with Dick Cheney.[4] He also has ties to various Muslim charities that have been accused of funding international terrorism.[5] In the wake of 9/11, al-Qadi was officially declared a Specially Designated Global Terrorist by the US government, and his assets were frozen.[6]

At the time, Ptech's owners and senior managers denied that al-Qadi was involved in any way other than his initial investment. But a 2007 indictment shows that the FBI believed them to be lying.[7] It alleges that al-Qadi had continued to invest millions of dollars in the company through various fronts and investment vehicles.[8] In 2002, al-Qadi's lawyers admitted that it was "possible" a representative for al-Qadi continued to sit on Ptech's board "until recently."[9]

Hussein Ibrahim, Ptech's vice president and chief scientist, was a former vice president of BMI, a New Jersey-based real estate investment firm that was also one of the initial investors in Ptech and that provided financing for Ptech's founding loan.[10] BMI leased computer equipment to Ptech[11] and accepted payments on behalf of Kadi International, owned and operated by none other than Yassin al-Qadi.[12] In 2003, counterterrorism czar Richard Clarke acknowledged that "[w]hile BMI held itself out publicly as a financial services provider for Muslims in the United States, its investor list suggests the possibility this facade was just a cover to conceal terrorist support."[13]

Another colourful character connected to Ptech was Suheil Laher, who served as Ptech's chief software architect. When he wasn't writing the code that would provide Ptech with detailed operational blueprints of the most sensitive agencies in the US government, he was writing articles in praise of Islamic holy war.[14] Laher was also fond of quoting Abdullah Azzam, Osama Bin Laden's mentor and the head of Maktab al-Khidamat, which was the precursor to Al-Qaeda.

That such an unlikely bunch was given access to some of the most sensitive agencies in the US federal government is startling enough. That they were operating software that allowed them to map, analyze, and access every process and operation within these agencies for the purpose of finding systemic weak points is even more astonishing. Most disturbing of all, though, is the connection between Ptech and the very agencies that are to blame for the events of September 11, 2001.

For two years prior to 9/11, Ptech was working to identify potential problems or weaknesses in the FAA's response plans to events like a terrorist hijacking of a plane over US airspace. According to its own business plan for the FAA contract, Ptech was granted access to every process and system in the FAA dealing with crisis response protocols. This included analyzing the FAA's "network management, network security, configuration management, fault management, performance management, application administration, network accounting management, and user help desk operation."[15] In other words, Ptech had free rein to examine every system and process the FAA uses to deal with the exact type of event that would come to pass on 9/11. As if that weren't astounding enough, Ptech was tasked with specifically analyzing the potential interoperability problems between the FAA, NORAD, and the Pentagon in the event of an emergency over US airspace.

The scope of its work with these agencies gave Ptech operational information about the systems that the FAA, the North American Aerospace Defense Command (NORAD), and others employed during crisis response exercises like Vigilant Guardian, the NORAD exercise that was taking place on 9/11.[16] These exercises included simulations of hijacked jets being flown into New York[17] and hijacked jets being flown into government buildings.[18] This is significant because there is every indication that the drills were devised to create confusion between them and the real-world events NORAD was responding to that day.

As researcher Michael Ruppert points out, a rogue agent

with access to a Ptech backdoor into the FAA's systems could have been deliberately inserting fake blips onto the FAA's radars on 9/11.[19] That scenario would explain the source of the "phantom Flight 11" that the FAA reported to NORAD at 9:24 a.m. (well after Flight 11 had already hit the World Trade Center), a report whose source the 9/11 Commission claims it was unable to find.[20]

In short, on the morning of 9/11, Ptech's software—designed for the express purpose of giving its users a complete overview of all the data flowing through an organization in real time—was running on the very systems that were supposed to defend against 9/11-style attacks. The father of enterprise architecture himself, John Zachman, explained that with Ptech-type software installed on a sensitive server, "[y]ou would know where the access points are, you'd know how to get in, you would know where the weaknesses are, you'd know how to destroy it."[21]

This is where the FBI enters the story.

In the late 1990s, Robert Wright—an FBI special agent in the Chicago field office—was running Vulgar Betrayal, an operation tracking terrorist financing.[22] From the very start, the probe was hampered by higher-ups; Wright and his associates were not even allocated adequate computer equipment to carry out their work.[23] Through Wright's foresight and perseverance, however, the investigation managed to score some victories, including the seizure of $1.4 million in US funds that traced back to Yassin al-Qadi.[24] Wright was pleased when a senior agent was assigned to help dig up info on "the founder and the financier of Ptech," but the agent did no work and merely pushed papers during his entire time on the case.[25]

Shortly after the 1998 African embassy bombings, Vulgar Betrayal began to uncover a money trail linking al-Qadi to that attack. Yet, according to Wright, when he proposed a criminal investigation into the al-Qadi links, his supervisor flew into a rage, saying, "You will not open criminal investigations. I forbid any of you. You will not open criminal investigations against any of these intelligence subjects."[26] Wright was taken off the Vulgar Betrayal case the next year, and the operation itself was shut down in 2000.

Meanwhile, in the aftermath of 9/11, Indira Singh was looking for enterprise architecture software to implement the next generation of risk management for JPMorgan Chase, where she worked as a risk management consultant. Impressed by Ptech's client list, Singh invited the firm to demonstrate its software to the bank. In performing her due diligence on the deal, though, she soon discovered the connections between Ptech and international terrorist financing.

Singh worked exhaustively to document and uncover these links in an effort to persuade the FBI agents in Boston to open their own investigation into Ptech. However, as she later related to Bonnie Faulkner on KPFA's *Guns and Butter* radio program, one Bureau agent told her that she herself was in a better position to get to the bottom of the case than was anyone inside the FBI.[27] Despite the persistent efforts of Singh and the testimony of company insiders, the FBI did not inform any of the agencies contracting with Ptech that there were concerns about the company or its software.[28]

Finally, in late 2002, Operation Green Quest—a US Customs Service-led multi-agency investigative unit that had been formed in October 2001 to do surveillance and interdiction of terrorist financing sources—raided the offices of Ptech, which it suspected had ties to al-

Qadi and terror financing. But that very same day, White House Press Secretary Ari Fleischer declared the company and its software safe. Mainstream news articles on the raid were at pains to include Ptech's denial that a raid had taken place. Instead, Ptech officials insisted they had "granted access" to investigators. They also claimed the government had assured them that "neither Ptech nor its officers or employees are targets of the government's investigation."[29]

The Ptech raid resulted in no indictments. Neither al-Qadi nor anyone else at the company was charged with any crime. Instead, Michael Chertoff, then head of the Department of Justice's Criminal Division, led a controversial effort to move Green Quest under the control of the FBI,[30] and, in June 2003, the operation was disbanded.[31]

For his efforts, Chertoff was rewarded with a position as a United States circuit judge and, in 2005, was appointed as United States Secretary of Homeland Security. Meanwhile, after years of legal wrangling, al-Qadi succeeded in having his name removed from the Specially Designated Global Terrorist list.[32] The Ptech cover-up now complete, the press went silent on the story.

The Final Report of the 9/11 Commission, released in 2004, does not mention Ptech. Given the remarkable information that had been uncovered about this company's links to both the US government and terror financing, Ptech's absence from the report is perplexing, to say the least. But the omission became positively ominous when it was discovered that 9/11 Commission co-chair Thomas Kean made $24 million dollars off a land deal with the Ptech-linked BMI.[33]

Seven years after the raid on Ptech, in July 2009, there finally appeared to be a break in the FBI case: the Bureau's

Boston Field Office unsealed a 2007 indictment of Oussama Abdul Ziade, Ptech's former CEO, and Buford George Peterson, its former CFO and COO. The indictment accused the pair of knowingly omitting the extent of al-Qadi's investments and ties with Ptech when they submitted a loan application to the US Small Business Administration (SBA), a federal agency.[34]

Peterson was arrested at John F. Kennedy Airport in New York the same day the indictment was unsealed. But his 2010 trial ended in a hung jury when the evidence showed that it was Ziade, not Peterson, who prepared the loan application to the SBA. In 2012, Peterson's indictment was dismissed by the United States Attorney for the District of Massachusetts.[35] Ziade, having fled to Lebanon, has never been arrested or faced trial under the indictment.

For over two decades, investigations into Ptech, its employees, and its investors have been stifled, suppressed, or derailed by people in positions of power. That suits the US Cyber Command, the NSA, the FBI, and all of their cronies in the terror-industrial complex just fine. For, as far as they're concerned, the entire Ptech affair—exposing as it does the culpability and potential complicity of the FBI and other federal agencies tasked with "protecting" the "homeland"—is best left swept under the rug and never spoken of again.

Nonetheless, the Ptech saga is proof that we have already endured one "cyber 9/11"—and that it happened on 9/11 itself.

NOTES

1. Corbin, Lisa. "Tools of the Trade." Government Executive. September 1, 1996. archive.is/jQQvs

2. "Raided al Qaeda-linked tech firm got Clinton clearance to work for FAA, FBI, Pentagon." Center for Security Policy. December 6, 2002. archive.is/J5hvF

3. Pope, Justin. "Software company tries to survive terrorism investigation." Daily Herald. January 4, 2003. archive.is/dhNO5

4. "Treasury action smacks of arrogance, violates human rights, says Al-Qadi." Saudia-Online. October 14, 2001. archive.is/eJUeF

5. Letter from David D. Aufhauser to M. Claude Nicati. "Re: Yassin A. Kadi." November 29, 2001. Pages 36-39. archive.is/FfF7O

6. "Treasury Department Releases List of 39 Additional Specially Designated Global Terrorists." U.S. Department of the Treasury. October 12, 2001. archive.is/QS0Y

7. "Former Ptech Officer Arrested for SBA Loan Fraud." U.S. Attorney's Office, District of Massachusetts. July 15, 2009. archive.is/l0NAf

8. "United States of America v. Oussama Abdul Ziade and Buford George Peterson." United States District Court, District of Massachusetts. Indictment. March 1, 2007. archive.is/fr8zp

9. Hosenball, Mark. "High-Tech Terror Ties?" Newsweek. December 5, 2002. archive.is/om7kz

10. Guidera, Jerry and Glenn R. Simpson. "U.S. Probes Terror Ties To Boston Software Firm." The Wall Street Journal. December 9, 2002. archive.is/AfPQ5

11. See endnote 3.

12. "Boim v. Quranic Literacy Institute." United States District Court for the Northern District of Illinois, Eastern Division. Complaint. May 15, 2000. The Investigative Project on Terrorism. bit.ly/2zcXnl9

13. "Statement of Richard A. Clarke Before the United States Senate Banking Committee." The Investigative Project on Terrorism. October 22, 2003. bit.ly/2yDrd5m

14. Ehrenfeld, Rachel. "The Business of Terror." Front Page Magazine. June 17, 2005. archive.is/RuleH

15. Kane, Michael. "Ptech, 9/11, and USA-Saudi Terror, Part II." From The Wilderness Publications. 2005. archive.is/Ywa9e

16. "Profile: Vigilant Guardian." History Commons. archive.is/Desx

17. Fenton, Kevin. "Two Days Before 9/11, Military Exercise Simulated Suicide Hijack Targeting New York." History Commons Groups. June 14, 2009. archive.is/5kkwP

18. Lumpkin, John J. "Agency planned exercise on Sept. 11 built around a plane crashing into a building." SFGate.com. August 21, 2002. archive.is/Xwmd8

19. See endnote 15.

20. "Improvising a Homeland Defense: Staff Statement No. 17." National Commission on Terrorist Attacks Upon the United States. Page 12. archive.is/voBHf

21. "The I Team Investigates P-Tech." WBZ 4. December 9, 2002. bit.ly/2fYrOmR

22. Crogan, Jim. "A Vulgar Betrayal." LA Weekly. August 26, 2004. archive.is/WMLAx

23. "Whistleblower Complains of FBI Obstruction." Fox News. May 30, 2002. archive.is/YgDtd

24. Johnson, Jeff. "Tearful FBI Agent Apologizes To Sept. 11 Families and Victims." CNSNews.com. May 30, 2002. archive.is/cNSHd

25. "Context of 'April 1998: FBI Agent Stifles Investigation into Ptech Figures.'" History Commons. archive.is/fwUjV

26. Ross, Brian and Vic Waler. "FBI Called off Terror Investigations." ABCNews. December 19, 2002. archive.is/DlSi9

27. "Ground Zero 9/11: Blueprint For Terror, Part One - Indira Singh, #66." Guns and Butter. Re-aired October 7, 2015. bit.ly/2yeHf4l

28. "How Much Did The FBI Know About P Tech?" cbs4boston.com. December 9, 2002. bit.ly/2yebWGV

29. See endnote 3.

30. Isikoff, Michael. "Terror Watch: Whose War on Terror?" Newsweek. April 8, 2003. archive.is/ykerE

31. "Subject: Investigations of Terrorist Financing, Money Laundering, and Other Financial Crimes." United States General Accounting Office. February 20, 2004. Page 16. bit.ly/3yPrAu2

32. "Counter Terrorism Designation Removals." U.S. Department of the Treasury. November 26, 2014. archive.is/xp3eA

33. Caylor, John. "Al-Qaeda/Hamas Financial Network Exposed." Insider-Magazine.org. bit.ly/3V884R2

34. See endnote 8.

35. "All Charges Dismissed Against Buford George Peterson, says Attorney Peter Parker." PR Newswire. May 3, 2012. archive.is/Z91Rn

Selling Your Soul for a Matrix Steak

IT MAY NOT BE the first scene that comes to mind when you think of *The Matrix*, but if you've seen the movie, you probably remember when Cypher is in the restaurant telling Agent Smith why he's selling out Neo and his friends. "I know that this steak doesn't exist," he says, eyeing a juicy red chunk of meat quivering on the end of his fork. "I know when I put it in my mouth, the matrix is telling my brain that it is juicy and delicious." And I bet you remember that moment when he stuffs the meat into his mouth, closing his eyes in delight as he mutters, "Ignorance is bliss."

Long story short for those who haven't seen the Hollywood action flick, the "matrix" is a computer-generated illusion designed to trick humans into believing that they are living in 1999. In the fictional world of the movie, however, it's actually the twenty-second century, and humanity has been enslaved by a swarm of dastardly robots.

Imprisoned in a vast network of pods, the humans' bodies are being harvested for electrical energy to power the very robots holding them in bondage. Everyone has been jacked into the matrix, a virtual reality role-playing game designed to prevent humans from ever learning the truth of their plight—much less ever doing anything about it.

In one sense, Cypher is completely correct: He is not in a restaurant, he is not eating a steak, and he is not, in fact, talking to anyone. All of the things he is experiencing are an illusion, conjured into existence by an elaborate computer program and fed into his central nervous system. But his brain is tricking him into believing that he's eating a delicious steak and drinking vintage wine, and that's good enough for him.

Now, what if I were to tell you that those dollars or pesos or euros or yen that you carry around in your wallet have all the unreality of a matrix steak? What if you've toiled your entire adult life in a store or an office or a factory, day in and day out, year after year after year, for something that isn't even real? And what if—just as in the film—someone, somewhere, someday could simply throw a switch, making all of those matrix steaks you've spent your whole life chasing simply disappear like that? Would that devastate you?

OK, I know what you're thinking: "*Whaaaaat?* You're comparing our monetary system to *The Matrix*? Next, you're going to tell us there's an army of robots pumping a fake reality into our brain to enslave us!"

Don't be ridiculous. I didn't say anything about *robots*.

But let's take a step back for a second. After all, no one can be told what the Matrix is. You have to see it for yourself.

So, take a look.

Open up your wallet. Go on, open it. If you're lucky enough to have one of those pieces of paper that passes for money where you live, take it out. What do you see? Is it merely a colourful slip of dyed cotton?

But how can this be?

People are turned to crime and vice in pursuit of this? Great loves are torn asunder for the lack of it? Wars are fought, murder committed, and honourable men brought to disgrace in the name of these pieces of paper?

Imagine a Martian landing on our planet for the first time and observing the human species. He watches us scrambling from home to office to home, day after day. He sees us stealing from the store, scamming our neighbours, betraying our loved ones. All for what? These elusive scraps of paper? It makes no sense to him. There must be more to this system than meets the eye, he speculates. The coloured cotton these humans carry around in their wallets must be of great worth. Why else would they value it so?

To get a handle on the real worth (or lack) thereof of these paper bills, let's consider an extreme example: counterfeit money. Counterfeit bills look like real money. They feel like real money. An inattentive shopkeeper may accept a crisp C-note from a customer and value it exactly as he would any other hundred-dollar bill he receives. But the moment it is revealed to be a counterfeit, it's rendered valueless. Not because the bill itself has changed but because the shopkeeper's perception of it has changed.

These observations are hardly revolutionary. We all know that money is simply coloured ink on paper, just as we all know that a Monet is simply oil on canvas. But we also understand that the ink on the paper and the oil on the canvas each represent something. In the case of a Monet, the brushstrokes may represent the French countryside or a bowl of fruit or a celebration of Bastille Day. In the case of money, the paper represents underlying value, a form of wealth. It's a nebulous product that results when we mix our time and labour with the world around us, whether in building a house or writing a computer program or refining a barrel of oil. In other words, that coloured paper you're holding in your hand is the physical representation of an idea.

"Yeah, well, so what?" you may be asking.

In order to understand why money as an idea is an important—even revolutionary—concept, we have to look into the origins of those pieces of paper. As we learned in history class, money didn't always look like the cash we use today. Many objects have been used as money at different times and in different places, from seashells to lengths of wood to playing cards.

Some types of objects have been used as money more often throughout history than others. Precious metals, for instance, by dint of their unique properties, have been used for trading not only within communities but also between communities. Portable, divisible, malleable, and durable, precious metals are scarce enough to be valuable in their own right, and they are also prized for their beauty as ornaments or jewelry. Precious metals don't just represent value, they contain value.

To "primitive" man it only made sense that coins forged from these precious metals would make an ideal medium of exchange. What could be easier than carrying a purse full of these coins to the marketplace and exchanging them for goods and services. Governments may come and go, civilizations may rise and fall, and the faces embossed on the coins may change, but the utility of gold and silver never disappears. Why would anyone need to use another form of money?

But then a funny thing happened. In 1095, Pope Urban II called for a Holy Crusade against the Turks, who were threatening the Christian Byzantine Empire. For the next two centuries, Crusaders and pilgrims traveled from far and wide to Jerusalem to prove their piety. In those days, it wasn't exactly a case of calling up your travel agent and booking the next flight. Travelling long distances was an expensive, arduous, and often dangerous proposition. Carrying around all the coins necessary for feeding, clothing, and lodging their small entourage as they made their way from town to town, the Crusaders were easy prey for highwaymen.

After a particularly bloody massacre of Christian pilgrims at the River Jordan in 1119, King Baldwin II of Jerusalem acceded to a request from Hugues de Payens, a French knight, to create an order of monk-knights who would protect the pilgrims in the holy land. With this act, the legendary Poor Fellow-Soldiers of Christ and of the Temple of Solomon—more commonly known as the Knights Templar—were born.

The strategy that the Knights Templar devised to protect the riches of the pilgrims and Crusaders on their perilous journey was as ingenious as it was devious. At the beginning of his trip, a Crusader would deposit his metal money with the Templars and would in turn receive a certificate for that money. Anywhere along the main routes, the Crusader could give his certificate to the local Templars and they would pay him back as much of his original deposit as he wanted. All the Templars asked in return was to hold a portion of the Crusader's land in his absence. They could sell whatever was produced from that land while he was away; that was their profit.

An idea was born.

The idea spread. Villagers began to store their gold in goldsmiths' vaults for safekeeping. In return, they would receive slips of paper showing how much gold they had deposited. Since it was easier to exchange the slips of paper than the coins themselves, before long the villagers began to regard the paper as money. The goldsmiths, realizing that only a fraction of the villagers ever wanted to withdraw their gold at any one time, began to print more certificates than they had gold in the vaults. As long as everyone didn't come to collect their gold at the same time, no one would notice that the goldsmiths were printing paper money out of thin air.

Do you smell that? Those goldsmiths just grilled the very first matrix steaks.

I'm sure I don't have to tell you the rest of the story. About how the central banks were formed. About how the financial system developed. About fractional reserve banking. Fiat money. Stock markets. Derivatives. Collateralized debt obligations. Subprime mortgages. Fannie and Freddie, Lehman Brothers. AIG. I think you all know how that narrative goes. And even if you don't, you can work it out *a priori*.

For, you see, it all goes back to the advent of paper bills. Once we've accepted them as money, once we've decided that the matrix steak is a steak, the rest of the story is inevitable. Today's Templars—the central bankers—can replace our paper dollars for paper stocks and bonds and Treasuries. They can tell us this matrix hamburger is just as tasty as the prime rib we used to have, and, deluded wage slaves that we are, we'll gladly eat it up. After all, one illusion is as good as another.

It's only when the stock market collapses that we find out all they really did was swap our matrix steaks for matrix ground beef. Not only is it not real, it doesn't even taste good.

From here, it's just a question of how long they can con us into accepting ever-less-substantial matrix money before the entire economic house of cards comes tumbling down. They've already replaced the matrix ground beef of stocks and bonds with the matrix spam of derivatives.

And they've served us the matrix "mystery meat" of collateralized debt obligations. And they've force-fed us a chemically processed meat substitute with cardboard filler and called it mortgage-backed securities. And on and on and on . . . .

Does any of what I've said bother you yet? Or are you still content with your lot despite knowing that all of the "wealth" in your wallet is nothing more than matrix money?

"It's just an illusion," you snort, a hunk of juicy, red matrix steak quivering on the end of your fork. "What does it really matter? As long as everyone believes in the illusion, no one's the worse off, right?" And, as if to prove your point, you shove the tender matrix meat into your mouth, savouring every bite. "Ignorance is bliss!"

But hold on a second. Before you swallow that steak, take a look at that bill in your hand one more time. Who issued it? It should say right on there. In Canada it's the Bank of Canada. In Japan it's the Bank of Japan. In England it's the Bank of England. In Europe it's the European Central Bank. In the US it's the Federal Reserve. The bank's name is on the bill because it belongs to the bank. Not to you.

I'll let you in on the real secret—the real key to the entire matrix of control. Starting with the Bank of England in the seventeenth century and spreading slowly around the globe, the central government of country after country has ceded its power to print debt-free fiat money to privately owned central banks. Let me repeat that: government after government in country after country has allowed private shareholders to set up unaccountable institutions headed by unelected bankers and granted them the power to create money out of thin air.

But wait, it gets worse. As everyone knows, governments have debts, and they have to pay money to service those debts. But to whom are these governments in debt? Why, to the bankers, of course!

Not only have governments given away the power to print money to private bankers, but they then turn around and borrow that same money from the banks. And since we live in a system where every new dollar is created as debt owed—*with interest*—to the bankers, as soon as the first paper bill goes into circulation, there is automatically more money owed to the bankers than there is money that exists. Meanwhile, when the money to pay the interest on that paper bill is created, the government goes *further* into debt to the banks. That accumulating debt includes more interest payable to (guess who?) the bankers, and so on, and so on, *ad infinitum*.

Since the money itself is created from debt, it is mathematically impossible to ever pay off the debt. It will never be retired. Your taxes will never go down—not because they actually pay for governmental "services," but because they are what the government uses to secure the debt. The debt that the government has created in your name. The debt that you now owe to the bankers.

You will have to work longer and longer hours to pay higher and higher taxes to service the larger and larger debt forever and ever until the day you die—as will your children, as will their children, all the way to the crack of doom.

There's no way to sugarcoat it: you've been a slave to the bankers since the day you were born. We all have. And you can blame it all on the innocent, colourful little pieces of paper you hold in your hand.

But we're not done with our catalogue of matrix woes

yet. It gets even worse. With a simple change in the public's perception, the entire monetary order can come crashing down—whether by a dollar crash, a bank run, a financial panic or some other dramatic event—and all the matrix steaks will disappear back into the abyss from which they were conjured. For those who think such a thing unlikely, I'm here to say that it is not only likely, *it's inevitable*. Every fiat currency eventually collapses.

In Weimar Germany, the *papiermark* became less valuable than toilet paper. People pushed wheelbarrows full of bills down to the store to buy a loaf of bread. If they went to a restaurant, they would pay for their food at the beginning of the meal, because they knew prices would rise before they finished eating. Germans in the 1920s knew the real value of a matrix steak.

And now, as the illusionary stability of the post-WWII monetary order—the order that has reigned since King Dollar took over as the world reserve currency—comes to an end and as more currency crashes and bank runs and digital money and all manner of monetary madness set in, where are we heading? Towards a revolution? A complete overthrow of the existing monetary system?

Yes, hopefully. But the system wasn't set up overnight, and it won't be dismantled overnight.

There will be a process of gradual change, and that change will only come about through organized, concerted, informed action.

It will require us to use complementary currencies, local exchange trading systems (LETS), mutual credit, and other means of transacting with one another .

It will mean supporting credit unions and alternative payment systems.

It will mean developing agoristic alternatives to the state-controlled markets.

It will mean exploring cryptocurrencies.

It will mean fostering community organizations and farmer's markets.

And it will mean finding a million other ways to harness the real wealth of our labour in order to help build the world we want to live in.

But something everyone can do right here, right now, is to make the conscious decision to see through the matrix. To recognize these pieces of paper for what they really are: eye-catching, mouth-watering, but completely valueless matrix steaks.

Because there will come a time in your life, as it does in everyone's life, when you will be asked to compromise your ideals, your beliefs—the very core of who you are—for a few of these coloured scraps of paper.

So, how about you? What lengths are you willing to go to in your quest for the almighty dollar? If someone asks you to sell your soul for a matrix steak, are you, like Cypher, going to close your eyes and take a blissful bite?

How to *Really* Defeat Globalism

IN JULY 2013, US Senator Dianne Feinstein presented a most unusual map during a meeting of the Senate Judiciary Committee. The map showed the geographical location of fifty-four "terror events" that the National Security Agency (NSA) claimed, without proof, to have disrupted under Section 702 of the FISA Amendments Act and Section 215 of the Patriot Act—two pieces of controversial post-9/11 legislation that granted the government sweeping new wiretap and data collection powers.[1]

What was unusual about this map was not that the NSA would create a visual aid to help a high-ranking senator promote tyrannical surveillance programs on the Senate floor. Sadly, that is exactly the type of behaviour we would expect from the NSA. No, what was peculiar about the map was that it was broken into four regions: Europe, Africa, Asia, and Homeland.

Homeland?

Yes, Homeland. That region of the globe formerly known as "North America and Central America," a section stretching from Ellesmere Island in Canada's Arctic all the way down to the tropical beaches of Panama on the equator, is now apparently referred to by the NSA as "Homeland."

Understandably, this cartographical curiosity caused a good deal of consternation in those formerly sovereign nations that were now suddenly designated as extensions of the USA's Homeland.

The mainstream media made merry with the situation. Canada.com tweeted, "We did it! Canada is now part of the American 'homeland,'"[2] and *The Atlantic* greeted its onetime-neighbours-turned-fellow-citizens with a hearty "Welcome to the Homeland, Mexico and Canada!"[3]

Levity aside, the incident did raise the question: What exactly is the "Homeland?" Does it have a legal definition?

Why, yes it does, actually, although you'd have a hard time finding it anywhere on the US Department of Homeland Security's (DHS) official website. Scattered throughout the mission statement, organizational chart, history, and other pages detailing DHS activities and listing its personnel, you'll see numerous references to "the nation," "the homeland," "the U.S. homeland," and various other designations, but nary a mention of what these phrases actually mean or of their actual territorial boundaries.

In order to discover what "the homeland" is, you'll have to turn to The Homeland Security Act of 2002.[4] There, in the definitions section, you'll find: "Each of the terms 'American homeland' and 'homeland' means the United States."

Well, that settles that, doesn't it?

Doesn't it?

If only. In reality, the NSA's reimagining of the Homeland's borders was no mere geographical gaffe. Rather, it reveals the desired end goal of a plan that is now being formulated to merge Canada, the US, and Mexico into a united "continental security perimeter." This merger, should it proceed as envisioned, would include standardized security procedures and information-sharing as part of an even-longer-term plot to ultimately synthesize the three countries into one European Union-like regional government.

The agenda to integrate the Americas was kick-started—like so many other despotic schemes, including the formation of the DHS itself—by the false flag terror events of September 11, 2001. The toxic dust was still settling on Ground Zero when then-Homeland Security Secretary Tom Ridge and then-Deputy Prime Minister John Manley signed the US and Canada Smart Border Declaration.[5] This declaration included vows to coordinate security and law enforcement efforts between the two nations.

Eventually, Smart Border was superseded by the Security and Prosperity Partnership (SPP), a trilateral framework between the governments of the US, Canada, and Mexico that began a process of regulatory integration. Documents obtained in 2007 by The Corbett Report revealed that the SPP was controlled by the North American Competitiveness Council (NACC)—a "body created by Leaders in 2006 to give the private sector a formal role in providing advice on how to enhance competitiveness in North America." Furthermore, the SPP process itself turned out to be an initiative launched by the Canadian Council of Chief Executives (CCOCE) in January 2003.[6]

The CCOCE, founded in 1976 but renamed in 2016 to the decidedly friendlier-sounding "Business Council of Canada," is comprised of the CEOs of 150 leading Canadian businesses. Together, these companies "account for more than half the value of the Toronto Stock Exchange."[7]

Based on its self-description, you'd be forgiven for cynically concluding that the Business Council of Canada has a number of high-level government officials from all three North American nations in its back pocket. You'd be forgiven, that is, because you'd be right. In fact, you don't have to look very hard to find evidence of this political collusion. The Council's President and CEO is none other than aforementioned Smart Border Declaration signatory and ex-Deputy Prime Minister of Canada John Manley.[8]

When some of these troubling connections came to light, Canadian Prime Minister Stephen Harper tried to laugh off accusations that the SPP represented a nascent North American Union. He insisted that conspiracy theories about "interplanetary" highways were untrue and that the pact was more concerned with "the rules for jelly bean contents" and other mundane matters.[9]

But the public was having none of it. After unprecedented protests at the SPP meeting in Montebello, Quebec, in late 2007 (including the now-infamous exposure of police *agents provocateurs* within the ranks of the protestors[10]), negotiations drew to a standstill. The SPP itself was subsequently shelved in 2009.

Needless to say, work on integrating the governments of North America continued behind the scenes under different auspices.

In February 2008, for instance, the Canadian and American militaries signed an agreement allowing troops of either country to cross the border and carry out operations in the other country in the event of an emergency, such as civil unrest.[11]

Then, in 2010, the two countries signed a shiprider agreement, allowing specially designated vessels to patrol the shared waterways of the two countries. The ships would be operated by a joint crew consisting of both

Canadian and American law enforcement.[12]

The following year, President Obama and Prime Minister Harper issued a declaration asserting a shared security perimeter for the two countries.[13] Broken into two "action plans," Beyond the Border[14] and the Regulatory Cooperation Council,[15] the 2011 agreement reaffirmed the commitment to a jointly policed security perimeter and to further harmonization of business regulations. Ominously, it also noted that Canada and the US "expect to work together with third countries and with international organizations" in order to "enhance standards that contribute to our overall security."

The deeper truth is that none of these agreements, pacts, partnerships, declarations, or resolutions spontaneously arose out of the ether. They are the result of decades of plans for a merging of national governments into regional entities that themselves will be subsumed behind the scenes by international trade pacts, treaties, and agreements, all of which will eventually form a de facto world government.

The plan to merge the US, Canada, and Mexico into a single "North American Community" was set in motion by three organizations: the Council on Foreign Relations (CFR), the Canadian Council of Chief Executives (now the Business Council of Canada), and the Consejo Mexicano de Asuntos Internacionales (COMEXI). In 2005 they released their blueprint for that consolidation, titled "Building a North American Community."[16] The document, created by a task force co-chaired by (surprise, surprise) John Manley, lays out two CFR visions—one for "Making North America Safer" by implementing a continental security perimeter; the other for "Creating a North American Economic Space" by harmonizing regulations and lowering barriers for workers looking to cross the borders for employment. Incredibly, the report even cites the Bilderberg Group as a model for the task force's proposed "North American Advisory Council," a body that would appoint "independent" advisors to "provide a public voice for North America." (For more on the Bilderberg Group, its history, and its activities, please see "Why We Must Oppose Bilderberg" elsewhere in this book.)

These three partners are advancing their concept of a "North American community" through a number of channels. As outlined in the CFR's own *Foreign Affairs* magazine in 2008, their plan is more than a political process. It is a cultural phenomenon, fostered by the creation of numerous "North American studies" programs at top-tier colleges and universities.[17]

Independent researcher Dana Gabriel provided details of this cultural conditioning in an article published on The Corbett Report in 2010:

> The Center for North American Studies at American University in Washington, D.C. "was established to educate a new generation of students, to promote policy debate among the governments and the public, and to undertake research on ideas for a continental future." Arizona State University has also created the North American Center for Transborder Studies, whose mission "is to advance greater understanding of border and trilateral issues in North America by supporting scholars who contribute to the development of innovative theory and actionable policy analysis regarding these issues." The North American Integration and Development Center based at the University of California, Los Angeles, "seeks to

build linkages among a wide variety of institutions, organizations, and community groups in order to promote North American integration." These various centers, along with other initiatives, are part of the ongoing efforts to further condition and train a new generation into accepting a North American consciousness.[18]

In other words, behind the feel-good blather about "advanc[ing] greater understanding" and "build[ing] linkages" is a stomach-turning reality: regional consolidation, despite donning the garb of education, is a purely politically motivated, corporate-driven, cronyist nightmare. Equally sickening is the realization that the process did not start with the consolidation of North America into a single administrative unit and that it will not stop at the borders of this reimagined "Homeland." Rather, it is a worldwide phenomenon with an end goal of nothing less than the consolidation of global political control in the hands of a few powerful oligarchs.

This process of global political consolidation is already underway and moving ahead, if fitfully, on other continents.

- Africa has already taken steps toward the creation of the African Union.[19]

- The leaders of the European Union continue attempting to expand their power over Europe despite a string of startling failures.[20]

- Vladimir Putin's Eurasian Economic Union was officially birthed in 2015.[21]

- The much-discussed "BRICS" association of Brazil, Russia, India, China, and South Africa, first dreamed up by the chairman of Goldman Sachs,[22] presses on with its own attempts to harmonize regulations and bring down borders.

All the while, the World Trade Organization, the World Health Organization, the United Nations, the International Monetary Fund, the World Bank, the Organisation for Economic Co-operation and Development, the World Customs Organization, and a thousand other international institutions, organizations, frameworks, and quasi-governmental structures persevere in the shadows, intent on achieving the "global governance" about which the arch-globalist oligarchs openly boast.

So, was the map of "the Homeland" that Senator Feinstein presented—a map spanning *all* of North America *and* Central America *and* the Caribbean—simply a case of a mapmaker's innocent mistake? Or a fanciful exaggeration? Or was this infographic one more attempt by the globalists to acclimate us to the inevitability of regional government?

Assuming we settle on the latter possibility, then the question is: how do we best oppose this globalist agenda? Shall we cling fast to the nation-state framework as our bulwark against the centralized control structure? Do we elect this or that president in the hopes that he or she will reverse the tide of this generations-old plan for world domination by the money printers, kingmakers, and oligarchs?

Certainly, either of these moves would make sense if the natural, rational, and defensible structure for the preservation of human freedom were the nation-state. But what if the nation-state is neither a natural institution nor one dedicated to the preservation of liberty for all?

What if regionalism and nationalism are not in fact opposites, as we are often told they are, but merely different sides of the same coin? And what if that coin is weighted, so that any battle between these two ideas is always going to arrive at the same conclusion: global government?

To answer these questions, let's go back in time to nineteenth-century Jena. History buffs will immediately recognize this modest city in the heart of modern-day Germany as the site of one of Napoleon's great battles, a crushing and decisive victory over the Prussian Army that resulted in the subordination of the Kingdom of Prussia to the French Empire. So humiliating was this defeat that it inspired one Nuremberg bookseller, Johann Philipp Palm, to distribute a pamphlet titled *Deutschland in seiner tiefen Erniedrigung* (*Germany in Its Deep Humiliation*), which urged the Germans to resist their French conquerors by force of arms. His reward? Palm was executed by a French firing squad.[23]

Palm's martyrdom became a rallying cry for the nascent German nation and inspired Johann Gottlieb Fichte, an influential philosopher with a reputation as a revolutionary firebrand, to deliver his *Reden an die deutsche Nation* (*Addresses to the German Nation*). In this landmark series of lectures, delivered between December 1807 and March 1808, Fichte laid the philosophical cornerstone of an idea that was just beginning to take shape at that time: the nation-state. Until the late Middle Ages, the Western world had been almost universally organized under monarchies, in which kings and queens claimed the divine right to rule. The revolutions in the United States and France at the end of the eighteenth century were expressions of the death throes of this form of government, though it was not yet clear on what basis the state would be organized in the post-monarchical, post-feudal world.

Speaking "for Germans only and of Germans only," Fichte outlined the role that he believed the nation-state should play in shaping and molding his countrymen—who were then living in a variety of small duchies, kingdoms, and principalities—into a single political whole:

> The aim of the state is positive law, internal peace, and a condition of affairs in which everyone may by diligence earn his daily bread and satisfy the needs of his material existence, so long as God permits him to live. All this is only a means, a condition, and a framework for what love of fatherland really wants, viz., that the eternal and the divine may blossom in the world and never cease to become more and more pure, perfect, and excellent. That is why this love of fatherland must itself govern the state and be the supreme, final, and absolute authority. Its first exercise of this authority will be to limit the state's choice of means to secure its immediate object—internal peace. To attain this object, the natural freedom of the individual must, of course, be limited in many ways.[24]

And how did Fichte propose to persuade his fellow Germans to embrace loyalty to the "fatherland," especially when doing so required restrictions on "the natural freedom of the individual"?

> [I] propose that you establish deeply and indelibly in the hearts of all, by means of education, the true and all-powerful love of fatherland, the conception of our people as an eternal people and as the security for our own eternity.[25]

The reforms laid out by Fichte after the Prussian Army's defeat at Jena became the basis for the Prussian education system, which in turn laid the groundwork for the confederation of modern-day Germany. He envisioned an educational model that eliminated individuality, independence, self-reliance, and concern for natural freedoms from the population in exchange for conformity, dependence, and subordination of individuals to the state.

Nearly two centuries later, the incomparable American historian of education, John Taylor Gatto, wrote a seminal essay on the subject, "The Public School Nightmare: Why fix a system designed to destroy individual thought?" in which he observed:

> In effect [Fichte] told the Prussian people that the party was over, that the nation would have to shape up through a new Utopian institution of forced schooling in which everyone would learn to take orders.
>
> So the world got compulsion schooling at the end of a state bayonet for the first time in human history; modern forced schooling started in Prussia in 1819 with a clear vision of what centralized schools could deliver:
>
> Obedient soldiers to the army; Obedient workers to the mines; Well subordinated civil servants to government; Well subordinated clerks to industry; Citizens who thought alike about major issues.[26]

The "achievements" of the Prussian system of education included the imposition, for the first time ever, of mandatory, year-round attendance at school, beginning with kindergarten. Other hallmarks of the Prussian system were the enforcement of a national curriculum, the introduction of standardized testing, and (of course) lessons designed to inculcate in the students a sense of national identity. This system was soon adopted by other nascent nation-states, including the United States of America.

Gatto went on to say:

> You need to know this because over the first 50 years of our school institution, Prussian purpose—which was to create a form of state socialism—gradually forced out traditional American purpose, which in most minds was to prepare the individual to be self-reliant.[27]

The "American purpose" is perhaps most famously present in the writings of Thomas Jefferson, who hailed the yeoman farmer as the most virtuous citizen of the republic, not because the farmer who cultivated his own land was interested in promoting nationalism but precisely because he "was far more concerned with fostering resistance to government [...] than he was with promoting the national defense."[28]

Opposed to Jefferson's vision of American purpose were the likes of Benjamin Rush, a co-signer of the Declaration of Independence who advocated the creation of public schools for the express purpose of turning children into state-loving automatons. Lest this characterization be mistaken for hyperbole, consider Rush's remarkably candid paper, "Of the Mode of Education Proper in a Republic," in which he wrote:

> Our schools of learning, by producing one general, and uniform system of education, will render the mass of the people more homogeneous, and thereby fit them more easily for uniform and peaceable government.[29]

Rush concluded:

> From the observations that have been made it is plain, that I consider it is possible to convert men into republican machines. This must be done, if we expect them to perform their parts properly, in the great machine of the government of the state. That republic is sophisticated with monarchy or aristocracy that does not revolve upon the wills of the people, and these must be fitted to each other by means of education before they can be made to produce regularity and unison in government.[30]

To be sure, the adoption of Prussian-style schooling in the US did not completely eliminate the previous style of education, nor was the original intent of that education—the preparation of self-reliant individuals for autonomous action—entirely abandoned. The classical subjects, instead of being repudiated, were taught exclusively to the children of the ruling elite, who literally saw themselves as existing for the purpose of managing and controlling the masses of workers.

This educational double standard was confirmed most astonishingly in a 1909 speech by then-President of Princeton University and soon-to-be-President of the United States Woodrow Wilson:

> We want one class of persons to have a liberal education, and we want another class of persons, a very much larger class, of necessity, in every society, to forego the privileges of a liberal education and fit themselves to perform specific difficult manual tasks.[31]

The idea of the nation-state did not spontaneously arise out of the soil in the mists of time, as nationalist mythology would have it. It was deliberately inculcated through generations of mandatory schooling, heavily promoted in national curricula, and rigorously reinforced through regular standardized testing. It led, piece by coercive piece, to a more docile, more complacent, more submissive population that was so far removed from the yeoman farmer of the Jeffersonian ideal as to be unrecognizable.

Most parents in the United States who are unhappy about the latest move to standardize their children's indoctrination, the Common Core State Standards Initiative, are probably unaware that the historical roots of the problem trace back to Prussia. They are therefore unaware that this "education" system was originally designed to instill nationalism in its victims and that this nationalist indoctrination is on the cusp of being swapped out for globalist indoctrination.

Parents who wish to inform themselves of these facts can visit The World Core Curriculum promoted on the website of the United Nations Educational, Scientific and Cultural Organization (UNESCO).[32] They may also wish to familiarize themselves with Obama Education Secretary Arne Duncan's description of UNESCO as a "global partner" in shaping a "cradle-to-career education agenda" that prepares students for "new global challenges."[33]

Thus informed, parents will understand at once how the public is being ushered from the age of Rush's "republican machines" directly into the age of UNESCO's "globalist machines."

The oligarchs of the past induced their indoctrinated minions to rally around a national flag, knowing that this made those minions more susceptible to parting with their natural freedoms. Now all the oligarchs of today have to do to lead their minions into the new globalist order is to change the colours on that flag. For, as they well know, once the population has been trained to pledge allegiance to an arbitrary collective, it is only a matter of switching out one collective (nation-states) for another (regional governments) for yet another (global government).

Springing from the same tyrannical seed of collectivism, in which individuals are merely cogs to be slotted into the machinery of the state, the ideologies of nationalism and globalism reveal themselves as different forms of the same idea. Globalism is not the *opposite* of nationalism. Quite the contrary. Globalism is the *logical conclusion* of nationalism.

So, if nationalistic fervour is not the solution to the globalist agenda, what is? To answer that question, we need only rephrase it: If surrendering individual freedom to the national collective is not the solution to surrendering individual freedom to the global collective, what is? Aha, there's our answer: individual freedom. We must protect our individual freedoms in the face of the collectivist onslaught, whether that onslaught be nationalist or regionalist or globalist in nature.

What do we mean by "individual freedom" in this day and age? Jefferson had his yeoman farmer, but that concept of economic and political freedom is nearly 250 years old. Are there new ways of organizing society that don't require us to surrender our identity or pledge our allegiance to massive, centralized bureaucracies? Of course there are. But to find them involves challenging our notions of "government" and "state"—notions that have circumscribed our political thought for thousands of years.

Think about it: For our entire lives, we've been taught to believe that living in a society without government is impossible. Many voters can't even contemplate the idea of opposing both Candidate A and Candidate B (let alone Candidates C through Z!). And if you dare mention the idea of not voting at all? "But isn't that *anarchy*?," they retort, quavering voices lowered to a whisper lest someone overhear them pronounce such a seditious word.

Ah, yes, *anarchism*. A word soaked in blood and written in flaming red letters in the imagination of the same people who have been conditioned to believe that voting for their next ruler is their noblest and most sacred duty.

The commonly held association between anarchy and violence is by no means new. In the 1920s, the fear aroused by the mere word "anarchism" was so strong among Americans and Europeans that anarchist philosopher Alexander Berkman felt he had to respond and allay that fear. In 1929 he published *What Is Anarchism?* whose Chapter 19, "Is Anarchism Violence?," addresses the issue head-on.

> Anarchism is the ideal of such a condition; of a society without force and compulsion, where all men shall be equals, and live in freedom, peace, and harmony.
>
> The word Anarchy comes from the Greek, meaning without force, without violence or government, because government is the very fountainhead of violence, constraint, and coercion.
>
> Anarchy therefore does not mean disorder and chaos, as you thought before. On the contrary, it is the very reverse of it; it means no government, which is freedom and liberty. Disorder is the child of authority and compulsion. Liberty is the mother of order.[34]

This is anarchism from the point of view of an anarchist: a society without compulsion, where order is the natural outgrowth of freedom.

Again, to those of us who have been programmed to see government as the fountainhead of law and order, it is almost incomprehensible that order (not to mention peace and harmony) is to be achieved by the dissolution of government. Yet the belief in the need for government, deeply ingrained by the Prussian education system, must be directly challenged.

One of the first to contest this indoctrination was Pierre-Joseph Proudhon, the nineteenth-century French thinker who was the first self-identified anarchist. In his 1851 treatise, *General Idea of the Revolution in the Nineteenth Century*, Proudhon dismantled the pieties of statist society with breathtaking ferocity:

> To be GOVERNED is to be kept in sight, inspected, spied upon, directed, law-driven, numbered, enrolled, indoctrinated, preached at, controlled, estimated, valued, censured, commanded, by creatures who have neither the right, nor the wisdom, nor the virtue to do so.... To be GOVERNED is to be at every operation, at every transaction, noted, registered, enrolled, taxed, stamped, measured, numbered, assessed, licensed, authorized, admonished, forbidden, reformed, corrected, punished. It is, under pretext of public utility, and in the name of the general interest, to be placed under contribution, trained, ransomed, exploited, monopolized, extorted, squeezed, mystified, robbed; then, at the slightest resistance, the first word of complaint, to be repressed, fined, despised, harassed, tracked, abused, clubbed, disarmed, choked, imprisoned, judged, condemned, shot, deported, sacrificed, sold, betrayed; and, to crown all, mocked,

ridiculed, derided, outraged, dishonored. That is government; that is its justice; that is its morality.[35]

Many of my readers will appreciate the overall sentiment of this Proudhon passage. What, though, of his assertion that these abuses are not just the failing of certain tyrannical governments but are endemic to government itself? Well, that may be a harder pill for my audience to swallow.

Nonetheless, it needs to be understood that not just the institution of government but the very concept of it is founded on injustice. Indeed, rooted in the poisonous soil of lies and violence, the fruit of government is itself cursed.

American political philosopher Lysander Spooner explained these lies and contradictions in his classic work, *No Treason*:

> [T]wo men have no more natural right to exercise any kind of authority over one than one has to exercise the same authority over two. A man's natural rights are his own against the whole world; and any infringement of them is equally a crime whether committed by one man or by millions; whether committed by one man calling himself a robber (or by any other name indicating his true character) or by millions calling themselves a government.[36]

The issue, then, is not whether the government of this or that country is likely to treat its subjects any better or worse than another country's government is, but whether these "subjects" are really "subjects" in the first place.

How, after all, did governments come into existence? Where did their authority over the land within their (arbitrarily defined) borders originate? What right does a government have to rule over "its" people, and what makes "its" people beholden to its laws? The obvious truth, of course, is that no would-be ruler—whether a single monarch or a handful of plutocrats or a military junta or a parliament or even one's next-door neighbour—has any intrinsic authority to rule over another human.

This principle has been presented and proven by many writers, activists, and thinkers over the centuries. Spooner, for example, writing *No Treason* nearly two centuries ago, carefully dismantled all the usual arguments for the authority of the US Constitution over the "citizens" of the US government.

A more contemporary writer making the same argument in equally clear, candid, compelling prose is Larken Rose, noted anarchist and author of the book, *The Most Dangerous Superstition*. In his essay, "My Deprogramming," Rose brilliantly articulates his thoughts on the illegitimate nature of government and its presumed authority over the people:

> By trying to reconcile contradictions in my own political beliefs, I proved to myself that "government" can NEVER be legitimate. It can never have "authority." However necessary it supposedly is, and however noble the stated goal might be, I eventually realized that it is utterly impossible for anyone to acquire the right to rule others, even in a limited, "constitutional" way.
>
> There are several ways to prove this, and each of them is astonishingly simple. For example, if a person cannot delegate a right he doesn't have, then it is impossible for those in "government" to have any rights that I

do not personally have. (Where and how would they have acquired such super-human rights?) Furthermore, unless human beings can actually ALTER morality by mere decree, then all "legislation" is pointless and illegitimate. If one accepts the principle of non-aggression, then "government" is logically impossible, because a "government" without the right to tax, regulate, or legislate (which are all threats of aggression) is no "government" at all.[37]

If one agrees with Rose's logic, then one is led to undertake a mission. No, not the mission—so often promoted in our schools, echoed by our media, and propounded by our politicians—of going to the ballot box and voting in better rulers. And not the mission—so often endorsed by mob leaders and rabble-rousers—of opening the ammo box to threaten the violent overthrow of the government. Rather, the mission of getting on a soap box and inspiring a revolution of consciousness.

A paradigm shift in our thinking about government is what is needed. The masses must discover that they are not "subjects" or "citizens" at all, but free human beings under no obligation whatsoever to follow the dictates of any governmental structure. It is only by raising awareness of the problem of political "authority" that we can hope to help the people discover this long-suppressed truth.

As Rose puts it:

> So now I spend much of my time trying to persuade others to give up the cult of statism. I do not advocate abolishing "government" any more than I advocate abolishing Santa Claus. I just want people to stop letting their perceptions and actions be so profoundly warped and perverted by something that DOES NOT

EXIST, and never did. That is why I refer to the belief in "government" and "authority" as "The Most Dangerous Superstition." If people could give up that superstition, even if they did not otherwise become any more wise or compassionate, the state of society would drastically improve. I don't pretend to have the ability to make anyone more virtuous, but by pointing out to them the contradictions in their own belief systems—the very same contradictions I struggled with for years—I hope to help some of them reclaim ownership of themselves, so they can start thinking and acting as rational, sentient beings, instead of as the well-trained livestock of malicious masters.[38]

At last, we discover the root of the problem. The real bugbear is not "government," after all, but our belief in the authority of whatever gang of criminals wears the mantle of "government official."

The hypocrisy that this belief gives rise to is galling. We rightly call an unelected man delusional if he believes his own dictates to be laws, yet we dutifully obey the dictates of our "legislators." Why?

We rightly castigate a common thief for stealing someone's money, yet we laud the thieves who call themselves our "government" and call their robbery "taxation." Why?

We rightly lock up a murderer who takes another's life, yet we praise a murderer dressed in uniform as a hero for spilling the blood of our "government's" enemies. Why?

Unravel the thread of this imaginary authority and you unravel the thread of statism—the belief that immoral actions can be made moral simply because they are committed in the name of the state.

According to the statist's twisted logic, people are inherently wicked and deceitful, so some of those wicked and deceitful people should become rulers so they can stop the others from being wicked and deceitful. By extension, since people tend to rob and kill others, some of those people should be authorized to rob and kill in order to stop the others from robbing and killing each other.

Contrast that muddied thinking with this lucid remark by American author Edward Abbey:

> Anarchism is founded on the observation that since few men are wise enough to rule themselves, even fewer are wise enough to rule others.[39]

Which brings us back to the beginning. The contention that any individual or group of individuals has a legitimately granted authority to govern any other individual against his will is a delusion, and a dangerous one at that. Thus, the notion that voting for Candidate B simply because the way he proposes to rule over you is more palatable than Candidate A's plan for ruling over you fundamentally misses the point. Even in the best-case scenario, where you vote for Candidate B and he actually gets into office, you are still a slave. The fact that you willingly put the chains around your own neck does not change the nature of the relationship.

In Spooner's words:

> The principle that the majority have a right to rule the minority practically resolves all government into a mere contest between two bodies of men, as to which of them shall be masters and which of them slaves: a contest, that—however bloody—can never, in the nature of things, be finally closed so long as man refuses to be a slave.[40]

Here, Spooner has pinpointed the underlying purpose of all (s)elections: to pick who will be masters and who will be slaves. Now, we can see why the ultimate power of the individual lies in refusing to be a slave and, equally, in refusing to accept the premise that electing a kinder master will stop the abuse inherent in that relationship.

Hence, voting for Candidate B is not the solution. Our true power lies in not complying with the dictates of any would-be authority. The best possible election, then, would be the one in which no one voted.

In the end, it should insult us no less if the NSA's "foiled terror plot" map showed only the fifty states of the Union as the "homeland." For, no matter how any political boundaries are drawn, no matter how far north or south or east or west they stretch, political boundaries merely reinforce the age-old belief in statism that constitutes the rotten core of both nationalism and globalism.

It is only in the rejection of this dangerous superstition that we can truly defeat the real threats to humanity: the globalist ideology that is being foisted upon us and the nationalist ideology that undergirds it.

NOTES

1. Daro, Ishmael N. "Canada now part of the American 'homeland.'" Canada.com. August 1, 2013. archive.fo/WIG79

2. @CanadaDotCom. "We did it! Canada is now part of the American 'homeland.'" Twitter. August 1, 2013. archive.fo/1aiMb

3. Bump, Philip. "Welcome to the Homeland, Mexico and Canada!" The Atlantic Wire. August 1, 2013. archive.fo/gBxWB

4. "Homeland Security Act of 2002." Electronic Privacy Information Center. archive.fo/3b5Rn

5. "US and Canada Smart Border Declaration (2001)." Legislationline.org. archive.fo/GX2hf

6. Corbett, James. "A Peek Behind Closed Doors." The Corbett Report. July 9, 2007. corbettreport.com/sppminutes

7. "About the Council." Business Council of Canada. archive.fo/i3LSJ

8. "President and CEO." Business Council of Canada. archive.fo/U4yCM

9. "President Bush Participates in Joint Press Availability with Prime Minister Harper of Canada, and President Calderon of Mexico." U.S. Department of State Archive. August 21, 2007. archive.is/G1MIq

10. "Quebec police admit they went undercover at Montebello protest." CBC News. August 23, 2007. archive.is/Buxgz

11. "U.S. Northern Command, Canada Command establish new bilateral Civil Assistance Plan." U.S. Northern Command. February 14, 2008. archive.fo/BuaD1

12. "Canada-U.S. Shiprider." Royal Canadian Mounted Police. archive.fo/qLzRs

13. "Declaration by President Obama and Prime Minister Harper of Canada — Beyond the Border." The White House. February 4, 2011. archive.fo/CmAnZ

14. "Beyond the Border: A Shared Vision for Perimeter Security and Economic Competitiveness." U.S. Department of Homeland Security. December 7, 2011. archive.fo/iFP3d

15. "U.S.-Canada Regulatory Cooperation Council." The International Trade Administration, U.S. Department of Commerce. February 4, 2011. archive.fo/8G5Ju

16. Andres Rozental, et. al. "Building a North American Community." Council on Foreign Relations Press. May 2005. archive.fo/v68Ey

17. Pastor, Robert A. "The Future of North America: Replacing a Bad Neighbor Policy." Foreign Affairs. July/August 2008. archive.is/hgZ3f

18. Gabriel, Dana. "A New Generation of North American Citizens." The Corbett Report. February 12, 2010. corbettreport.com/nacitizens

19. "About the African Union." African Union. archive.is/7JYmT

20. Corbett, James. "EU Unmasked: After Brexit, Plans for Full EU Superstate Revealed." The Corbett Report. June 28, 2016. corbettreport.com/euunmasked

21. "EAEU." Ministry of Foreign Affairs of the Republic of Kazakhstan. October 16, 2019. archive.is/6viCn

22. Ro, Sam. "Goldman's Jim O'Neill Reflects 10 Years After Coining 'BRIC.'" Business Insider. November 27, 2011. archive.fo/gWPtd

23. Holmberg, Tom. "The Execution of Johann Philipp Palm." The Napoleon Series. August 2005. archive.fo/lYKW9

24. Fichte, Johann Gottlieb. *Addresses to the German Nation.* Translated by R. F. Jones, M.A. and G.H. Turnbull, M.A., Ph.D. (London: The Open Court Publishing Company, 1922.) Page 138.

25. See endnote 24. Page 151.

26. Gatto, John Taylor. "The Public School Nightmare: Why fix a system designed to destroy individual thought?" The Kossor Education Newsletter. Volume 4 Number 11. 1996. archive.fo/q1D4K

27. See endnote 26.

28. Pyne, Charlynn Spencer and Barbara Bryant. "Jeffersonian Ideals: Symposium Focuses on First 'Education President.'" The Library of Congress Information Bulletin. Volume 52 Number 15. July 26, 1993. archive.fo/GN22M

29. Rush, Benjamin. "Of the Mode of Education Proper in a Republic." The Founders' Constitution. Volume 1, Chapter 18, Document 30. Page 686. (Chicago: The University of Chicago Press, 1987.) archive.fo/8XUlv

30. See endnote 29.

31. Wilson, Woodrow. "The Meaning of a Liberal Education." Wikisource. January 9, 1909. archive.fo/7h1I0

32. The World Core Curriculum. UNESCO. archive.fo/HHHZN

33. Duncan, Arne. "The Vision of Education Reform in the United States." United States Mission to UNESCO. November 4, 2010. bit.ly/3yc9Etj

34. Fellner, Gene, editor. *Life of an Anarchist: The Alexander Berkman Reader* (New York: Seven Stories Press, 2005.) Page 272.

35. Proudhon, Pierre-Joseph. General Idea of the Revolution in the Nineteenth Century. Translated by John Beverley Robinson. (New York: Haskell House Publishers, 1969.) Page 294.

36. Spooner, Lysander. *No Treason, no. 1.* Mises Institute. archive.fo/cpNMC

37. Rose, Larken. "My Deprogramming." Voluntaryist.com. archive.fo/XJfdC

38. See endnote 37.

39. Abbey, Edward. *A Voice Crying in the Wilderness (Vox Clamantis in Deserto): Notes from a Secret Journal.* (New York: St. Martin's Press, 1989.) Page 23.

40. See endnote 36.

Biotech Billionaires and GMO Doomsday

A CURIOUS DOUBLE STANDARD pervades mainstream thinking about corporations these days. On the one hand, it is not at all uncommon to hear corporate fat cats referred to as devils incarnate—men and women who are prepared to do anything, up to and including destroying the very planet itself, in pursuit of their financial goals. On the other hand, merely questioning the motives of the corporate fat cats behind the genetic modification (GM) of our food supply is enough to get you dismissed as an anti-science kook.

This double standard is fraught with irony. As evidence of the dangers of genetically modified crops continues to mount, it is the bought-and-paid-for scientists shilling for the GM industry who increasingly find themselves on the anti-science side of the debate.

GM crops have long been sold to the public as the answer to our food security problems. For decades now, the "biotech industry" (as the companies that genetically engineer food refer to themselves) has assured us that GM crops are safe for human consumption, that they will produce higher yields, that they will require less pesticide, and that they will be the safest, most effective way to feed the world's population as we head into times of severe instability in the global food supply.

Contrary to what the biotech giants say in their corporate PR materials, however, GM crops do *not* produce greater yields. A comprehensive 2009 report by the Union of Concerned Scientists demonstrated that there was no increase in intrinsic yield between genetically modified strains of soybean and corn and their non-modified varieties.[1] This discovery was confirmed by a 2016 National Academy of Sciences report, which found "no evidence that GE [genetically engineered] crops had changed the rate of increase in yields" in soybean, cotton, or maize in the US.[2] The same year, an extensive *New York Times* investigation examined approximately thirty years of United Nations (UN) data and found no discernible difference in yields between Western Europe, where GM crops are not planted, and North America, where they are.[3]

For its part, the biotech sector likes to tout the research of Dr. Matin Qaim of the University of Göttingen, which suggests that GM crops do in fact enjoy larger yields. According to a meta-analysis of 147 separate studies co-authored by Dr. Qaim, adoption of GM technology increased crop yield by an average of 22 percent.[4] When questioned on this finding, however, Dr. Qaim admitted that these yields were possible only in the developing world, where modern farming techniques are not widely implemented. "Currently available GM crops would not lead to major yield gains in Europe," he told *The New York Times*.[5] "I don't consider this to be the miracle type of technology that we couldn't live without."

In the biotech industry's eyes, another key selling point of GM crops is that, being genetically engineered to resist pests, they allow farmers to use less pesticide. But what the biotech boosters don't like to admit is that the crops, which are also being engineered to resist herbicides, *eventually require farmers to greatly increase their use of these agrichemicals.*

The best example of this phenomenon is Roundup, the weed killer that was originally manufactured by the Monsanto Company and that accounted for nearly half of that company's profit before it was taken over by Bayer AG in 2018.[6] Glyphosate, the main ingredient in Roundup, is now the most-used agrichemical in history, with over 1.6 billion kilograms of the chemical having been applied between 1974 and 2016.[7]

A 2016 study found that 72 percent of that forty-two-year total was applied in the ten years from 2006 to 2016, a clear indication that the introduction of Monsanto's Roundup Ready GM Crops—engineered to be resistant to glyphosate—has led to a dramatic increase in the use of that very chemical.[8] In fact, a 2009 study, which attempted to quantify this increase, estimated that the use of GM crops has led to US farmers applying 383 million *more* pounds of herbicide in the 1996-2008 period than they would have sprayed had *no* GM crops been planted.[9]

This trend is especially worrying because multiple scientific studies have linked glyphosate to a range of negative health effects on humans. A 2015 study, for example, found that Roundup was both cytotoxic and endocrine-disrupting.[10] Also in 2015, the International Agency for Research on Cancer (IARC)—part of the World Health Organization (WHO)—listed glyphosate as a probable human carcinogen.[11]

In 2017, California became the first state in the US to list glyphosate as a carcinogen,[12] and in 2020—following a series of judgments holding Monsanto and its new owner, Bayer AG, responsible for the non-Hodgkins lymphoma of various California residents—Bayer settled a class-action lawsuit of 95,000 similar cases for a startling $10 billion.[13]

To make matters worse for proponents of the pesticide, a 2012 paper[14] confirmed that the biotech revolution has given rise to "superweeds" that are themselves resistant to glyphosate.[15] Naturally, their resistance necessitates the use of even more herbicides as farmers look for Roundup alternatives to eliminate the superweeds. Following their standard operating procedure, the biotech behemoths have used these setbacks not to reevaluate their position on GM technologies and harmful pesticides but to offer a phoney "solution" that promises to make them even more money.

This time, their "solution" is 2, 4-dichlorophenoxyacetic acid, an herbicide commonly known as 2, 4-D. As weeds have begun to develop resistance to glyphosate, farmers are finding that most weeds are still vulnerable to 2, 4-D, so the biotech industry is now creating GM crops that are resistant to this new pesticide.[16] In 2014, the US Department of Agriculture approved a number of 2, 4-D-resistant GM corn and soybean crops for commercial planting.[17] Studies have estimated that the USDA's decision could drive up overall use of agrichemicals in the US by 50 percent from current levels.[18]

So, what's the problem with 2, 4-D? As it turns out, 2, 4-D, just like glyphosate, has been clinically associated with a range of human illnesses. The research shows that 2, 4-D is a potential endocrine-disruptor[19] and a suspected neurotoxin.[20] And—again, just like glyphosate—it has been recognized by the IARC as "possibly carcinogenic to humans."[21]

But as head-spinning as all this is, the most disingenuous part of the biotech industry's PR campaign is its claim that genetically modified crops are themselves perfectly safe to eat. This pronouncement is particularly galling since in reality the US Food and Drug Administration (FDA) doesn't even test the safety of GM crops.[22] Instead, government regulators assume all GM foods to be safe unless and until there is proof to the contrary. In other words, the FDA bases its assessment of a GM product's safety on self-reported data from the very companies that manufacture the product.

Even more abominable, legal and copyright restrictions surrounding patents on genetically modified organisms (GMOs) force independent scientists to ask the biotech companies' permission before publishing research on their products.[23] As a result, almost all of the long-term animal feeding studies that have ever been conducted on GMOs have been carried out by the biotech companies themselves, using their own rules and with their own standards of reporting. What few independent studies have been conducted show a range of adverse health effects associated with the consumption of genetically modified foods (and the pesticides they have been engineered to resist), from reduced fertility[24] to immune system dysfunction,[25] liver failure,[26] obesity,[27] and cancer.[28]

From the falsehoods told about the benefits of GM crops to the cover-up of their ill effects on the environment and human health, it seems there is plenty of evidence to give even the staunchest defenders of GM crops cause for concern. Sadly, however, the social stigma against raising these concerns in public is severe. Those brave enough to do so are roundly accused of being "anti-scientific"—a term that itself perverts the meaning of the word "science."

It's hardly a mystery why these scientific refutations of GM myths have not penetrated the public consciousness.

After all, the continued existence of Bayer-Monsanto and its biotech brethren depends on their ability to convince the public of their products' safety. These corporations, Monsanto chief among them, have fought a long and protracted campaign to smear, undermine, and cover up any and all studies that point out the disastrous consequences of genetically engineering the food supply.

Indeed, we no longer have to speculate on this point: the consequences *are* disastrous. As we have already seen, tens of thousands of lawsuits have been filed against Bayer's Monsanto since the IARC's 2015 determination that glyphosate is a "probable human carcinogen."[29] In October 2016, a number of these lawsuits were consolidated into a single trial, formally known as "In re: Roundup Products Liability Litigation (MDL No. 2741)."[30]

One of the many remarkable facts to emerge from the discovery process of that trial is the existence of an internal Monsanto public relations program, dubbed "Let Nothing Go," which, as the name suggests, aimed to let absolutely no criticism of the company—even individual Facebook posts—go unaddressed. According to one of the documents filed in the case, "through a series of third parties, it [Monsanto] employs individuals who appear to have no connection to the industry, who in turn post positive comments on news articles and Facebook posts, defending Monsanto, its chemicals, and GMOs."[31]

The same document also details how supposedly independent think tanks like the Genetic Literacy Project and the American Council on Science and Health give a scientific gloss to blatantly biotech-friendly propaganda. As an illustration, after the WHO's IARC declared glyphosate a probable carcinogen, the Genetic Literacy Project responded with an editorial that wrestled with the question of whether the agency's cancer classification scheme can be reformed or whether it needs to be abolished altogether.[32]

Other documents to emerge from the trial confirm long-held suspicions of collusion between Monsanto and the US Environmental Protection Agency (EPA)— the regulatory body charged with assessing the potential cancer risks of chemicals like glyphosate. Specifically, these documents show that the head of the EPA's Cancer Review Committee, Jess Rowland, was in regular contact with Monsanto, providing insider information that helped shape the company's PR strategy.[33] He even warned Monsanto about the IARC's determination that glyphosate was a probable carcinogen months before the information became public, giving the company plenty of time to craft its propaganda plan.

In one especially egregious email, a Monsanto official discussed Rowland's efforts to quash a US Department of Health and Human Services (HHS) review of glyphosate safety. The official quoted Rowland as saying, "If I can kill this [safety review,] I should get a medal."[34]

Also coming to light during the trial was an excoriating letter written in 2013 to Rowland by Marion Copley, an EPA whistleblower who left the agency when she herself fell ill with cancer. In her letter, Copley pleaded for the serious problems in the EPA's cancer review process—the glyphosate review, in particular—to be addressed before she went to her grave. She also chastised Rowland for his obvious attempts to manipulate the science in Monsanto's favour for his own monetary gain:

> For once in your life, listen to me and don't play your political conniving games with the science to favor the registrants. For once do the right thing and don't make decisions based on how it affects your bonus.[35]

Just nine months later Copley was dead and none of her concerns had been addressed.

But of all the documents to emerge from the trial, none are more revealing than those that detail the incredible lengths Monsanto went to in order to smear the work of Gilles-Éric Séralini, a French scientist who published a groundbreaking study showing an increase in tumours among rats fed genetically modified corn and Monsanto's Roundup herbicide.

The controversy started in 2012, when a team of researchers led by Dr. Séralini at the University of Caen published a study, "Long term toxicity of a Roundup herbicide and a Roundup-tolerant genetically modified maize," in the *Journal of Food and Chemical Toxicology*.[36] The paper detailed the results of an experiment in which Séralini's team followed 200 rats through a two-year feeding study. They divided the rats into ten groups of twenty each (ten male rats and ten female rats). Rats in three of the groups were fed Monsanto's patented NK603 GMO corn alone. Rats in another three groups were fed the corn treated with Roundup herbicide. Rats in three other groups were fed Roundup-treated water but no GMO corn. And rats in the tenth group, a control group, were fed neither GMO corn nor Roundup herbicide. The researchers' results indicated that the rats fed the Roundup or the GMO corn, either separately or combined, were more likely to experience a range of adverse health effects than were the rats in the non-GMO control group.

Immediately upon the release of the study, another team—this one organized by third-party think tanks in the orbit of the biotech industry—kicked into overdrive in an attempt to cast doubt on Séralini et al's conclusions. Critics pointed to perceived flaws in the collection, reporting, and analysis of the study's findings. Some of the key voices driving the campaign against the Séralini study included the aforementioned Genetic Literacy Project, along with the American Council on Science and Health and other industry-sponsored organizations. One, a supposedly neutral party called the Science Media Centre, connects journalists to scientists when important scientific discoveries are in the headlines. The Science Media Centre is actually far from neutral. It is funded by bodies like CropLife International, a biotech trade association that promotes the interests of biotechnology companies worldwide, and Syngenta AG, one of the key biotech seed giants. The Centre has also received funding directly from Monsanto UK.[37]

Of all the Séralini detractors, the European Food Safety Authority (EFSA)—the European Union (EU) equivalent of the FDA—was particularly vociferous. In 2009, the EFSA had recommended NK603 corn to the EU for regulatory approval—the very strain of proprietary GMO corn that Séralini's results were calling into question.[38] The EFSA responded to the study with a blistering twenty-two-point press release in which it defended its own assessment of the GM corn's safety and concluded that Séralini's work "does not meet acceptable scientific standards and there is no need to re-examine previous safety evaluations of genetically modified maize NK603."[39] Conspicuously absent from the press release was the fact that the EFSA had *not* examined the safety of Monsanto's corn in the first place. That is, it had conducted no animal tests itself, instead relying on "information supplied by the applicant" (i.e. Monsanto).

As researcher William Engdahl noted in his op-ed on the controversy:

> EFSA argued that Séralini had used the wrong kind of rats, not enough rats and that the statistical analysis was inadequate. By these standards, all toxicity studies on glyphosate and GMOs should be retracted because they used the same type and approximate number of rats as those in the Séralini study.[40]

Nonetheless, the Monsanto-led PR blitz, consisting of numerous letters to the editor and even an online petition calling on Séralini to voluntarily withdraw the study, had its intended effect. The editor of the *Journal of Food and Chemical Toxicology* (FCT), where the study had been published, seemingly bowed to the whirlwind of pressure by making the unprecedented decision to retract the study. "Unprecedented" because the move went against the FCT's publisher's own express principles and guidelines.

The journal's publisher, Elsevier, is a member of the Committee on Publication Ethics, whose criteria for retracting a paper are: clear evidence that the findings are unreliable due to misconduct (e.g., data fabrication) or honest error; plagiarism or redundant publication; or unethical research.[41] The editor who oversaw the paper's retraction, Dr. A. Wallace Hayes, admitted that it met none of these criteria. In his own statement on the retraction, he confirmed that he "found no evidence of fraud or intentional misrepresentation of the data."[42] Yet the paper was retracted because, according to Hayes, "the results presented (while not incorrect) are inconclusive"—apparently a new standard for article retraction that seems to apply specially to articles critical of the GMO industry in general and of Monsanto products in particular.

The first clue as to what prompted Hayes' unusual behaviour appeared when Dr. E. Ann Clark, a former associate professor in the Department of Plant Agriculture at the University of Guelph, noted that the FCT had created an entirely new position ("deputy editor in biotechnology") shortly after the Séralini paper was published.[43] The journal proceeded to staff that position with Richard E. Goodman, a University of Nebraska allergy specialist who just happened to have worked as an allergy program manager for the safety assessment of GM crops at Monsanto from 1997 to 2004 and who, by his own admission, received 50 percent of his 2012 salary from a project funded by Monsanto, Bayer, BASF, Dow, DuPont, and Syngenta.[44]

As part of his role in the newly created deputy editor spot at FCT, Dr. Goodman helped identify and ultimately retract two studies that were widely seen as "problematic" by the biotech industry: Séralini's rat feeding study and a similar study from Brazil that demonstrated the toxic effects on mice of the *Bacillus thuringiensis* insecticide that forms the basis of a wide variety of GM crops.[45]

Outraged by the way the Séralini paper had been treated by the Monsanto PR spin machine, a team of independent scientists and researchers from across the globe wrote an open letter pointing out how the Séralini affair underscored a long history of attacks on research whenever it uncovered the adverse health effects of GM foods. "The Séralini publication, and resultant media attention, raise the profile of fundamental challenges faced by science in a world increasingly dominated by corporate influence," the scientists wrote. They concluded:

> When those with a vested interest attempt to sow unreasonable doubt around inconvenient results, or when governments exploit political opportunities by picking and choosing from scientific evidence, they jeopardize public confidence in scientific methods and institutions, and also put their own citizenry at risk. Safety testing, science-based regulation, and the scientific process itself, depend crucially on widespread trust in a body of scientists devoted to the public interest and professional integrity. If instead, the starting point of a scientific product assessment is an approval process rigged in favour of the applicant, backed up by systematic suppression of independent scientists working in the public interest, then there can never be an honest, rational or scientific debate.[46]

When the retraction was issued, the Séralini affair appeared to be yet one more example of the biotech industry's tried-and-true tactic of bashing, belittling, and besmirching its opposition. Evidence has emerged from the Monsanto trial in California, however, demonstrating that the company itself was in fact squarely behind the coordinated attempt to get the study retracted. The same evidence also reveals the ties between Monsanto and the FCT journal were even more direct than was known at the time.

One document released during the trial, for instance, features Monsanto scientist David Saltmiras boasting that he personally "facilitated numerous third-party expert letters to the editor [of the FCT]" that criticized the Séralini paper.[47] Another document demonstrates that a different Monsanto employee had pressured Bruce

Chassy, an "independent" professor of food safety, to join the campaign against the study and that Chassy had capitulated by co-authoring a *Forbes* article parroting the Monsanto viewpoint.[48] Even more incriminating, the *Forbes* piece was co-authored by Henry I. Miller, a Hoover Institution medical researcher and columnist who is a prolific apologist for GMOs and who, other documents reveal, has published pro-glyphosate articles ghostwritten by Monsanto itself.[49]

But the most explosive revelation from the released court documents concerns A. Wallace Hayes, the aforementioned FCT editor who oversaw the Séralini paper's retraction. Specifically, there is a letter detailing a consulting agreement that Hayes entered into with Monsanto in August 2012, just weeks before the paper was published— and just weeks before the year-long campaign to get the paper retracted began.

That Hayes didn't acknowledge this relationship with Monsanto, let alone recuse himself, during the time that the Séralini paper was being reviewed by the very journal Hayes was editing is nothing short of scandalous. Hayes defended himself by telling *The New York Times* that "he had not been under contract with Monsanto at the time of the retraction."[50] Yet, as independent biotech watchdog group GMWatch points out, "since it took the journal over a year to retract the study after the months-long second review, which Hayes oversaw, it's clear that he had an undisclosed conflict of interest from the time he entered into contract with Monsanto and during the review process."[51]

Ultimately—even incredibly, given the formidable corporate resources that Monsanto and its biotech cohorts spent in smearing the study—Séralini's conclusions were validated. In 2014, his paper was republished in another journal. Then, in 2015, Séralini won two separate court cases defending his work.

The whole sordid affair, now amply detailed in a series of court documents that have received scant attention in the mainstream press, serves as a case study in how the biotech industry uses its clout to cast doubt on research that points to the unhealthy consequences of its GM products.

Why this system exists as it does, with the rules of the game seemingly being written for the benefit of the big biotech multinationals, is not difficult to fathom: the playbook was written by the players themselves.

The concept of "regulatory capture," wherein government regulators are beholden to the very entities they are supposedly regulating, is not a new one. But perhaps nowhere is the ability of the private sector to control the very government agencies that are tasked with regulating it more apparent than in the biotech industry. Indeed, of all the companies in the US, Monsanto is perhaps the most notorious for the "revolving door" between its top management and the key staffers of the federal agencies that write the rules governing its products.

Literally dozens of Monsanto officers, lobbyists, and consultants have walked through this spinning door— in both directions. Among the notable examples of this phenomenon are Linda Fisher, who held four senior management positions in the US Environmental Protection Agency (EPA) before leaving to become Monsanto's Vice President of Government and Public Affairs, and US Supreme Court Justice Clarence Thomas, who was a corporate lawyer for Monsanto in the 1970s. A less-famous but more blatant user of this revolving door was Michael

Taylor, whose career path has included, chronologically, positions at the US Food and Drug Administration, at a private law firm that included Monsanto among its clients, and at Monsanto itself (where he was Vice President for Public Policy), followed by a return trip to the FDA, where he served until 2016.[52]

So, what exactly do these "public servants" *do* for their biotech masters? They make sure that the regulatory bodies adopt practices that turn out in their paymasters' favour.

Take the "substantial equivalence" principle, for example. As a 1996 joint consultation on GM food safety from the UN's Food and Agricultural Organization (FAO) and the World Health Organization (WHO) explains, this principle holds "that if a new food or food component is found to be substantially equivalent to an existing food or food component, it can be treated in the same manner with respect to safety." The idea—which, conveniently enough for the biotech companies, reduces the burden of proving the safety of novel genetically engineered foods—was suggested in a series of joint consultations on "Biotechnology and Food Safety" between the FAO and the WHO in the early 1990s[53] and was subsequently touted by the Organisation for Economic Co-operation and Development.[54] It is now employed by the FDA, the Canadian Food Inspection Agency, and Japan's Ministry of Health, Labour and Welfare as an underlying principle in GM food safety assessment.[55]

The logic of "substantial equivalence" is viciously circular: how can a new food, such as a GM corn or soybean (created by transfusing genes from bacteria or other organisms that are not endemic to that crop), be deemed substantially equivalent *without* testing how its differences affect its safety?

The aforementioned FAO/WHO consultations wave away this obvious paradox by simply asserting that the determination of substantial equivalence is an "analytical exercise" which "may be a simple task or be very lengthy depending upon the amount of available knowledge and the nature of the food or food component under consideration." After citing characteristics that can be compared between GM crops and their non-modified counterparts—including "molecular characterization, phenotypic characteristics, key nutrients, toxicants and allergens"—the report on those consultations then goes on to declare that the actual determination of substantial equivalence "need[s] to be flexible and will change over time in accordance with the changing needs of processors and consumers and with experience."

In 1998, geneticists Mae-Wan Ho and Ricarda A. Steinbrecher issued a scathing critique of the FAO/WHO report:

> This principle [of substantial equivalence] is
> unscientific and arbitrary, encapsulating a dangerously permissive attitude toward producers, and at the
> same time it offers less than minimalist protection for
> consumers and biodiversity, because it is designed to
> be as flexible, malleable, and open to interpretation
> as possible. [...] All the signs are that the producers
> are handed carte blanche to do as they please for
> maximum profitability, with the regulatory body
> acting to allay legitimate public fears and opposition.[56]

If this decidedly *un*scientific principle seems like a dream come true for biotechs trying to slip their GM foods through the regulatory approval process with a minimum of friction, that's because it is.

First formulated by the FDA in 1976 to regulate (or, more accurately, *not* regulate) new medical devices that were essentially the same as medical devices already approved for sale, "substantial equivalence" became an official part of the FDA's approach to (not) regulating GM foods in 1992, when it was enshrined in a policy statement on "Foods Derived from New Plant Varieties."[57]

Unsurprisingly, this policy statement was co-authored[58] by none other than the previously cited Michael Taylor, an attorney who practiced food and drug law, whose clients included Monsanto, and who was brought into George H. W. Bush's FDA to fill the newly created position of "Deputy Commissioner for Policy."[59] After achieving this coup for Monsanto and his biotech buddies, Taylor, as noted above, left the FDA and became a Monsanto VP. Then, as we already recorded, he returned to the FDA to take first one,[60] then two,[61] prominent positions. Taylor's curriculum vitae reads like a case study in how to make the most of the revolving door.

There are many more examples of this two-way door between the biotech industry and government regulators, but in focusing on particular people and their positions we run the risk of losing sight of a much more insidious but much lesser-known fact: the biotech sector as a whole emerged, not organically, but through the coordinated efforts of a handful of corporate foundations and billionaire-backed non-governmental organizations (NGOs), with the full cooperation of governments around the world.

An even more pernicious fact is that the "Gene Revolution" that birthed this multibillion-dollar industry and its genetic engineering of the food supply is part of a much darker agenda than the mere amassing of corporate profit.

In order to understand the story of the so-called Gene Revolution, however, we have to first understand the true history of the so-called "Green Revolution," an explosion in crop production in the 1950s and 1960s that was facilitated by new agricultural technologies.

The sanitized version of this story is that the Green Revolution sprang from the pioneering research of Norman Borlaug, an American scientist who began experimenting with disease-resistant, high-yield varieties of wheat in Mexico in the 1940s.[62] His research, combined with an increased use of mechanized tools in industrial farming practices, is credited with "staving off world hunger." It also led to his receiving a Congressional Gold Medal, a Nobel Peace Prize, and a Presidential Medal of Freedom (making him one of only five people to receive all three honours).[63]

Contrary to the praises of his modern-day hagiographers, however, *Borlaug did not single-handedly "save a billion lives."* He was, in fact, funded in his efforts by wealthy benefactors, and the fruits of his labour on their behalf were not exactly a boon to humanity.

Generous support for Borlaug poured in from "philanthropic" organizations, notably the Ford Foundation and the Rockefeller Foundation. These foundations not only footed the bill for Borlaug's research, they also established such institutions as the International Maize and Wheat Improvement Center,[64] which made that research possible in the first place. Glowing articles on the Green Revolution—largely penned by these foundations themselves or by purportedly objective outsiders who were secretly on their payroll—are always careful to note that these billionaires were motivated to support Borlaug's work by only the noblest of humanitarian intentions.

The real story, though, is more nuanced and paints an altogether different picture. In actuality, the Rockefeller dynasty—led at the time of Borlaug's work by third-generation patriarch John D. Rockefeller III—was not only largely responsible for bringing about the Green Revolution and the subsequent Gene Revolution, *its motives were far from humanitarian.* Driven by their egomaniacal desire to monopolize the world's resources, the Rockefellers sought to expand the global market for their family's petrochemical empire and to consolidate control over the global food supply.

In *Seeds of Destruction*, a comprehensive overview of the Green Revolution and the Gene Revolution, author William Engdahl reports that Nelson Rockefeller set up the Mexican American Development Corp. in the 1940s and used the Rockefeller-owned Chase National Bank—then under the stewardship of Winthrop Aldrich, Nelson's uncle—to set up Chase Bank's Latin American division in Mexico. As Engdahl observes, Nelson's primary motive was to "regain a foothold in Mexico through the guise of helping to solve the country's food problems."[65]

With their business ducks now in a row, the Rockefellers were ready to get down to the corporate "philanthropy" that had increased the family's fortune (not to mention their reputation) ever since John D. Rockefeller, Sr. had plowed his oil money into the establishment of their eponymous foundation. In this case, the Rockefellers' "philanthropy" took the form of the newly established Mexican Agricultural Program (MAC), headed by George Harrar, who would go on to become the president of the Rockefeller Foundation.[66] It was from MAC that Norman

Borlaug and the fabled Green Revolution were to emerge.

Next, the Green Revolution expanded into Brazil, where another of the Rockefellers' seemingly infinite corporate extensions—the International Basic Economy Corporation (IBEC), set up by Nelson in 1947—was employed in transforming that nation's agricultural industry. According to the Rockefeller Archive Center:

> The Corporation was developed as a private business enterprise that would focus on upgrading the "basic economies" of lesser-developed nations by lowering food prices, building sound housing, mobilizing savings, and fostering industrialization. The objective was for the business to be profitable and sustainable, and to encourage others, especially nationals, to establish competitive businesses and thereby establish a "multiplier" development effect.[67]

But the real insight into what the IBEC (and the Green Revolution in general) *actually* cared about comes from Lester Brown, another beneficiary of Rockefeller largesse whose Worldwatch Institute was founded in 1974 with the aid of a $500,000 grant from the Rockefeller Brothers Fund.[68] In *Seeds of Change*, his 1969 book on the subject, Brown admitted the business motivations that were really driving this supposedly "humanitarian" venture.

> Fertilizer is only one item in the package of new inputs which farmers need in order to realize the full potential of the new seeds. Once it becomes profitable to use modern technology, the demand for all kinds of farm inputs increases rapidly. And only agribusiness firms can supply these new inputs efficiently. This means that the multinational

corporation has a vested interest in the agricultural revolution along with the poor countries.[69]

This is the basis of the so-called Green Revolution: multinational corporations profiting handsomely from "developing" the agricultural sector of Third World countries by selling them fertilizers, chemicals, and capital-intensive technology. It's no surprise, then, to learn that the very term "agribusiness" emerged from the Harvard Business School[70] out of research conducted by Wassily Leontief under a Rockefeller Foundation grant.[71]

From the Rockefeller family's perspective, the Green Revolution project was a runaway success. By the 1970s, the satellite of companies in the orbit of their Standard Oil network, including their cronies in the nitrogen fertilizer industry (DuPont, Dow Chemical Company, and Hercules Powder Company), had broken into new markets around the world. More precisely, these markets had been pried open for this oligopoly by the US government under President Lyndon B. Johnson's Food for Peace (FFP) program,[72] which handed the reins of US food aid over to USAID, a CIA front organization.[73] And, as a happy "coincidence" for the Rockefellers, the FFP program *also* happened to encourage the use of petrochemical-dependent agricultural technologies (fertilizers, tractors, irrigation, etc.) by aid recipients.

Out of this monopolistic morass sprang a cartel of grain companies—the so-called "ABCD" cartel of Archer Daniels Midland, Bunge, Cargill, and Louis Dreyfus[74]— and other agribusiness giants, all of which continue to dominate the global food trade to this day.[75]

Although its crony corporate- and foundation-funded champions insist otherwise, the Green Revolution has in fact exacerbated, rather than reduced, the disparity between rich feudal landowners and poor farming peasants in countries like India. The propaganda narrative that paints this transformation as a "miracle" also neglects to mention how the expensive farming technologies behind this revolution were funded on the back of loans from the World Bank[76] and how these loans further impoverished India and other developing countries. Indeed, the end result of the Green Revolution was the convenient creation of indebted, captive markets for American-dominated petrochemical-dependent agribusiness.

From this historical soil, a modern GM seed cartel has sprung. It consists of the biotech branches of Big Ag and Big Pharma: Dow AgroSciences, DuPont/Pioneer Hi-Bred, Syngenta, and—now that Monsanto has been swallowed by Bayer—Bayer CropScience. And, like the ABCD cartel before them, these companies, too, have secured a dominant position in the new genetically engineered global food chain.[77]

One lowlight of the biotechs' seed saga was the complete agribusiness neocolonialization of Argentina, where Monsanto ran an elaborate "bait-and-switch" to get the country hooked on its technology before demanding royalties on the crops that were already growing,[78] and where DuPont magnanimously began a "Protein for Life" programme to foist its GM soybeans on Argentina's poor.[79]

Another horrific consequence of this cartel showed up in the aftermath of the illegal invasion of Iraq in 2003. Under the occupation government, "Administrator" Paul Bremer III enacted a series of 100 new "orders" designed to open up Iraq to foreign "investment." These orders included changes to the tax code, the easing of restrictions on contracts and leases for foreign corporations and banks, the lifting of restrictions on foreign ownership of the country's natural resources, and a series of other rules designed to benefit foreign (mostly American) banks and corporations that were descending like locusts on the newly "liberated" country.

The most incredible of these mandates was Order 81, a wholesale change in the country's patent laws.[80] It contained a provision allowing companies holding the registration of a "protected plant variety" to sue farmers who were found to be saving, reusing, or planting these seeds without the explicit approval of the patent holder. Iraq, the former breadbasket of the Middle East, was now being deprived of its food sovereignty and reduced to a mere plantation presided over by a syndicate of seed producers.[81]

The convergence of corporate, "philanthropic," governmental, and inter-governmental interests promoting GM crops around the world can be seen in the bewildering array of research institutes, industry associations, and "consultative groups" that have invaded this field. They include the Rockefeller-founded International Rice Research Institute (IRRI),[82] the Rockefeller/Monsanto/USAID brainchild International Service for the Acquisition of Agri-biotech Applications (ISAAA),[83] the Rockefeller/Ford/World Bank-created Consultative Group of International Agricultural Research (CGIAR),[84] and dozens of other bland and benign-sounding organizations set up for the sole purpose of creating and popularizing GM crops. Through the combined efforts of public and private groups in funding and publicizing GM research, the GM cartel has succeeded in sowing its synthetic seed all across the planet.

One sign, if any were needed, that the ultimate aim of this cartel may not be benign is the Svalbard Global

Seed Vault. Like something out of a James Bond movie, the seed vault is carved into the side of a mountain on a remote archipelago halfway between Norway and the North Pole. And, as the vault's own website informs us, it is designed "to store duplicates (backups) of seed samples from the world's crop collections" as "the ultimate insurance policy for the world food supply." Specifically, the permafrost and thick rock of the Arctic tundra are meant to ensure that the seed samples will remain frozen and preserved even without power, meaning that the vault and its contents will survive in the event of a worldwide disaster.

The vault contains more than 1,000,000 non-GMO seed samples from all over the world and has the capacity to store as many as 4.5 million varieties of crops within its icy walls. It is administered by the Crop Trust, an organization founded by the aforementioned CGIAR[85] and funded by the Bill & Melinda Gates Foundation,[86] along with the Rockefeller Foundation, Dupont/Pioneer Hi-bred, Syngenta AG, and a score of governments, UN-affiliated organizations, and other corporations and foundations.[87]

So, what exactly *is* the Crop Trust? Long story short, in 2001, the FAO adopted the International Treaty on Plant Genetic Resources for Food and Agriculture[88] (shortened to "the plant treaty"), which "aims to improve global food security by making it easier for scientists and farmers to obtain and use seeds and other plant material for crop improvement, research, and training."[89] The treaty created a mechanism called the "Multilateral System" to make sixty-four valuable food crops available in "an easily accessible global pool of genetic resources that is freely available to potential users in the Treaty's ratifying nations for some uses." To help it reach this lofty goal, the governing body of the plant treaty entered into an agreement with the Global Crop Diversity Trust (aka "the Crop Trust"), an international nonprofit organization charged with raising and disbursing funds to preserve crop diversity, to provide tools and financial support for genebanks worldwide, and to conserve genebank specimens *ex situ*—i.e. buried in the side of a mountain in Svalbard's icy Arctic tundra.

Until 2012, the Crop Trust was chaired by Margaret Catley-Carson,[90] a former president of the J. D. Rockefeller III-founded Population Council[91] (the American Eugenics Society by another name[92]). Her connections prove that no matter where you turn in the realm of genetics you always end up back at the doorstep of the same elitist, eugenics-obsessed families and the corporate oligopoly they have nurtured into existence.

What on earth are the eugenicists preparing for with the seed vault? Why does humanity need a backup of millions of seed varieties that have presumably been around (for the most part) throughout human history? What kind of environmental catastrophe could possibly contaminate the gene pool to the point where we would need to repopulate the earth with heirloom, non-GMO seeds?

The answers you receive to these questions depend, as usual, on whom you ask.

The Crop Trust itself has offered some scenarios that appear to justify the existence of the seed vault.

"There are big and small doomsdays going on around the world every day," the trust's former executive director, Marie Haga, told TIME in 2017. "Genetic material is being lost all over the globe." To which one property manager in charge of overseeing the vault's day-to-day operations added: "It is away from the places on earth where you have war and terror, everything maybe you are afraid of in other places."[93]

Two years earlier, in 2015, the Crop Trust announced that the Svalbard seed bank had had its first-ever withdrawal that year after a gene bank in war-torn Aleppo was damaged by the US-backed terrorist insurgency in Syria. At the time, Crop Trust spokesman Brian Lainoff opined that "the withdrawal actually serves as proof that such a vault is necessary."[94]

More recently, the case has even been made by the *Independent* that the vault is required to protect the world's genetic heritage "in times of global catastrophe, like the raging COVID-19 pandemic."[95] Who knew that COVID was such a threat to crop diversity?

War? Terrorism? COVID? True, geopolitical turmoil and natural disasters *do* present a threat to crop diversity in various locales, but these threats alone could not be the *real* reason that the multibillion-dollar foundations and NGOs behind the Gene Revolution are creating a disaster-proof seed bank.

No. There must be something more than these concerns to explain their obsession with repopulating the earth with heirloom, non-GMO seeds in the wake of a worldwide catastrophe.

The only logical conclusion is that the very eugenicists who have spearheaded the genetic engineering of the food supply are aware that their Machiavellian machinations threaten life on earth to such an alarming extent that a "backup" of the natural world may be needed to one day "reboot" the planet.

Our first reaction to this sobering information and its implication might be to panic. Then a feeling of helplessness might set in, causing us to simply cave to the seemingly unstoppable GMO takeover. After all, how could there possibly be a solution to an agenda as meticulously planned, massively funded, and monumentally overwhelming as this one?

It has been suggested that governments should be lobbied to institute national bans on the planting or cultivation of GM crops. Yet, given that these national governments are increasingly ensnared in a web of international treaties and organizations—the FAO, the WHO, the UN, the World Trade Organization, the plant treaty, the Crop Trust, etc.—and given that these organizations and agreements are themselves tied in to the biotech agenda through groups like IRRI and ISAAA and CGIAR, it seems unlikely that individual nation-states will be able to buck the onslaught of the multibillion-dollar, multidecade, multi-national agenda of the agribusiness giants for very long.

On an even more fundamental level, though, the answer to bad science is not to ban science, any more than the answer to hate speech is to ban speech. Giving governments the power to ban (or, by implication, permit) this or that field of research is to assign the power over the future direction of society to the very eugenicists and corporate fat cats who control the legislatures of each nation-state.

Certainly, by all means, we should be engaged in whatever efforts we can to stop state funds from underwriting this type of research, but lobbying for laws to ban the research altogether would almost certainly backfire. The ban hammer *may* strike in the direction we want (banning GM crops, for example), *but it may just as easily swing in a direction we don't want* (approving GM crops for cultivation). And, given the resources at the disposal of the GMO-crazed eugenicists, it is difficult to imagine how we citizens would ever win that political fight.

So, then, *is* there a way to stop the scourge of GMOs from taking over the planet? Thankfully, that isn't a rhetorical question. And, thankfully, the answer is a resounding "Yes." In fact, it has already been demonstrated that we *can* win this war by employing one of the simplest weapons at our disposal: the boycott.

Let me explain. Posilac is the trade name for Monsanto's genetically engineered recombinant bovine growth hormone (rBGH), which is injected into lactating dairy cows to increase milk production.[96] In 1993, Posilac was approved by the FDA for use in the dairy industry despite warnings from medical researchers about the potential dangers it posed to humans who consume the milk from cows treated with these injections.[97]

The milk from Posilac-treated cows was sold unlabeled, despite being chemically, nutritionally, and pharmacologically different from non-treated milk. Not only did the rBGH milk contain significantly higher levels of the cancer-accelerating hormone IGF-1 (Insulin-like Growth Factor) than does regular dairy milk, but it also contained pus and antibiotics from the mastitis caused by the use of the drug.[98]

Multiple FDA insiders were warning in the 1990s that safety data about the rBGH milk was being manipulated by compromised FDA staffers to help Posilac pass the agency's approval process. Nonetheless—and unsurprisingly—the approval went ahead anyway. Equally unsurprisingly, the whistleblowers who raised these concerns about the process were forced out of the agency and their testimony was disregarded.[99]

But the suppression of this data did not stop there.

In a case made famous by the 2003 documentary *The Corporation*, two investigative reporters at a Fox News channel affiliate television station produced an exposé on the rBGH scandal. After Monsanto put pressure on the network, their story never aired, and the two were fired.

By 2004, however, the public had begun to become informed about the issue and consumers began to put massive pressure on stores to stop selling rBGH milk. This movement scored success after success, with major national retailers—including Kroger,[100] Safeway,[101] Starbucks[102] and Walmart[103]—and producers—including Breyers,[104] Byrne Dairy,[105] and General Mills[106]—agreeing to stop selling or producing milk from cows treated with artificial growth hormones. Today, rBGH milk, once nearly ubiquitous across America, is a rarity in the dairy section.

This change didn't come about through sweeping government action. It didn't come about through violence or coercion. Instead, it came about when consumers educated themselves about the problem, put pressure on the producers to address the problem, and continued that pressure until their demands for rBGH-free milk were met.

Granted, the overall struggle against GM foods will not be won as easily or as straightforwardly as it was in the specific instance of rBGH. Yet we can take the kernel of wisdom found in the story of the struggle against rBGH milk and plant that kernel in the rich seedbed of the struggle against GMOs.

Because it is within our power as consumers to reject products that we have concerns about, whether on health or safety or moral grounds, there is really no one else to blame but ourselves for the fact these GMO foods are so prevalent on our plates today. It is our responsibility to know what is in the products we are eating and to withhold our support from the companies that are using genetically engineered ingredients in their products.

Thankfully, technologies are coming online that will make coordinated consumer action against GMOs easier than it was even a decade ago.

The Buycott app, for example, promises to allow users to join the "buycotting" of non-GMO products—that is, to commit to buying only certified non-GMO goods— and also to join a boycott campaign that targets producers of GMO products.[107] An Organic Consumers group on the Buycott website has organized a "Pro-GMO? Or Pro-Right to Know?" campaign that lists 243 companies to either avoid or back based on those companies' opposition to or support of GMO labeling laws. Of the million-plus members of the Buycott site who are voting with their wallets, more than half of them are signed up to champion the GMO labeling campaign.[108]

Other initiatives include the Institute for Responsible Technology's Non-GMO Shopping Guide, which lists thousands of consumer products that have been verified as GMO-free.[109]

There's also the no-tech solution to GMOs: guerrilla gardening. This approach encompasses a wide variety of actions—from growing food on your own land to participating in a community garden to sourcing organic food from local producers via the local farmer's market.

If all of this sounds like a lot of work, it is.

If it sounds like the switch to 100 percent non-GMO foods will be a gradual process of weaning yourself off of certain products and sourcing appropriate alternatives, it will.

If it sounds like there's no one else to blame but ourselves if we don't start taking these steps toward securing a non-GM world for our children, there isn't.

In the end, we can't directly determine what happens in our neighbour's house (let alone what happens in other countries or on other continents), but the buck stops where it has always stopped: at our own kitchen table.

For the most part, we still have the freedom to choose what we eat—and what we won't eat. But, unless we start taking that freedom seriously and treating it as the grave responsibility it is, the Gene Revolution just might be the planet-wide disaster that makes the seed vault in the frozen tundra of Norway a necessity.

NOTES

1. "Failure to Yield: Evaluating the Performance of Genetically Engineered Crops." Union of Concerned Scientists. 2009. archive.fo/Ac0k

2. "Distinction Between Genetic Engineering and Conventional Plant Breeding Becoming Less Clear, Says New Report on GE Crops." The National Academies of Sciences, Engineering, and Medicine. May 17, 2016. archive.fo/XCuNg

3. Hakim, Danny. "Doubts About the Promised Bounty of Genetically Modified Crops." The New York Times. October 29, 2016. archive.fo/4EBkk

4. Klümper, Wilhelm and Matin Qaim. "A Meta-Analysis of the Impacts of Genetically Modified Crops." PLOS ONE. November 3, 2014. archive.fo/jknGO

5. See endnote 3.

6. Chatsko, Maxx. "How Much Money Does Monsanto Make From Roundup?" The Motley Fool. May 26, 2016. archive.fo/rp3kD

7. Main, Douglas. "Glyphosate Now the Most-Used Agricultural Chemical Ever." Newsweek. February 2, 2016. archive.fo/9BiNZ

8. Benbrook, Charles M. "Trends in glyphosate herbicide use in the United States and globally." Springer Open. February 2, 2016. archive.fo/1yJMN

9. "Impacts of Genetically Engineered Crops on Pesticide Use in the United States: The First Thirteen Years." The Cornucopia Institute. November 18, 2009. archive.fo/Uh46B

10. Young, Fiona, et al. "Endocrine disruption and cytotoxicity of Glyphosate and Roundup in human JAr cells in vitro." Open Access Text. archive.fo/4Ra1a

11. "IARC Monographs Volume 112: evaluation of five organophosphate insecticides and herbicides." International Agency for Research on Cancer. March 20, 2015. bit.ly/2JtN1nP

12. Hogue, Cheryl. "California to list glyphosate as a carcinogen." Chemical & Engineering News. archive.is/HUqQx

13. Cohen, Patricia. "Roundup Maker to Pay $10 Billion to Settle Cancer Suits." The New York Times. June 24, 2020. archive.is/0UbBT

14. Benbrook, Charles M. "Impacts of genetically engineered crops on pesticide use in the U.S. — the first sixteen years." Environmental Sciences Europe 24, Article number: 24. September 28, 2012. archive.md/GSIGw

15. Gillam, Carey. "Pesticide use ramping up as GMO crop technology backfires: study." Reuters. October 2, 2012. archive.md/R3gJN

16. Keim, Brandon. "The Next Generation of GM Crops Has Arrived—And So Has the Controversy." Wired. June 24, 2014. archive.md/tpcm2

17. Pollack, Andrew. "Altered to Withstand Herbicide, Corn and Soybeans Gain Approval." The New York Times. September 17, 2014. archive.is/sISTJ

18. See endnote 14.

19. "UN List of Identified Endocrine Disrupting Chemicals." Chem Safety Pro. archive.md/fjXYE

20. Bjørling-Poulsen, Marina, et al. "Potential developmental neurotoxicity of pesticides used in Europe." Environmental Health 7, Article number: 50. October 22, 2008. archive.md/wWuPU

21. "IARC Monographs evaluate DDT, lindane, and 2,4-D." International Agency for Research on Cancer. June 23, 2015. bit.ly/2NfMHKs

22. Weise, Elizabeth. "Genetically engineered foods Q & A." USA TODAY. October 28, 2012. archive.md/SY0zd

23. "Do Seed Companies Control GM Crop Research?" Scientific American. July 20, 2009. archive.md/fBBXx

24. Chiu, Yu-Han, et al. "Association Between Pesticide Residue Intake From Consumption of Fruits and Vegetables and Pregnancy Outcomes Among Women Undergoing Infertility Treatment With Assisted Reproductive Technology." JAMA Internal Medicine. January 2018; 178(1): 17-26. archive.md/P7Y8o

25. Finamore, Alberto, et al. "Intestinal and Peripheral Immune Response to MON810 Maize Ingestion in Weaning and Old Mice." Journal of Agricultural and Food Chemistry. November 14, 2008. archive.is/Vh6pN

26. "Scientists Warn on CSIRO GM Wheat Threat." Safe Food Foundation & Institute. September 11, 2012. archive.md/byT1S

27. Foss, Arild S. "Growing fatter on a GM diet." ScienceNorway. July 17, 2012. archive.md/c2LUy

28. "IARC Monograph on Glyphosate." International Agency for Research on Cancer. archive.is/BoBdv

29. "Bayer faces skyrocketing US lawsuits over glyphosate." Deutsche Welle. July 30, 2019. archive.is/Njzjr

30. "In re: Roundup Products Liability Litigation (MDL No. 2741)." United States District Court Northern District of California. archive.is/biMzo

31. "In re: Roundup Products Liability Litigation (MDL No. 2741). Case 3:16-md-02741-VC Document 246-2." United States District Court Northern District of California. April 20, 2017. bit.ly/2V7Ocjw

32. Boobis, Alan, et. al. "WHO's IARC under fire for ignoring exculpatory data on glyphosate: Should it be reformed or abolished?" Genetic Literacy Project. June 16, 2017. archive.is/yEMdx

33. Hakim, Danny. "Monsanto Weed Killer Roundup Faces New Doubts on Safety in Unsealed Documents." The New York Times. March 14, 2017. archive.is/Fg56R

34. "Case 3:16-md-02741-VC Document 189-4." U.S. Right to Know. March 14, 2017. bit.ly/2VeLKro

35. "Case 3:16-md-02741-VC Document 141-1." U.S. Right to Know. February 10, 2017. bit.ly/32iWUg8

36. Séralini, Gilles-Éric, et al. "RETRACTED: Long term toxicity of a Roundup herbicide and a Roundup-tolerant genetically modified maize." Food and Chemical Toxicology. Volume 50, Issue 11, November 2012, Pages 4221-4231. archive.is/M0lh6

37. "Funding." Science Media Centre. archive.is/CFugb

38. "Applications (references EFSA-GMO-NL-2005-22, EFSA-GMO-RX-NK603) for the placing on the market of the genetically modified glyphosate tolerant maize NK603 for cultivation, food and feed uses, import and processing and for renewal of the authorisation of maize NK603 as existing products, both under Regulation (EC) No 1829/2003 from Monsanto[1]." European Food Safety Authority. June 11, 2009. archive.is/LsORZ

39. "Séralini et al. study conclusions not supported by data, says EU risk assessment community." European Food Safety Authority. November 28, 2012. archive.is/R9ZN8

40. Engdahl, William. "Ratted out: Scientific journal bows to Monsanto over anti-GMO study." RT. December 2, 2013. archive.is/GdKlq

41. Wager, Elizabeth, et al. "Retraction Guidelines." Committee on Publication Ethics. September 2009. archive.ph/kLQD7

42. See endnote 36.

43. "Orwellian airbrushing of scientific record." GMWatch. November 30, 2013. archive.is/3xYwt

44. Foucart, Stéphane. "La discrète influence de Monsanto." Le Monde. July 10, 2016. archive.is/xbHHS

45. Mezzomo, Bélin Poletto, et al. "WITHDRAWN: Effects of oral administration of Bacillus thuringiensis as spore-crystal strains Cry1Aa, Cry1Ab, Cry1Ac or Cry2Aa on hematologic and genotoxic endpoints of Swiss albino mice." Food and Chemical Toxicology. November 9, 2012. archive.is/QezvC

46. Bardocz, Susan, et al. "Seralini [sic] and Science: an Open Letter." Independent Science News. October 2, 2012. archive.is/H9YiW

47. Saltmiras, David Anthony. "FY2013." Baum Hedlund Aristei & Goldman, PC, Trial Lawyers. August 20, 2013. bit.ly/2TbEXgH

48. Sachs, Eric S., et al. "RE: Letters to the Editor?" Baum Hedlund Aristei & Goldman, PC, Trial Lawyers. September 26, 2012. bit.ly/2vwBMHk

49. Hakim, Danny. "Monsanto Emails Raise Issue of Influencing Research on Roundup Weed Killer." The New York Times. August 1, 2017. archive.is/22aGQ

50. See endnote 49.

51. "Uncovered: Monsanto campaign to get Séralini study retracted." GMWatch. August 2, 2017. archive.is/1a6th

52. Kenfield, Isabella. "Michael Taylor: Monsanto's Man in the Obama Administration." Organic Consumers Association. August 14, 2009. archive.is/FwSTZ

53. "Joint FAO/WHO Expert Consultation on Biotechnology and Food Safety." Food and Agricultural Organization. October 4, 1996. bit.ly/3O3Eh9t

54. "Safety evaluation of foods derived by modern biotechnology: concepts and principles." CiteSeerX. archive.is/ondHG

55. "Substantial Equivalence." Wikipedia. archive.is/UeKH6

56. Ho, M.W. and R. Steinbrecher. "The Principle of Substantial equivalence is Unscientific and Arbitary." Institute of Science in Society. 1998. archive.is/o1ReJ

57. "Statement of Policy — Foods Derived from New Plant Varieties." FDA. May 1992. archive.is/yGLWe

58. Nestle, Marion. "Michael Taylor appointed to FDA: A good choice!" Food Politics. July 7, 2009. archive.is/VLSqB

59. Murphy, Dave. "20 Years of GMO Policy That Keeps Americans in the Dark About Their Food." HuffPost. July 30, 2012. archive.is/B5Izz

60. "Noted Food Safety Expert Michael R. Taylor Named Advisor to FDA Commissioner." FDA. July 7, 2009. archive.is/aEBnY

61. "Meet Michael R. Taylor, J.D., Deputy Commissioner for Foods." FDA. October 19, 2011. archive.is/kMuqy

62. Briney, Amanda. "History and Overview of the Green Revolution." ThoughtCo. January 23, 2020. archive.is/CVa1e

63. "Dr. Norman Borlaug: He Saved A Billion Lives." American Council on Science and Health. May 7, 2020. archive.is/ZxeI2

64. "Our history." International Maize and Wheat Improvement Center. archive.is/yhzMW

65. Engdahl, William F. Seeds of Destruction: The Hidden Agenda of Genetic Manipulation. (Montreal, QC: Global Research, Centre for Research on Globalization, 2007.) Page 110.

66. "Jacob George Harrar." The Rockefeller Foundation: A Digital History. archive.is/oqvL9

67. "International Basic Economy Corporation (IBEC) records 1945-1977." Rockefeller Archive Center. archive.is/zTMTM

68. "The Worldwatch Institute." Rockefeller Brothers Fund. 1974. archive.is/NK669

69. Brown, Lester R. Seeds of Change: The Green Revolution and Development in the 1970's. [sic] (New York: Praeger Publishers, 1970.) Page 59.

70. Hamilton, Shane. "Revisiting the History of Agribusiness." Cambridge University Press. December 13, 2016. archive.is/EMBpN

71. Golden, Soma S. "Loentief [sic] Relates Economic Theory to Fact." The Harvard Crimson. December 17, 1959. archive.is/79mZW

72. "USAID and PL-480, 1961-1969." Office of the Historian, Foreign Service Institute, United States Department of State. archive.is/dYgLA

73. Corbett, James. "Beware Americans Bearing Gifts: NGOs as Trojan Horses." The Corbett Report. August 9, 2015. corbettreport.com/?p=15895

74. Murphy, Sophia, et al. "Cereal Secrets: The world's largest grain traders and global agriculture." OXFAM International. August 3, 2012. archive.is/z6tqc

75. Farmer Jon. "Meet the Behemoths of Modern Grain Trading." Medium. January 28, 2017. archive.is/62qUp

76. "Agriculture & the World Bank." The Whirled Bank Group. 2003. archive.is/bxPuJ

77. Roseboro, Ken. "The GMO Seed Cartel." The Organic & Non-GMO Report. February 1, 2013. archive.is/XSEmB

78. "Monsanto's royalty grab in Argentina." GRAIN. October 8, 2004. archive.is/uc9H6

79. Joensen, Lilian and Stella Semino. "Argentina's torrid love affair with the soybean." GRAIN. October 26, 2004. archive.is/7o5gt

80. Bremer, L. Paul. "Coalition Provisional Authority Order Number 81: Patent, Industrial Design, Undisclosed Information, Integrated Circuits and Plant Variety Law." Coalition Provisional Authority. April 26, 2004. bit.ly/2StKCBc

81. Gershman, John. "Iraq's New Patent Law." Institute for Policy Studies. October 3, 2005. archive.is/Xwol3

82. Anderson, Robert S. "The Origins of the International Rice Research Institute." Minerva, Vol. 29, No. 1 (March 1991), pp. 61-89. JSTOR. archive.is/mCnO2

83. "International Service for the Acquisition of Agri-biotech Applications." SourceWatch. October 27, 2011. archive.is/fn7lt

84. "CGIAR." Wikipedia. April 30, 2021. archive.is/a3d1Y

85. "About Us." Crop Trust. archive.is/1fJwG

86. "Foundation Funds Efforts to Rescue 95 Percent of Endangered Crop Biodiversity." Bill & Melinda Gates Foundation. April 2007. archive.is/xX0N8

87. "Donors and Funding Status." Crop Trust. archive.is/w1esS

88. "About Us." International Treaty on Plant Genetic Resources for Food and Agriculture. Food and Agriculture Organization of the United Nations. archive.is/JSY2I

89. "The Plant Treaty: Q&A with Crop Trust Director of Science, Luigi Guarino." Crop Trust. November 4, 2019. archive.is/xOfMn

90. "Crop Trust Announces New Board." Crop Trust. February 16, 2007. archive.is/YAXwX

91. "About — 1990s." Population Council. Archived December 3, 2008. archive.is/ZL6lh

92. See "They Don't Want Your Genes in the Pool" elsewhere in this volume.

93. Duggan, Jennifer. "Inside The 'Doomsday' Vault." TIME. April 2017. archive.is/rWHoM

94. Palermo, Elizabeth. "'Doomsday' Seed Vault: The Science Behind World's Arctic Storage Cube." LiveScience. September 24, 2015. archive.is/3Jfzm

95. Boyle, Louise. 'The 'Doomsday' seed vault protecting the world's crops amid catastrophes like coronavirus." Independent. March 27, 2020. archive.is/FYOme

96. "General Information." Posilac Bovine Somatotropin by Monsanto. 2007. archive.is/71ivE

97. "Dr. Samuel Epstein's 20 Year Fight Against Biotech, Cancer-Causing Milk." Organic Consumers Association. October 28, 2009. archive.is/94RYw

98. Ewall, Mike. "Bovine Growth Hormone: Milk does nobody good..." EJNet. archive.is/xtaST

99. Smith, Jeffrey M. "Got Hormones — Monsanto's GM hormones for cows cause controversy." GMWatch. December 5, 2004. archive.is/vzjOc

100. "Kroger to Complete Transition to Certified rBST-free Milk by Early 2008." The Kroger Co. August 1, 2007. archive.is/DDEiu

101. "Safeway milk free of bovine hormone." Seattle PI. January 21, 2007. archive.is/LbnJ

102. Adamy, Janet. "Starbucks Less Organic." The Wall Street Journal. January 16, 2008. archive.is/Z8ZFL

103. "Wal-Mart Offers Private Label Milk Produced without Artificial Growth Hormone." Walmart Corporate. March 21, 2008. archive.is/nogZn

104. Paley, Rachel Tepper. "Breyers Ice Cream Nixes Dairy Treated With Artificial Growth Hormones." yahoo!life. February 3, 2015. archive.is/DOK5R

105. "Frequently Asked Questions." Byrne Dairy. Archived May 3, 2015. archive.is/Upbk1

106. McKinney, Matt. "General Mills to stop use of rBGH milk in Yoplait." Star Tribune. February 9, 2009. archive.is/1bEGs

107. Buycott. buycott.com

108. "Pro-GMO? Or Pro-Right to Know?" Buycott.com. archive.md/lVDg2

109. "Non-GMO Shopping Guide... And When You Dine Out." Institute for Responsible Technology. nongmoshoppingguide.com

How to Enjoy Your Servitude

CAN YOU IMAGINE trying to explain the twenty-first century to someone from the 1950s?

1950s: So, let me get this straight: this magic box you carry around in your pocket...

2020s: It's called an iPhone.

1950s: ... this magic box creates a list of every place you've been?

2020s: Yes, and what time I went there and how long I was there for!

1950s: And this log is automatically sent to a corporation in California?

2020s: Yes.

1950s: Aren't you afraid of what that company will do with all those records on you? What if it turns everything over to the government?

2020s: Oh, I'm not worried about that happening.

1950s: But why not?

2020s: Because the government already has all that data! Don't you know about the PATRIOT Act?[1]

1950s: *Of course* I know how a patriot would act in the face of such tyranny! I mean, this is your private information! It's unthinkable that you could be so careless about it!

2020s: It's not careless. It's convenient! Why, just today I used Foursquare to check in at the restaurant where I ate lunch, updated my Facebook status while waiting for my afternoon Pilates class, and tweeted a selfie at the ball game this evening.

1950s: I have no idea what any of that even means.

2020s: It means I'm not concerned about my privacy.

1950s: Then I guess the commies have won.

2020s: Come again?

1950s: The Reds. You know, the Russkies! Clearly the Soviets have taken over the US and you've all lost your minds. Brainwashed by those crafty pinkos, no doubt.

2020s: Oh, you mean the Soviet Union? I think I learned about that in history class. No, we're in the land of the free here.

1950s: In what sense, exactly, are you free?

2020s: Well ... uh ....

And that would be just the *start* of the conversation.

How would you even begin to explain that your identity cards and your passport are being digitized, loaded with your biometric data, and used against you as a tool of governmental surveillance and control?[2]

Or that an extrajudicial presidential kill list euphemistically referred to as a "disposition matrix" presumes to grant the President of the United States the authority to kill anyone he wants anywhere in the world at any time?[3]

Or that an international treaty permits your personal banking details to be shared among the OECD nations as the first step toward an envisioned global tax grid?[4]

Or that secret DNA databases store blood samples collected from your newborn at birth—samples that are owned by private companies and studied by researchers without your knowledge or consent?[5]

How, indeed, would you explain the million other infringements on basic personal liberties that have taken place in the past half-century? After all, you wouldn't simply be listing the encroachments on your liberty that have been wrought by technological advances. You'd be explaining the fundamental shift in the *conception* of these liberties and their importance in our lives that has taken place in recent decades. Even assuming you could teach this imaginary time traveller the technical details of the systems that are stripping us of our rights and freedoms, could you ever really explain the *mindset* of our generation?

Doubtless, the very liberties we are so cavalier about losing are the self-same liberties that, fifty years ago, were considered so sacrosanct that no one even thought to articulate them—let alone protect then. Explaining their loss to someone of that era, then, might be well-nigh impossible.

1950s: What you're saying reminds me of that English chap, Orwell. Just died recently, I hear. Did you read his final work? What was it called again? *1994*?

2020s: *Nineteen Eighty-Four.*

1950s: Oh, right, that's it. Chilling, wasn't it?

2020s: I guess so. A bit clichéd, though, don't you think? Besides, Huxley was closer to the mark.

Although your 1950s interlocutor would be familiar with Aldous Huxley's 1932 book, *Brave New World*, he wouldn't have heard Huxley's 1962 speech at Berkeley, ambitiously titled "The Ultimate Revolution." It was in that speech that Huxley really pulled back the curtain on the myriad of technological and pharmacological techniques of mental manipulation that the technocrats and social engineers of modern times have at their disposal.[6]

Huxley contrasted George Orwell's nightmare vision of the tyrannically controlled 1984 society—"a projection into the future of a society where control was exercised wholly by terrorism and violent attacks upon the mind-body of individuals"—with his own vision of a *Brave New World* of control through manipulation and reward:

> [I]f you can get people to consent to the state of affairs in which they're living—the state of servitude, the state of being, having their differences ironed out, and being made amenable to mass production methods on the social level—if you can do this, then you are likely to have a much more stable and lasting society. A much more easily controllable society than you would if you were relying wholly on clubs and firing squads and concentration camps.[7]

American media critic Neil Postman touched on these contrasting methods of control in his 1985 book, *Amusing Ourselves to Death*. He pointed out how the nature of television news reporting—contextless, frantic, constantly shifting in focus—placates viewers and blunts their reaction to even the most brazen violations of personal liberty and public liberty.

> For all his perspicacity, George Orwell would have been stymied by this situation; there is nothing "Orwellian" about it. The President does not have the press under his thumb. *The New York Times* and *The Washington Post* are not *Pravda*; the Associated Press is not Tass. And there is no Newspeak here. Lies have not been defined as truth nor truth as lies. All that has happened is that the public has adjusted to incoherence and been amused into indifference. Which is why Aldous Huxley would not in the least be surprised by the story. Indeed, he prophesied its coming. He believed that it is far more likely that the Western democracies will dance and dream themselves into oblivion than march into it, single file and manacled. Huxley grasped, as Orwell did not, that it is not necessary to conceal anything from a public insensible to contradiction and narcoticized by technological diversions. Although Huxley did not specify that television would be our main line to the drug, he would have no difficulty accepting Robert MacNeil's observation that "Television is the soma of Aldous Huxley's *Brave New World*." Big Brother turns out to be Howdy Doody.[8]

1950s: I knew it! Television is the culprit! It's been a tool of commie brainwashers all along, and here we are inviting it into our homes and letting it rot the minds of our children!

2020s: TV? That's so twentieth century. Now we have Netflix and Hulu and Peacock and Prime. We can check our TikTok feed while we're on the john listening to a podcast. We can even download Huxley's 1962 speech just like that! And for free! But why be a nerd and waste time listening to that boring old Brit? Hey, I hear the new Taylor Swift song just got leaked online!

Ah, yes. Bread and circuses. As our articulate, time-travelling interlocutor might observe (once Netflix, Hulu, Peacock, Prime, TikTok, and Taylor Swift are explained to him): "*plus ça change* . . . ."

But mere distraction is not the primary tool of societal control at the disposal of modern-day social engineers. Other elements of psychological manipulation are at work as well.

There are, for instance, what Huxley in his speech identified as "the techniques of terrorism"—that is, techniques of inflicting mental or physical violence, pain, or stress on a target in order to manipulate or condition his behaviour.

These techniques—the modus operandi of Big Brother and the *Nineteen Eighty-Four* boot-on-the-face-style police state—have been around since time immemorial, and, Huxley insists, are only becoming more effective as scientific methods are applied to refine them. One need only study the modern types of brainwashing, for example, to see how these modern techniques of terror constitute "a real refinement on the older methods of terror" because they end up "inducing a kind of voluntary acceptance of [. . .] the state of affairs in which [a given target] finds himself."[9]

But beyond systems of control that rely on brute force and naked aggression, there exists what Huxley describes as an array of "non-terroristic techniques for inducing consent and inducing people to love their servitude."

Such "non-terroristic" control tactics include the use of psychopharmaceuticals[10] and TV screen flicker rates[11] and social media algorithms[12] to induce "voluntary" consent in targeted individuals. Like the techniques of terror, these subtler methods of manipulation, too, are being constantly refined through empirical study and are now incredibly effective in swaying the opinions of vast swaths of the population.

One need only witness the remarkable feats of pretzel logic that supporters of the establishment's geopolitical narratives are capable of to understand just how effective this form of mind control can be. The average establishment news junkie, for example, can go from hailing Osama Bin Laden and his band of Al Qaeda agents as "warriors for peace" in 1990s Afghanistan[13] to reviling them as the epitome of evil responsible for the September 11, 2001, terror attacks to accepting them as necessary allies in the war against Bashar al-Assad in Syria in the 2010s[14]— all without experiencing cognitive whiplash.

That the masses are capable of holding these flatly contrary positions at various times is itself a testament to the power of these non-terroristic techniques of persuasion. But what's even more remarkable is that the people who are molded by these master manipulators don't even notice these contradictions as contradictions. They're too entranced by the latest bells and whistles on their fondleslabs to be very aware of the world around them.

1950s: So, wait, you're saying many Americans think a military coup would be a *good* thing?[15]

2020s: Mm hmm.

1950s: And you're all becoming used to the idea of giving up your fingerprints like common criminals just so you can cross the borders between countries?[16]

2020s: Mm hmm.

1950s: And you'd rather members of Congress be randomly selected from the phone book than put your trust in the crooks voted into office?[17]

2020s: Mm hmm.

1950s: And you're all perfectly happy with this?

2020s: Mm hmm.

1950s: Why aren't you outraged? Why aren't you throwing these damn magic boxes in the trash? Why aren't you soaking up the sweet summer sunshine and talking with your neighbours and *living life* anymore?

2020s: Mm hmm.

1950s: Are you even listening to me?

2020s: Sorry, what was that? I was texting my friend about this viral video I just watched.

1950s: Never mind. I give up. Send me back to the '50s!

NOTES

1. "PATRIOT Act." Electronic Privacy Informaton Center. archive.is/4vdqU

2. Corbett, James. "Episode 415 - The Global Digital ID Prison." The Corbett Report. March 12, 2022. corbettreport.com/digitalid

3. Becker, Jo and Scot Shane. "Secret 'Kill List' Proves a Test of Obama's Principles and Will." The New York Times. May 29, 2012. archive.fo/QE3mz

4. "Interview 742 - New World Next Week with James Evan Pilato." The Corbett Report. September 6, 2013. corbettreport.com/?p= 7938

5. Corbett, James. "Announcing the DNA Control Grid." The Corbett Report. February 27, 2009. archive.fo/ofM22

6. "Aldous Huxley 1962 U.C. Berkeley Speech on 'The Ultimate Revoluton.'" Public Intelligence. archive.fo/OZLj9

7. See endnote 6.

8. Postman, Neil. Amusing Ourselves to Death: Public Discourse in the Age of Show Business. (New York: Penguin, 2006.) Page 111.

9. See endnote 6.

10. Deegan, Gordon. "Psychiatrist calls for lithium to be added to water." The Irish Times. December 2, 2011. archive.is/u2Inl

11. Nelson, Joyce. The Perfect Machine: Television and the Bomb. (Philadelphia: New Society Publishers, 1992.) Pages 69-73.

12. Booth, Robert. "Facebook reveals news feed experiment to control emotions." The Guardian. archive.is/nBsbt

13. Fisk, Robert. "Anti-Soviet warrior puts his army on the road to peace: The Saudi businessman who recruited mujahedin now uses them for large-scale building projects in Sudan. Robert Fisk met him in Almatig." Independent. December 6, 1993. archive.is/ePAFy

14. Freeman, Elliot. "From 2012: Senior CFR official: Free Syrian Army needs al-Qaeda support." Syria Resources Archive. August 27, 2012. archive.is/qb1vo

15. Foa, Roberto and Yascha Mounk. "Across the Globe, a Growing Disillusionment With Democracy." The New York Times. September 15, 2015. archive.fo/iDWsl

16. Corbett, James. "Japan to Fingerprint Foreigners on Entry." The Corbett Report. October 8, 2007. corbettreport.com/japanfingerprints

17. "U.S. Congress no better than random choices from a phone book: poll." Daily News. February 9, 2012. archive.is/FDTfW

The Three Types

There are those who watch Building 7 falling and see a progressive collapse caused by office fires.

There are those who watch Building 7 falling and see a controlled demolition.

And there are those who don't know what Building 7 is.

Which one are you?

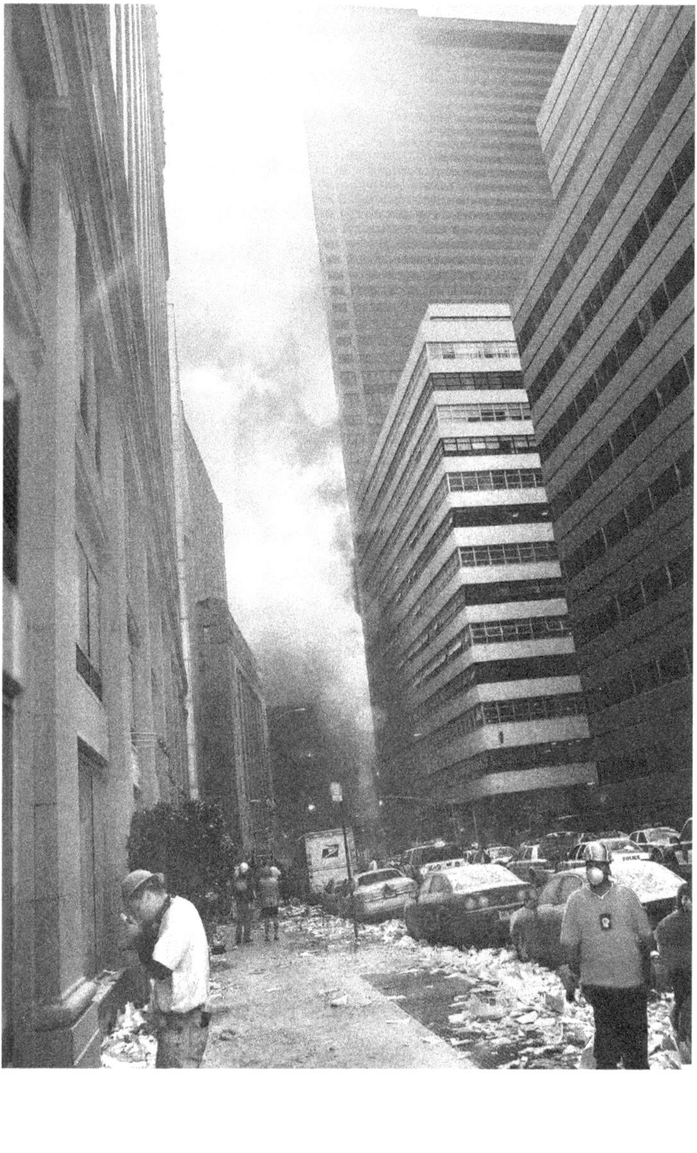

The Strange Life of Maurice Strong

THIS IS WHAT Maurice Strong's obituary would have looked like in any reasonable world:

> Disgraced kleptocrat Maurice Strong died in 2015 at the age of 86. He was shunned from polite society and forced into a life of exile in Beijing after his decades of business intrigues, crimes against humanity, and environmental destruction unraveled. His savagery culminated with an attempt to profit off the death of starving Iraqi children.
>
> His funeral was a quiet affair, attended only by those few family members who could not find it in their heart to ignore him completely. Former friends and business associates like Paul Martin, James Wolfensohn, Kofi Annan, Conrad Black, and Al Gore all avoided calls for comments on their disgraced colleague's passing.

But this is not a reasonable world, so we were handed this instead:

> On Wednesday, hundreds will gather across from Parliament Hill for an extraordinary commemoration. The Governor General, the Prime Minister, the Minister of the Environment, the former president of the World Bank—among other dignitaries, in and out of office—will pay homage to one of the great Canadians of his generation.

They will celebrate the life of Maurice Frederick Strong, who died on November 27. His passing brought the obligatory obituaries and personal tributes. But in a country that often hides its light under a barn, Maurice Strong—and the feverish, consequential life he led at home and abroad—should not go uncelebrated.[1]

And the accolades just kept pouring in.

From Canadian Prime Minister Justin Trudeau: "Maurice Strong was a pioneer of sustainable development who left our country and our world a better place."[2]

From Klaus Schwab, the co-founder of the World Economic Forum at Davos: "He was a great visionary, always ahead of our times in his thinking."[3]

From author and philosopher John Ralston Saul: "He changed the world."[4]

In fact, a whole gaggle of globalists showed up to pay their respects at Strong's memorial service in Ottawa in January 2016—from former World Bank president James Wolfensohn to under-secretary-general of the United Nations Achim Steiner to the former secretary-general of the Club of Rome, Martin Less. Written condolences poured in from other prominent globalists, including Mikhail Gorbachev, Gro Harlem Bruntland, and Kofi Annan.

And why exactly was Maurice Strong so beloved by his globalist peers? Oh, that's right:

INTERVIEWER: Maurice Strong doesn't have any ambition for the United Nations to become the world's government?

STRONG: No, and it's not necessary, it's not feasible, and certainly we are a long way from any such thing. But we do need—if we are going to have a more peaceful world, a more secure world— we need a more effective system of cooperation, which is what I call "system of governance." And the United Nations, with all its difficulties, is the best game in town.[5]

President of Power Corporation of Canada. President of the Canadian International Development Agency. Chair of Petro Canada. Chair of Ontario Hydro. Head of the United Nations Environment Programme. Founding member of the World Economic Forum at Davos. Father of the Intergovernmental Panel on Climate Change (IPCC). Committed globalist.

No, it is not difficult to see why fellow globalists love arch-globalist Maurice Strong. But how did this man, a dirt-poor high school dropout from Oak Lake, Manitoba, rise through the ranks of political power to become an international wheeler-dealer who shaped many of our modern-day globalist institutions?

To answer that question, we need to take a closer look at the man himself. This unlikely tale is the story of Maurice Strong's remarkable life, and it wends its way from the heart of Alberta's oil patch right to the corridors of power in the United Nations.

But in order to understand the Maurice Strong story, first we have to note the equally remarkable story of his aunt, Anna Louise Strong. Born in Nebraska in 1885, Anna Louise was a fervent anti-capitalist whose passions led her, in the 1920s, to the newly formed Soviet Union, where she helped found Moscow's first English-language newspaper, then to China, where she met with China's labor and women's movement leaders. Along the way, she befriended the Communist luminaries of her day, including Vladimir Lenin and Leon Trotsky (with the latter actually writing the preface for her 1925 book on the fledgling USSR[6]) and Mao Zedong and Zhou Enlai.

As Anna Louise lay on her death bed in Beijing in 1970, Zhou (then premier of communist China) paid her a personal visit, encouraging her to cooperate with the doctors because, he said, "You have important things to do for us and the rest of the world."[7] But she died a few days later. Anna Louise Strong was buried in Beijing's famed Babaoshan Revolutionary Cemetery, a resting place reserved for China's "highest- ranking revolutionary heroes, high government officials, and, in recent years, individuals deemed of major importance due to their contributions to society."[8]

Unfortunately for humanity, the Maurice apple didn't fall far from the Strong family tree. Born in rural Manitoba in 1929 and suffering through the worst of the Great Depression, Maurice Strong dropped out of school at age fourteen in search of a job. He worked his way around as a deck hand on various ships and then, at age sixteen, as a fur buyer for the Hudson's Bay Company in Canada's North. There he met "Wild" Bill Richardson, whose wife, Mary McColl, hailed from the family behind McColl-Frontenac, one of Canada's largest oil companies.

Through Richardson, Strong made contacts that propelled him into his unlikely career. As Wikipedia puts it:

> Strong first met with a leading UN official in 1947 who arranged for him to have a temporary low-level appointment, to serve as a junior security officer at the

UN headquarters in Lake Success, New York. He soon returned to Canada, and with the support of Lester B. Pearson, directed the founding of the Canadian International Development Agency in 1968.[9]

From junior security to head of an international development agency in two sentences. As far as massive narrative gaps and cryptic cover-ups of detail go, that paragraph is a masterpiece.

Yet the truth behind the concealment is even weirder. That "leading UN official" referred to by Wikipedia? None other than Treasurer Noah Monod. In fact, Monod didn't just get Strong a job, he gave him a place to live; the two roomed together during Strong's time in the Big Apple. But most importantly, Monod introduced Strong to the man who, more than any other, would aid his meteoric rise to international superstardom: David Rockefeller.

Maurice Strong liked to boast that he was confrontational with Rockefeller at the start. According to Strong, some of his first words to David were, "I'm deeply prejudiced against you and all your family stands for." Oddly, David doesn't remember the meeting that way, recalling instead that the two had "a strong working relationship."[10]

Either way, from that moment on, Strong was a made man. And from that moment on, wherever Strong went, Rockefeller and his associates could be found hovering somewhere in the background, opening doors, making connections, and pulling strings.

When Maurice Strong quit that lowly UN security job to return to Canada, it was a Standard Oil veteran, Jack Gallagher, who gave him his big break in the Alberta oil patch. Gallagher had been hired to create a new oil and gas exploration company by Henrie Brunie, a close friend of Rockefeller associate John J. McCloy. Strong signed on as Gallagher's assistant.[11]

Then, after Strong unaccountably decided to quit his job, sell his house, and travel to Africa, there was Rockefeller waiting for him with a position at CalTex Oil Kenya in Nairobi.[12]

When he left Kenya in 1954 to start his own company back in Canada, Strong hired Brunie to manage it and appointed two Standard Oil of New Jersey reps to its board. By this point he was in his late twenties and already a multi-millionaire.[13]

After considerable networking with Canada's political elite, Strong was appointed head of Power Corporation, the baby of the powerful "Canadian Rockefellers," the Desmarais family.[14] Power Corporation had long been a political kingmaker in Canadian politics, and under Strong's stewardship it continued to foster the next generation of political superstars. One of Strong's best-known appointees was a fresh-faced Harvard MBA named James Wolfensohn, future president of the World Bank. Another hand pick: Paul Martin, future Prime Minister of Canada.

Strong left Power Corporation to head up Canada's External Aid Office, which he reorganized into the Canadian International Development Agency (CIDA). Separately, he chaired the similarly named Canada Development Investment Corporation (CDIC) and the Board of Governors of the International Development Research Centre (IDRC). As journalist Elaine Dewar, who interviewed Strong for her groundbreaking book *Cloak of Green*, explains:

IDRC had a clause in its enabling legislation allowing it to give money directly to individuals as well as to governments and private organizations. It was set up as a corporation, reporting to Parliament through the minister of external affairs. Its board of governors was designed to include private and even foreign persons. [...] Since IDRC was not created as an agent of the Crown (as CIDA is), it was able to receive charitable donations from corporations and individuals as well as government funds.[15]

Naturally, those "corporations and individuals" generously "donating" their money to IDRC included Rockefeller's Chase Manhattan Bank and the Rockefeller Foundation itself. Naturally, too, Strong used the IDRC for political purposes: He even admitted to Dewar that the Centre peddled influence in the Third World under its quasi-governmental guise.[16]

His quasi-business, quasi-governmental, quasi-"philanthropic" career reached an even more rarified level in 1969. That's when the Swedish ambassador to the UN called up Strong to see if he wanted to head the forthcoming United Nations Conference on the Human Environment, which was due to take place in Stockholm in 1972. The summons came not because of Strong's supposed love for the environment, but because, by then, the 40-year-old Strong was renowned as a human Rolodex of political, business, and financial connections that spanned the developed and developing world.

By this point it will come as no surprise to learn that before departing for the Stockholm summit, Strong was duly appointed a trustee of the Rockefeller Foundation,[17] which promptly funded his office for the conference and also supplied Carnegie Fellow Barbara Ward and Rockefeller ecologist Rene Dubos for his team. Strong commissioned Ward and Dubos to write *Only One Earth*, a foundational text in the sustainable development arena that is heavily touted by globalists as a key for promoting the global management of resources.[18]

That 1972 summit in Sweden is still hailed as a landmark moment in the history of the modern environmental movement. It led not only to the first governmentally administered environmental action plans in Europe but to the creation of an entirely new UN bureaucracy: the United Nations Environment Programme, or UNEP.[19] As Dewar explains:

> Like so many of the organizations Strong has made, this one too had multiple uses. In 1974, UNEP rose out of the undeveloped soil of Nairobi, Kenya, Strong's old stomping ground. Placing UNEP in Africa was explained as a sop to the developing countries, who had been suspicious of Western intentions. But it was also useful for the big powers to have another international organization in Nairobi. After the Yom Kippur War in 1973, Nairobi became the key spy capital of Africa.[20]

The Yom Kippur War referenced by Dewar and the resulting OPEC oil embargo (magically foretold by the Bilderberg Conference in Sweden earlier that year and arranged by David Rockefeller's agent, Henry Kissinger[21]) had another spin-off effect that ended up benefiting Strong. The embargo hit eastern Canada hard, prompting Prime Minister Pierre Trudeau to create a publicly run national oil company. As a result, Petro-Canada was born in 1975. And who do you suppose Trudeau appointed to head it? You guessed right: Maurice Strong, by now the single most powerful member of the global(ist) environmental movement, became the first president of Canada's national oil company.

And David Rockefeller was there with Strong yet again in Colorado in 1987 for the "Fourth World Wilderness Congress," a meeting of world-historical importance that almost no one had even heard of. Attended by the likes of not only Rockefeller and Strong but also James Baker, President Reagan's then-Secretary of the Treasury, and, yes, Edmund de Rothschild himself, the conference ultimately revolved around the question of how to finance the burgeoning environmental movement that Strong had shaped from the ground up through his work at UNEP.

It was at that conference (recordings of which are available online, thanks to whistleblower George Hunt[22]) that Rothschild called for a World Conservation Bank, which he envisioned as the funding mechanism for a "second Marshall Plan" that would be used for Third World "debt relief" and for that favourite globalist dog whistle, "sustainable development."

Rothschild's dream came true when Strong presided over another high-level UN environment summit: the 1992 Rio de Janeiro "Earth Summit." Although the Earth Summit is best known as the conference that birthed Agenda 21, an overlooked fact is that it allowed the World Conservation Bank to become a reality.

Started on the summit's eve as a $1 billion World Bank pilot program, the World Conservation Bank, now known as the Global Environment Facility (GEF), is the largest public funder of global environmental projects. To date, it has made more than $23 billion in grants and has cofinanced a further $129 billion.[23] The bank is the financial mechanism for the United Nations Framework Convention on Climate Change (UNFCCC), the organizing convention directing the Intergovernmental Panel on Climate Change (IPCC).

With Agenda 21 under his belt and Rothschild's GEF dream bank in the can and the IPCC already twinkling in his eye, Strong's remarkable career showed no signs of stopping or even slowing down. After wrapping up in Rio, he took on a series of appointments so bewildering, exhaustive, and frankly exhausting, that it almost defies credulity. From his official website comes the following list:

> After the Earth Summit, Strong continued to take a leading role in implementing the results of Rio through establishment of the Earth Council, the Earth Charter movement, his Chairmanship of the World Resources Institute, Membership on the Board of the International Institute for Sustainable Development, the Stockholm Environment Institute, the African-American Institute, the Institute of Ecology in Indonesia, the Beijer Institute of the Royal Swedish Academy of Sciences, and others. Strong was a longtime Foundation Director of the World Economic Forum, a Senior Advisor to the President of the World Bank, a Member of the International Advisory of Toyota Motor Corporation, the Advisory Council for the Center for International Development of Harvard University, the World Business Council for Sustainable Development, the World Conservation Union (IUNC), the World Wildlife Fund, Resources for the Future, and the Eisenhower Fellowships.[24]

There is no doubt that Strong led a charmed life. The persistent presence of Rockefeller interests throughout that life leaves no doubt as to why doors automatically opened for him wherever Strong went in the world.

But still, one has to ask how and why a high school dropout who made it big in the oil patch thanks to his Big Oil connections would go on to become the single most important figure in the international environmental movement. Was he genuinely interested in protecting the environment?

Consider Strong's acquisition of the Arizona Colorado Land & Cattle Company from Saudi arms dealer Adnan Khashoggi in 1978. As part of that acquisition, Strong gained control of a ranch in the San Luis Valley in Colorado called the Baca Grande. As Henry Lamb details in a 1997 article:

> The ranch, called Baca, sat on the continent's largest fresh water aquifer. Strong intended to pipe the water to the desert southwest, but environmental organizations protested and the plan was abandoned. Strong ended up with a $1.2 million settlement from the water company, an annual grant of $100,000 from Laurance Rockefeller, and still retained the rights to the water.[25]

But Strong's interest in the site had nothing to do with preserving the pristine environment of the San Luis Valley. His motives were altogether stranger. According to a report by John Izzard published in *Quadrant Online*, Strong had been told by a "mystic" that:

> The Baca would become the centre for a new planetary order which would evolve from the economic

collapse and environmental catastrophes that would sweep the globe in the years to come.

Izzard's article continues:

> As a result of these revelations Strong created the Manitou Foundation, a New Age institution located at the Baca ranch—above the sacred waters that Strong had been denied permission to pump out. This hocus-pocus continued with the foundation of The Conservation Fund (with financial help of Laurance Rockefeller) to study the mystical properties of the Manitou Mountain. At the Baca ranch there is a circular temple devoted to the world's mystical and religious movements.[26]

Indeed, Strong's missionary zeal for spreading his environmental message of doom and destruction for so many decades can be more easily explained as a quasi-religious zeal for preparing the way for the "New World Order" that this environmental doom supposedly foretells.

Further insights into Strong's own mystic New Age beliefs are found in what he considered to be his most important achievement: the creation of the Earth Charter. The Earth Charter was an outgrowth of Strong's Earth Council Institute, which he founded in 1992 with the help of Mikhail Gorbachev, David Rockefeller (of course), Al Gore, Shimon Peres, and a host of Strong's other globalist friends.[27]

Strong's website describes the Earth Charter as "a widely recognized, global consensus statement on ethics and values for a sustainable future,"[28] but the Charter's co-founder, former Soviet leader Mikhail Gorbachev, saw it as a religious document, which he hoped would replace the Ten Commandments.[29] Strong, in an uncharacteristic display of modesty, merely compared the Charter to the Magna Carta.[30]

So, what exactly does the Earth Charter say? Why, the predictable mealy-mouthed platitudes one would expect about "social and economic justice" and other political buzzwords, of course. But beyond that, the document also serves as a love letter to world government:

> In order to build a sustainable global community, the nations of the world must renew their commitment to the United Nations, fulfill their obligations under existing international agreements, and support the implementation of Earth Charter principles with an international legally binding instrument on environment and development.[31]

The physical Earth Charter itself rests in the "Ark of Hope," a literal ark that was constructed specifically to house the original document. An obvious reference to the ark of the covenant from the Old Testament, the Ark of Hope was unveiled in a ceremony in Vermont presided over by none other than Steven C. Rockefeller (son of Nelson Rockefeller) on September 9, 2001. Two days later, when news of the events of September 11th rocked the world, the 200-pound ark was carried 350 miles to the United Nations Headquarters in New York City.[32]

While this quasi-religious quest for global government is wrapped in feel-good language about strengthening communities and preserving the planet, the underlying reality reveals a much more Machiavellian agenda. In her aptly named book *Cloak of Green*, Elaine Dewar writes of the 1992 Rio Earth Summit:

Advertised as the World's Greatest Summit, Rio was publicly described as a global negotiation to reconcile the need for environmental protection with the need for economic growth. The cognoscenti understood that there were other, deeper goals. These involved the shift of national regulatory powers to vast regional authorities; the opening of all remaining closed national economies to multinational interests; the strengthening of decision making structures far above and far below the grasp of newly minted national democracies; and, above all, the integration of the Soviet and Chinese empires into the global market system. There was no name for this very grand agenda that I had heard anyone use, so later I named it myself—the Global Governance Agenda.[33]

Exactly twenty years before Rio, during a 1972 BBC interview introducing the United Nations Conference on the Human Environment in Stockholm, Strong himself offered an insight into what this agenda would entail for the average man or woman. Discussing the "overpopulation problem" then being hyped as the environmental cause du jour, Strong admitted to his musings on the potential for reproductive licenses:

> Licenses to have babies, incidentally, is something that I got in trouble for some years ago for suggesting even in Canada that this might be necessary at some point ... at least some restriction on the right to have a child. I'm not proposing this, I was simply predicting this as one of the possible courses that society would have to seriously consider should we get ourselves into this kind of situation.[34]

That Strong was so successful in promoting this Global Governance Agenda for so long testifies not to his own visionary leadership, which so many globalists profess to have, but to the incredible resources of the Rockefellers and Rothschilds and others who have been funding the agenda into existence and pushing it along every step of the way.

It is some measure of good fortune for humanity, then, that Strong's decades of deceit finally came to an end (more or less) in 2005, when he was finally caught "with his hand in the till." As *Quadrant Online* reported:

> Investigations into the UN's Oil-for-Food-Program found that Strong had endorsed a cheque for $988,885 made out to M. Strong—issued by a Jordanian bank. The man who gave the cheque, South Korean business man Tongsun Park, was convicted in 2006 in a US Federal court of conspiring to bribe UN officials. Strong resigned and fled to Canada and thence to China where he has been living ever since.[35]

Although still making appearances at various events around the world, Strong kept a much lower profile for the last decade of his life, likely due to the ravages of advancing age. But now that he has passed away, we can more clearly see the many globalist institutions that constitute his real legacy.

So, no, it is not difficult to understand why Maurice Strong was so beloved by the globalist jet set. Just don't expect any of those jet-setters to relate the finer points of the Strong saga.

NOTES

1. Cohen, Andrew. "Cohen: Maurice Strong was the Earth's Mr. Fix-It." Ottawa Citzen. January 26, 2016. archive.fo/bjyOI

2. Semeniuk, Ivan. "Maurice Strong remembered for putng environmental issues on global stage." The Globe and Mail. January 27, 2016. archive.fo/8CMEC

3. Schwab, Klaus. "Maurice Strong: an appreciaton." November 29, 2015. World Economic Forum. archive.fo/jNkHT

4. "'A truly great citzen of Canada': Maurice Strong remembered in Ottawa." CTV News. January 28, 2016. archive.fo/RGkZt

5. "Life and Times: Maurice Strong (Complete)." YouTube, uploaded by GBPPR2, April 16, 2011. youtu.be/fhkxC1Q2FNU

6. Strong, Anna Louise. *The First Time in History*. Marxists.org. archive.fo/zxr1

7. "Anna Louise Strong." Knox County Historical Society. archive.fo/tFaCZ

8. "Babaoshan Revolutonary Cemetery." Wikipedia. archive.fo/3pZLo

9. "Maurice Strong." Wikipedia. archive.is/Ukil0

10. Dewar, Elaine. Cloak of Green. (Toronto: James Lorimer & Company, Publishers, 1995.) Pages 259- 260.

11. Thompson, Scot. "Maurice Strong Discusses His Pal Al Gore's Dark Age 'Cloak of Green.'" Executve Intelligence Review. January 29, 1999. archive.fo/igOQp

12. See endnote 10. Page 267.

13. See endnote 10. Page 268.

14. "Episode 240 - Power Corporaton Exposed." The Corbett Report. August 27, 2012. corbettreport.com/?p=5481

15. See endnote 10. Page 274.

16. See endnote 10. Page 274.

17. "The President's Review and Annual Report." The Rockefeller Foundaton. 1972. bit.ly/4cgJHaz

18. Vitachi, Anuradha. "Only One Earth." New Internatonalist. September 2, 1980. archive.fo/h3u8D

19. "The United Natons Conference on the Human Environment." GEO: Global Environment Outlook 3. archive.fo/sVj7y

20. See endnote 10. Page 279.

21. "How Big Oil Conquered The World." The Corbett Report. December 28, 2015. corbettreport.com/bigoil

22. "UN UNCED Earth Summit 1992 by George Hunt." YouTube, uploaded by Canada Live, February 16, 2015. youtu.be/r8c-NKjOOA0

23. "Who We Are." Global Environment Facility. archive.is/vgJoa

24. "Short Biography." MauriceStrong.net. archive.fo/slqcf

25. Lamb, Henry. "Maurice Strong: the new guy in your future!" Citizen Review Online. January 1997. archive.fo/y4n3i

26. Izzard, John. "Maurice Strong, Climate Crook." Quadrant Online. December 2, 2015. archive.fo/zOjZD

27. "Earth Council: how did it start?" MauriceStrong.net. archive.fo/lcVPM

28. "Earth Council Alliance." MauriceStrong.net. archive.fo/iXmxF

29. "Mikhail Gorbachev: New Moses for the masses." Canada Free Press. December 9, 2002. archive.fo/ZfvE1

30. "Maurice Strong thoughts on the Earth Charter (1/5)." YouTube, uploaded by Earth Charter Internatonal, November 27, 2009. youtu.be/O5rf6NTVHMU

31. "The Earth Charter." Earth Charter Initiative. archive.fo/dGwx0

32. "Ark of Hope." Ark of Hope. archive.is/jjvup

33. See endnote 10. Page 249.

34. "Maurice Strong Interview (BBC, 1972)." YouTube, uploaded by MDJarv, May 16, 2009. youtu.be/1YCatox0Lxo

35. See endnote 26.

The Real Meaning of "Independence"

EVERY FOURTH OF JULY, people the world over watch as the United States of America celebrates its Independence Day. Every country has its own national day, but American Independence Day has a certain mystique. Here the fireworks and festivities are not mindless celebrations of an abstract "nationhood." Rather, they're reminders of the war that was fought in the name of liberty to cast off an oppressor.

In the course of human events, nothing has been more dangerous to the ruling class than the concept of freedom. I'm not referring to the *documents* that have encapsulated and encouraged freedom and charted the development of this idea—the Magna Carta, the Declaration of Independence, the Emancipation Proclamation, or any of the other pieces of paper upon which the concept of freedom has been inscribed—*but to the idea itself.*

The idea that all human beings are born equal. That there exist inalienable rights which no self-proclaimed authority is ever justified in usurping. That our life, our liberty, and our property are inviolable, and that it is our duty to resist those who seek to violate them. These are the truths we hold to be self-evident here in the twenty-first century. We stand on the shoulders of the philosophical giants who possessed not only the intuition and understanding to grasp that living under tyranny is not the natural condition of humanity but the courage to fight and die for those convictions.

The idea of freedom has been dangerous to those who aim to dominate others *precisely because it is an idea*—a fire in the minds of men that, once lit, can never be put out. The torch of freedom cannot be imprisoned, stabbed, shot, or guillotined, although the heroic souls who have carried this torch are routinely subjected to such punishments. The documents which enumerate these ideals can be ignored, amended, or destroyed altogether, but the light of freedom shines eternally.

Yes, the idea of freedom is dangerous precisely because it is innate, indestructible, and, ultimately, irrepressible.

Not that the tyrants haven't tried to suppress our inborn will to be free. For as long as there have been ordinary men and women willing to defy their would-be rulers and assert their rights as individuals, there have been autocrats intent on snuffing out the flickering flame of freedom.

In 73 BC, Spartacus sparked a slave rebellion against the Roman Republic. Using nothing more than kitchen implements, he led a small band of fellow slave-gladiators in a plot to escape their bondage in Capua. They seized supplies from some wagons full of gladiatorial weapons and armour, plundered the area, and escaped to Mount Vesuvius, along the way recruiting other slaves to join them in their uprising. Defeating wave after wave of militia sent to subdue them, the ranks of the Spartacan rebellion swelled to 70,000 former slaves. Beset by eight legions of Roman troops under the command of the feared Marcus Crassus, Spartacus made a valiant last stand at Lucania. There, he and his followers were decimated by the disciplined, well-armed Roman forces.[1] The six thousand rebels who survived were captured and crucified by Crassus' legions.[2]

In 1381, King Richard II of England levied a deeply unpopular poll tax on the British serfs, who were already living in abject poverty under the English feudal system. When the villagers of Fobbing in Essex refused to pay, John Bampton, a former sheriff of that county, was sent to collect the tax for the king. In a violent confrontation, the villagers turned Bampton away empty-handed.[3] Next, the king dispatched his soldiers to re-establish his rule over the villagers, but they were likewise turned away.[4] Soon the Peasants' Revolt spread to nearby villages, then into the neighbouring county of Kent, and an armed uprising began to march on London. They stormed the Tower of London, killing the nobles ensconced there, including the Lord Chancellor and the Lord Treasurer. Desperate to contain the rebellion, King Richard agreed to negotiations with the rebel leader, Wat Tyler. But during their bargaining, Tyler was killed and his decapitated head impaled upon a stick as a warning to the peasants. The revolt was quashed.[5]

In 1869, the newly established government of Canada negotiated the purchase of Rupert's Land from the Hudson's Bay Company and appointed an English-speaking lieutenant governor to rule over the French-speaking Métis-dominated region. Louis Riel led an uprising of Métis, known as the Red River Rebellion, that resulted in a provisional government and the establishment of the province of Manitoba. As a condition of the entry of Manitoba into the Canadian Confederation, the rebels drafted a List of Rights for the people of the former territory.[6] The bill staked out a number of the rebels' claims, including the right to their own legislature; the right to elect their own sheriffs, magistrates, constables, and other officials; the right to full representation in the Canadian Parliament; and the right to all privileges and customs at the time of the transfer. In 1875, Riel was banished to the US for his role in what the government of Canada branded a treasonous act. After he returned to lead a new rebellion in the 1880s, he was captured and hung by the Canadian government.[7]

The path from the first flowering of human freedom to its full bloom is a long and winding one, to be sure, and many of the early steps along that path were halting and imperfect. Even so, the annals of this awakening have no shortage of martyrs. Emanating from every race, every creed, every corner of the globe, and every walk of life, these martyrs have been united in a passion for freedom and a pursuit of those ideals which are anathema to every despot: the rights to life, liberty, and property. Rights that no "official" in whatever post, dressed in whatever uniform, claiming to speak with whatever authority, can take away.

But the tyrants of the twenty-first century are not stupid. They do not suffer from the same delusion as the tyrants of old—namely, the idea that human freedom can be suppressed by the barrel of a gun. Granted, there remain repressive regimes throughout the world that employ the infrastructure of a police state to encroach further and further upon the rights of the people. Yet more insidious by far is the way that the deep state operators, the powers-behind-the-throne of today's democratic dictatorships, use psychological warfare to convince us that slavery is freedom. That the answer to the problems created by centralized forms of control is *to impose even greater centralization of control.* That people are most independent when they are in a state of utter dependency, relying fully on these systems of ever-more-centralized control.

So, what does the tyranny of 73 BC or the tyranny of 1381 or the tyranny of 1869 look like in a modern context? We have watched as the world has been brought to the brink of economic collapse by the concerted actions of bankers and politicians, supranational bodies and intergovernmental organizations. We have witnessed the plundering of developing nations by political pirates, who have enriched themselves at the public trough and then run to the IMF for the privilege of selling their country into debt-bondage. We have seen our so-called "leaders" and their mouthpieces in the establishment press drag us into war after war based on ill-defined mandates from international bodies, like the UN and NATO, which we have not created and in which we have no say. And when we protest that each of these actions has left us more impoverished and enslaved than before, we're told that the answer is to give the same "leaders" and "authorities" even more power over our lives.

In the wake of the worldwide cataclysm of the 2008 financial meltdown, we were told that only a "New World Order" of ever-tightening financial cooperation and coordination could save us from another crisis.[8]

In the midst of the Eurozone panic of 2010-2012, Europeans were told that the solution to the crisis was not to *curtail* the EU's power and influence, but to *expand* it by creating a European finance ministry with the power to intervene in the economies of individual member states.[9]

In the aftermath of 9/11, Americans were told that only greater government intervention in their daily lives could prevent another attack. They stood by, defenseless, as a formidable new cabinet department, the Department of Homeland Security, was set up. And ever since, they have watched helplessly as their government's tools of surveillance and propaganda have been systematically deployed not on "enemy nations" but on US citizens themselves.

The would-be tyrants, globalists all, have only the hammer of centralization to "fix" the problems they devise. And, from their perspective, every expression of human liberty that pops up anywhere is a nail in need of hammering.

Those of us who claim our independence from the system and stake out for ourselves those rights that our progenitors fought and died for are dubbed "extremists" and are socially demonized for our refusal to go along with our own enslavement. Those of us who grow our own gardens to free ourselves from dependence on the multinational food conglomerates are derided as "doomsday preppers." Those of us who invest in precious metals or alternative currencies against the devaluation of the debt-based fractional-reserve derivatives-backed central-bank-issued funny money that serves as the basis of our system of economic dependence are dismissed as "goldbugs" or "bitcoin bros." Those of us who refuse to recognize the authority of the government to impose limits on our freedom from unlawful searches and seizures—and even freedom from violation of our own bodies—are branded "dangerous subversives."

From our viewpoint, it is increasingly clear that the next stage in the unfolding expression of the ideal of liberty will not be found at the ballot box. The belief that voting for another politician to come down from Mount Olympus and fix the problems that the political class has created is not only the most childish of fantasies, it is, in and of itself, an abrogation of the very freedom we are seeking.

Indeed, the political system into which we have been born is itself just another kind of enslavement. And the slave masters of our political system are even more fearsome than the slave masters in Capua or the troops of King Richard. Why? Because, unlike their predecessors, they pretend to be our friends, our advocates, our "representatives."

Sure, we're free. After all, that's what they tell us, isn't it?

Sure, we have control over our own destiny. After all, if we want to change the world, we only have to wait four years for our next chance to push a button or pull a lever or touch a screen. *Yes We Can!*

Who today could believe in such a fairy tale?

Ironically, discovering that we have been politically enslaved all our lives is in itself liberating. Once we see through the propaganda and platitudes of the modern-day tyrants, the chaos and tumult of the political system come into sharp focus.

We are *not* cogs in a machine called "society" to be dictated to by some nebulous entity we have been taught to call "the government" or "the authorities." Instead, we are freeborn men and women. We are free to interact with whomever we want in pursuit of our common interests. We are bound by the ethical injunction not to initiate force against others or to take things from others against their will. We are accountable for our actions and their consequences, whether those consequences are positive or negative. We are responsible for what we do or don't do to help others in our community. We can heed the moral imperative to make the world better, or we can ignore that imperative and leave the planet to rot.

No, there is no political messiah who will descend from the heavens to tell us what to do or to protect us from the bad guys. Instead, *there is only us*—the community of like-minded liberty-lovers we foster by exercising our freedom in cooperation with those around us.

In reality, we *do* vote each and every day, not for some false political saviour, but for whomever we choose to associate with, whatever we choose to spend our money on, and however we choose to invest our time and energy. *This* is the essence of freedom.

It is strange, then, to watch Americans celebrating Independence Day in these times. We see the political puppets of all stripes line up to pay lip service to the ideals of human freedom even as they seek to strip those freedoms from the very public they are addressing. The crowds, lulled into a stupor by patriotic fervour, are happy to go along with these shibboleths. They have their hot dogs and their fireworks, they celebrate their independence just as their forebears did, and so, in their minds, all is well.

But all is not well. Now, as in every generation throughout human history, the ideals of liberty are under attack, and it is up to the vanguard to protect those ideals—with their very lives, if necessary.

It is time for people the world over to ask themselves if they stand with the ideals enshrined in the Declaration of Independence, a document that reminds us:

> [W]hen a long train of abuses and usurpations, pursuing invariably the same Object evinces a design to reduce them under absolute Despotism, it is their right, it is their duty, to throw off such Government, and to provide new Guards for their future security.

Our liberty is not a vague concept to be reaffirmed on occasion, when it suits us. Our liberty is a decision that we make each and every day—a decision to live in independence . . . or in slavery.
Every day is Independence Day.

NOTES

1. Plutarch. *The Lives of the Noble Grecians and Romans*. Translated by John Dryden. (New York: Modern Library, 1864.) Pages 655-658.

2. Appian. *Roman History*, Volume III. Translated by Horace White. The Loeb Classical Library. (London: William Heinemann, Ltd., 1964.) Page 225.

3. "The Peasants' Revolt." Voices of the Powerless. BBC Radio 4. August 1, 2002. archive.is/kKy8

4. Johnson, Ben. "Wat Tyler and the Peasants Revolt." Historic UK. archive.is/pEKmr

5. Oman, Charles William Chadwick. *The Great Revolt of 1381*. (Oxford: Clarendon Press, 1906.) Pages 202-203.

6. Begg, Alexander. *The Creation of Manitoba, or, A History of the Red River Troubles*. (Toronto: A. H. Hovey, 1871.) Pages 255-259.

7. Thomas, Lewis H. "RIEL, LOUIS (1844-85)." Dictionary of Canadian Biography, vol. 11, (University of Toronto/Université Laval, 2003.) archive.is/72F0k

8. Porter, Andrew, et al. "G20 summit: Gordon Brown announces 'new world order.'" The Telegraph. April 3, 2009. archive.is/Ou4op

9. Torobin, Jeremy and Brian Milner. "ECB chief pushes for European finance ministry." The Globe and Mail. June 2, 2011. archive.is/lSeKB

The 9/11 Whistleblowers

"**B**ut someone would have talked."

We've all heard that cliché tumble from the lips of a self-styled "skeptic" who, having been cornered by facts, reason, and evidence, is on the verge of losing an argument with a conspiracy realist.

"Someone would have talked" is a logical fallacy, of course, but that doesn't stop people whose whole public persona revolves around debunking these fallacies from employing such a tactic themselves. People like Michael Shermer, for instance, who is considered a leading light of the so-called "skeptic" movement. In 2009, Shermer wrote:

> Complex conspiracies are difficult to pull off, and so many people want their quarter hour of fame that even the Men in Black couldn't squelch the squealers from spilling the beans. So there's a good chance that the more elaborate a conspiracy theory is, and the more people that would need to be involved, the less likely it is true.[1]

Or, in other words: "But someone would have talked."

Never mind that any vast conspiracy that *has* been successfully squelched would not, by definition, be available as evidence to counter such a claim. Never mind that, in fact, we *do* have numerous examples of large-scale conspiracies—notably the Manhattan Project, which involved hundreds of thousands of workers, none of whom uttered a peep.

"No, large-scale conspiracies *always* involve a whistleblower, and that's that!" insists our stubborn self-proclaimed "skeptic."

As frustrating as this fallacious argument is, it is even more vexing when our "skeptic" employs it to dismiss the mounds of evidence that refute the official conspiracy theory of September 11, 2001. Because, in this case, someone *did* talk. *Many* "someones" talked, in fact. And the tales they told put them in the pantheon of the 9/11 whistleblowers.

Take the story of Barry Jennings. He was the Deputy Director of Emergency Services for the New York City Housing Authority. On the morning of 9/11, he rushed to the city's Office of Emergency Management in World Trade Center Building 7 (WTC 7) with NYC Corporation Counsel Michael Hess. Discovering the office had been abandoned, they attempted to flee the building but got stuck in the stairwell. In an interview years after the events, Jennings revealed what he had heard and seen inside the building that day as he and Hess were attempting to find a way out:

> All this time I'm hearing explosions. And I'm thinking that maybe it's the buses around me that were on fire, the cars that were on fire, but, I don't see no... you know, but I'm still hearing these explosions. When they [the rescuers] finally got to us, and they took us down to what they called the lobby... Because I asked them when we got down there I said, "Where are we?" He said, "This was the lobby." And I said, "You've got to be kidding me." Total ruins.

Total ruins. Now keep in mind when I came in there, the lobby had nice escalators, it was a huge lobby. And for me to see what I saw, was unbelievable.[2]

Jennings' testimony directly contradicts the claim made by the National Institute of Standards and Technology (NIST) that there was "no evidence supporting the existence of a blast event" in WTC 7 and thus no need to investigate the possibility of pre-planted explosives or controlled demolition of the building.[3] Jennings died on August 19, 2008, under extremely suspicious circumstances just two days before NIST released a draft report on its investigation of WTC 7's collapse, which it attributed to ordinary office fires.[4]

Or there's the story of J. Michael Springmann. After heading the visa section at the US consulate in Jeddah, Saudi Arabia, for eighteen months in the late 1980s, Springmann attempted to blow the whistle on a visas-for-terrorists scheme that was being run by CIA personnel in the consulate. This operation—conducted on behalf of CIA asset Osama bin Laden—funneled Afghan mujahedeen into the US for training.[5]

> They [Osama Bin Laden's associates] received visas to travel to the United States, usually from Saudi Arabia, for training, debriefing, and other purposes. In enabling their passage, American government officials violated the Immigration and Nationality Act as well as the State Department's regulations, codified in its Foreign Affairs Manual. I know. I was there. I issued the visas, and I objected to gross violations of law and regulation. As a result, as happens to nearly all whistle-blowers, I was fired.[6]

The State Department retaliated by not renewing Springmann's contract. Years later, the Jeddah consulate would issue visas to fourteen of the nineteen alleged 9/11 hijackers.[7]

Then there is the story of Richard Andrew Grove. In 2000, Grove was working for SilverStream Software, a business specializing in enterprise architecture software. By October of that year, he had landed the largest client in SilverStream's history: Marsh & McLennan Companies. Upon finding evidence that SilverStream was overbilling Marsh by nearly $7 million, Grove aired his concerns. But both his own managers and those he confided in at Marsh advised him to keep his mouth shut.

> I first noticed fiscal anomalies with respect to the Marsh.com project when I was in a meeting on the 98th floor in October of 2000 with a gentleman named Gary Lasko. Gary was Marsh's North American Chief Information Officer, and that particular afternoon a colleague and I helped him identify about $10,000,000 in suspicious purchase orders—after I recognized that certain vendors were deceiving Marsh and specifically appeared to be selling Marsh large quantities of hardware that were not necessary, as this was later confirmed by Gary.
> [...]
> I brought my concerns up to executives inside of SilverStream, and I was urged to keep quiet and mind my own business. I went to an executive at Marsh, and he advised me to do likewise.[8]

Despite having won the company its biggest client, Grove was fired from SilverStream shortly after revealing the evidence of these suspicious transactions. After his termination, Grove was invited to present his evidence at a staff meeting in Marsh's offices on the 98th floor of the North Tower. Only the Marsh employees who, like Grove, were suspicious of those transactions were invited to attend that meeting, held on the morning of September 11, 2001. The executive who called the meeting was attending remotely. Everyone in the room perished.

Grove, who was stuck in traffic and late for the meeting, saw the South Tower fall—and promptly fled Manhattan. The crime he witnessed, as well as subsequent events, led him to start piecing together how 9/11 had enabled financial institutions and insurance companies to cover up billions of dollars in fraud—by eliminating whoever had been asking questions about it.

Another story that has been swept under the rug by the purveyors of the official 9/11 coincidence theory is told by Kevin Ryan. At the time of 9/11, Ryan was working as a site manager at a division of Underwriters Laboratories (since renamed UL), the worldwide safety consulting and certification company headquartered in Northbrook, Illinois. In fact, he was present when, a few weeks after 9/11, then-CEO Loring Knoblauch made a surprise visit to the South Bend, Indiana, laboratory and told workers that UL "had certified the steel in the World Trade Center buildings" and that "we should all be proud that the buildings had stood for so long under such intense conditions."[9]

That remark piqued Ryan's interest, and two years later he began following the ongoing investigation into the destruction of the Twin Towers. He wrote to Knoblauch, whose reply reassured him that the company had indeed "tested the steel with all the fireproofing on" and that "it did beautifully." However, UL's Fire Protection division manager, Tom Chapin, contradicted Knoblauch's assertion, insisting that UL did not certify structural steel but instead merely tested the assemblies of which steel was a component. Ryan likens this distinction to "we don't crash test the car door, we crash test the whole car."[10]

The issue came to a head in 2004, when UL performed fire-resistance tests on models of the WTC floor assemblies for NIST's official report on how the Twin Towers fell. The tests showed that the floor assemblies "were able to sustain the maximum design load for approximately 2 hours without collapsing." Instead of prompting NIST engineers to question whether jet fuel fires really did cause the towers to "collapse," the tests instead led them to question whether their model was scalable to a larger floor system like that found in the WTC.[11]

Realizing that the then-working hypothesis for the towers' destruction—namely, that the fires had caused the buildings' steel cores to soften and melt—was untenable, Ryan wrote a letter to Frank Gayle, the head of NIST's World Trade Center investigation.

> This story just does not add up. If steel from those buildings did soften or melt, I'm sure we can all agree that this was certainly not due to jet fuel fires of any kind, let alone the briefly burning fires in those towers. That fact should be of great concern to all Americans. Alternatively, the contention that this steel did fail at temperatures around 250°C suggests that the majority of deaths on 9/11 were due to a safety-related failure. That suggestion should be of great concern to my company.

There is no question that the events of 9/11 are the emotional driving force behind the War on Terror. And the issue of the WTC collapse is at the crux of the story of 9/11. My feeling is that your metallurgical tests are at the crux of the crux of the crux. Either you can make sense of what really happened to those buildings, and communicate this quickly, or we all face the same destruction and despair that come from global decisions based on disinformation and "chatter."[12]

Given the importance of the issue, Ryan allowed his letter to be published online. UL immediately denied ever certifying the WTC steel and five days later fired Ryan.[13]

There are scores of similar stories from whistleblowers digging into other aspects of the 9/11 story. Like Robert Wright, the Federal Bureau of Investigation (FBI) Special Agent whose investigation—code-named "Vulgar Betrayal"—into the financing of terror events was shut down when it came close to exposing the US government's own relationship with the terrorist financiers. Or Indira Singh, the risk management consultant for JPMorgan Chase who tried to warn the FBI about a software company with some very strange ties to both known terrorist financiers and powerful US government agencies and who was told by one FBI agent that she was in a better position to investigate the case than the Bureau was. (For more information on the Wright and Singh stories, please see "The Ptech Story" elsewhere in this book.)

But of all the 9/11 whistleblowers, perhaps the most noteworthy are the 9/11 Commissioners themselves.

The 9/11 Commission (formally "The National Commission on Terrorist Attacks Upon the United States") was established to investigate the 9/11 attacks. President George W. Bush dragged his heels a full 441 days after 9/11 before finally setting it up. But it was not just a case of Bush being slow to act. He actively resisted any investigation for as long as he could,[14] taking the extraordinary and unprecedented step of personally asking Senate Majority Leader Tom Daschle to limit Congress' investigation into those events.[15]

It was only when the political pressure to form a commission of inquiry became too great for Bush to resist that he nominated a chairman: Henry Kissinger. Kissinger's reputation as a cover-up artist and tool of the political establishment was such that even *The New York Times* speculated that his nomination showed that the president wanted to contain the investigation into 9/11, not enable it.[16]

Family members of the 9/11 victims, similarly concerned that Kissinger was being appointed to run a cover-up commission, asked him to his face to release the client list of his political consulting business (specifically, to disclose any clients named "Bin Laden"). Kissinger was reportedly so unnerved by the question that he "spill[ed] his coffee and nearly f[ell] off his sofa."[17] The next morning he resigned, and former New Jersey Governor Thomas Kean and former Indiana Congressman Lee Hamilton were appointed chairman and vice-chairman, respectively, to take his place.

Remarkably, the suggestions of political cover-up did not end there, nor were they confined to a marginalized "lunatic fringe" of "conspiracy theorists" derided by the establishment media. Six out of the ten commissioners—Kean[18] and Hamilton,[19] as well as Bob Kerrey,[20] Tim Roemer,[21] John Lehman[22] and Max Cleland[23]—all expressed concern that the commission was misled, stymied, hampered by conflicts of interest, and, ultimately, forced to participate in a politically motivated cover-up.

In their book, *Without Precedent: The Inside Story of the 9/11 Commission*, Kean and Hamilton famously remarked that the commission had been "set up to fail."[24] Commission members considered bringing criminal charges against Pentagon officials who had deliberately lied to them about the military's complete lack of response on that day.[25] One of them, Max Cleland, even resigned because the commission had been "deliberately compromised by the president of the United States."[26] Bob Kerrey, meanwhile, cryptically commented that 9/11 was a thirty-year conspiracy. No mainstream reporter has ever followed up with him to clarify this statement.[27]

Yet none of these repeated attempts by the 9/11 commissioners to blow the whistle on their own commission has ever dissuaded the mainstream press from treating the 9/11 Commission's final report as the last word on the 9/11 attacks. And, despite the fact that the majority of Americans believe the government is concealing what it knows about the attacks of September 11th from the public,[28] to this day anyone who raises questions about the commission or its findings is treated as a conspiratorial loony by the major media.[29]

It should be apparent by this point that the old argument that "someone would have talked" is not just fallacious, but factually incorrect. As we've just read, there have been numerous whistleblowers with documentable evidence of the frauds and fictions that have been constructed around the official 9/11 narrative. Their disclosures put the "someone would have talked" doubters in an uncomfortable predicament: Either they are lazy—boldly pronouncing on issues they have not themselves bothered to investigate—or they are lying.

What's especially galling when the so-called "skeptics" use the "someone would have talked" fallacy is that the whistleblowers *have* in fact done everything possible to publicize their stories—holding press conferences, filing formal appeals, joining whistleblower organizations, and making themselves available for interviews. For their heroic efforts, these brave men and women have been fired from their jobs, shunned by former colleagues, smeared by the mainstream media, and ignored by the public.

"Someone would have talked." Indeed, numerous "someones" *have* talked. Some of them have even screamed. But when their cries are ignored, the stories of the 9/11 whistleblowers sound like the proverbial trees falling with no one in the forest to hear them.

NOTES

1. Shermer, Michael. "Paranoia Strikes Deep." Michael Shermer. September 2009. archive.is/1yMAu

2. McMahon, Dennis P., JD, LLM. "Barry Jennings Revisited." Architects & Engineers for 9/11 Truth. May 31, 2012. archive.is/oOOts

3. "FAQs - NIST WTC 7 Investigation." NIST. September 19, 2011. archive.is/qgzlb

4. "NIST WTC 7 Investigation Finds Building Fires Caused Collapse." NIST. August 21, 2008. archive.is/x5nHM

5. "Interview 1019 - Michael Springmann on Visas for Terrorists." The Corbett Report. March 31, 2015. corbettreport.com/?p=14061

6. Springmann, J. Michael. *Visas for Al Qaeda: CIA Handouts That Rocked the World*. Daena Publications LLC. Kindle Edition. (Kindle Location 149)

7. Eldridge, Thomas R. et al. "9/11 and Terrorist Travel: Special Report of the National Commission on Terrorist Attacks Upon the United States." National Commission on Terrorist Attacks Upon the United States. August 21, 2004. bit.ly/2BpgASw

8. "9/11 Whistleblower: Richard Andrew Grove (Transcript)." Scribd. June 1, 2006. bit.ly/2SryGed

9. Ryan, Kevin. "Propping Up the War on Terror: Lies about the WTC by NIST and Underwriters Laboratories." 9/11 Review. March 28, 2006. archive.li/GwSfC

10. See endnote 9.

11. Gross, John, et al. "NIST NCSTAR 1-6B. Federal Building and Fire Safety Investigation of the World Trade Center Disaster. Fire Resistance Tests of Floor Truss Systems." NIST. September 2005. archive.is/qvh9N

12. "UL Executive Speaks Out on WTC Study." 911Truth.org. November 12, 2004. archive.is/Zc6Jp

13. "Ryan's Hometown Paper Reports on Letter and Firing." 911Truth.org. November 24, 2004. archive.is/CAHtK

14. Brush, Pete. "Bush Opposes 9/11 Query Panel." CBS News. May 23, 2002. archive.is/arUyp

15. "Bush asks Daschle to limit Sept. 11 probes." CNN. 2002. January 29, 2002. archive.is/vEPzy

16. "The Kissinger Commission." The New York Times. November 29, 2002. archive.is/i4afd

17. Thomas, Evan. "Tragicomic Tale of the 9/11 Report." The New York Times. February 4, 2008. archive.is/m7oRK

18. May, Ernest R. "When Government Writes History: The 9-11 Commission Report." History News Network. archive.is/RSJVh

19. "Truth, Lies and Conspiracy - Interview with Lee Hamilton." 911Truth.org. August 21, 2006. archive.is/cuL0Z

20. bbruhwiler8. "Truth Squad: 9-11 Commissioner Bob Kerrey finally confesses 9-11 Commission could not do it's [sic] job." 911Blogger.com (site inactive). November 29, 2009. archive.is/rvRLI

21. "9/11 panel distrusted Pentagon testimony." CNN. August 2, 2006. archive.is/jdwOL

22. "Lehman: Commission Purposely Set Up So that 9/11 Staff Had Conflict of Interest." George Washington's Blog. February 4, 2008. archive.is/UcUwY

23. "'The White House Has Played Cover-Up'-Former 9/11 Commission Member Max Cleland Blasts Bush." DemocracyNow!. March 23, 2004. archive.is/nd7rx

24. Kean, Thomas H. and Lee Hamilton. Without Precedent: The inside Story of the 9/11 Commission. (New York: Vintage Books, 2006.) Page 14.

25. Eggen, Dan. "9/11 Panel Suspected Deception by Pentagon." The Washington Post. August 2, 2006. archive.is/BYb7i

26. Arnold, Laurence. "9/11 panel to get access to withheld data." Boston.com. November 13, 2003. archive.is/Xs1OP

27. See endnote 20.

28. "What Aren't They Telling Us? Chapman University Survey of American Fears." Chapman University. October 11, 2016. archive.is/hzdj4

29. Bell, Chris. "The people who think 9/11 may have been an 'inside job.'" BBC News. February 1, 2018. archive.is/jJNPv

Why We Must Oppose Bilderberg

DID YOU KNOW that each year one hundred and fifty of the richest and most powerful corporate chieftains from Europe and North America meet behind closed doors with top government officials, influential financiers, media mavens, and even members of royalty? Or that these off-the-record meetings involve discussions on pressing political and economic matters and result in decisions that—according to the attendees of this shadowy conference—are then implemented by the same powerful figures?

Well, just such an event does take place each year, and it has a name: the Bilderberg Meeting.

If you aren't aware of this annual conclave, don't worry. You're not alone. In fact, even though seventy of these globalist conferences have been held since the first one took place at the Hotel de Bilderberg in Oosterbeek, Netherlands, in 1954, there has been a near-total media blackout on reporting about the event. As a result, most of the public has never heard of the Bilderberg Group.

However, thanks to the tireless efforts of a handful of independent journalists ringing the alarm about this secretive meeting over the past two decades, that veil of ignorance is starting to lift. Prompted by growing public awareness of the group's existence, not only has the mainstream media begun to give the Bilderberg Meeting some cursory press coverage in recent years, but the organization itself has even launched its own website where one can learn more about the Bilderberg Group and its activities:

> Since its inaugural meeting in 1954, Bilderberg has been an annual forum for informal discussions, designed to foster dialogue between Europe and North America. Every year, between 120-150 political leaders and experts from industry, finance, academia and the media are invited to take part in the meeting. About two thirds of the participants come from Europe and the rest from North America; one third from politics and government and the rest from other fields. The meeting is a forum for informal discussions about megatrends and major issues facing the world. The meetings are held under the Chatham House Rule, which states that participants are free to use the information received, but neither the identity nor the affiliation of the speaker(s) nor of any other participant may be revealed. Thanks to the private nature of the meeting, the participants are not bound by the conventions of their office or by pre-agreed positions. As such, they can take time to listen, reflect and gather insights. There is no detailed agenda, no resolutions are proposed, no votes are taken, and no policy statements are issued.[1]

The website's matter-of-fact description fails, though, to give a sense of both the gathering's significance and the cloak of secrecy behind which this clique operates. Convening each year at a different five-star hotel within driving distance of a major international airport, Bilderberg is no mere talking shop for the rich and powerful. By the admission of former NATO Secretary-General and two-time Bilderberg attendee Willy Claes, participants at the meetings are expected to implement the group's decisions in their area of influence.[2]

That the Bilderberg Group does indeed reach decisions and implement agenda items is by now undeniable. Some of the independent journalists who have researched these confabs over the years have even used confidential information leaked by attendees to predict the course of world events. In June 2002, the late Jim Tucker—an intrepid reporter who observed Bilderberg's annual encampments for decades—reported that then-US Secretary of Defense Donald Rumsfeld had been summoned from the Pentagon to the nearby Bilderberg meeting in Chantilly, Virginia, to assure participants that there would be "no immediate" strike on Iraq, despite what was being widely conjectured at the time.[3] In 2005, Daniel Estulin, the best-selling author of *The True Story of the Bilderberg Group*, was able to tap his sources inside the organization to correctly predict the spike in oil prices that took place the following year.[4]

But, having learned about the existence of this shadowy cabal, some are inclined to dismiss it as a nothingburger. A "Bilderberger with cheese," if you will. After all, why should we care about a talking shop for corporate bigwigs and politicians? Don't they have these types of conferences and meetings all the time?

One first response to those so curiously incurious about this closed-door conspiracy is to point out the most obvious problem with such secretive meetings: the hypocrisy of the attendees.

We can point, for example, to Barack Obama, who, when campaigning for president in 2008, promised to lead one of the most transparent administrations ever—

and slammed his predecessor for having one of the least:

> It's no coincidence that one of the most secretive administrations in our history has favoured special interests and pursued policies that could not stand up to the sunlight.[5]

Or we can steer them to Hillary Clinton, who, in delivering remarks at the Transparency International-USA's Annual Integrity Award Dinner, said:

> Before government officials spoke as openly and loudly about these issues, Transparency International was already bringing corruption out of the shadows, sunlight being the best disinfectant.[6]

Or how about referring them to this declaration by then-newly elected British Prime Minister David Cameron:

> It is our ambition to be one of the most transparent governments in the world, open about what we do and, crucially, about what we spend.[7]

Transparency, indeed.

So dedicated to the cause of openness and accountability are the Obamas and Clintons and Camerons of the world that the very idea that such a surreptitious network of secretive string-pullers even exists must be repugnant to them. Surely it rankles their transparency-loving hearts to learn that politicians are meeting behind closed doors with corporate lobbyists and . . .

Wait! As it turns out, all three of these politicians have graced the Bilderberg Meeting with their presence at least once.

Cameron attended Bilderberg in 2013, when the annual

soiree alighted on Watford, a town and borough in Hertfordshire, England.[8] Just to add insult to injury, Cameron's appearance at the closed-door, off-the-record meeting came just one week after Mr. "Open About What We Do" renewed his pledge to achieve "open government" at an "Open Government Partnership Summit."[9]

Obama and Clinton's joint Bilderberg attendance in 2008, meanwhile, represents an even more galling display of hypocrisy. Not only did they mouth platitudes about openness and transparency while attending this secretive gathering, but they even went to extreme lengths of duplicity to hide their presence.

In fact, the story of these two politicians' conspiracy to commit a conspiracy reads like it was ripped straight from the pages of a true crime novel. It was in the heat of the 2008 Democratic primaries, when Obama and Clinton were going head-to-head for the right to seize the crown from lame-duck George W. Bush. Man of his word that he is, Obama let his press corps believe he was on his campaign plane, then sent it off to Chicago with the hapless reporters aboard.[10] Clinton, meanwhile, ditched her own entourage for a "secret late-night meeting" with her erstwhile campaign competitor. Their rendezvous was originally reported to have taken place at the Washington, D.C., home of Senator Dianne Feinstein.[11] But that was before *The New York Times* clarified that the location of the Obama-Clinton face-to-face was never, in fact, clarified. (The paper also duly noted that it couldn't confirm that Feinstein even has a property in the district).[12]

If they didn't get together at Feinstein's Washington abode (which may or may not exist), then *where did they meet?* Could their powwow perchance have taken place at the Bilderberg conference, which was going on at that precise moment in that precise area? The Westfields Marriott Washington Dulles hotel in Chantilly, Virginia, is located, as its name suggests, a convenient eleven miles away from the Washington Dulles International Airport, where Obama kidnapped his press corps. If the armed Secret Service convoys caught on film entering the Bilderberg venue are any indication, then, yes, *that's exactly where Hillary and Barack met*.[13]

But that's not all.

In 1991, a then-unknown Governor of Arkansas by the name of Bill Clinton attended the Bilderberg meeting in Baden-Baden, Germany.[14] The next year he blew onto the national stage from the comparative sticks of Little Rock and won an upset election victory over George H. W. Bush to become President of the United States.

In 1993, Tony Blair, then the shadow Home Secretary for the Labour opposition, attended the Bilderberg meeting in Vouliagmeni, Greece.[15] The next year he became Leader of the Opposition and, three years later, Prime Minister of the United Kingdom.

In 2003, Canadian Opposition Leader Stephen Harper attended the Bilderberg meeting in Versailles, France.[16] One year later Harper became Leader of the Conservative Party and, two years after that, Prime Minister of Canada.

Right wing or left wing, obscure backbencher or rising star, political candidates of all stripes find the Bilderberg Meeting a perfect venue to hobnob with the global elite before hitting the big time.

But as galling as the hypocrisy of transparency-touting politicians conspiring in off-the-record meetings might be, it is not the worst thing about the Bilderberg Group.

Indeed, to understand why the Bilderberg conspiracy is so pernicious, we have to unearth its hidden history.

To really get a handle on where this sinister organization comes from, we must go back to the Second World War, when the Council on Foreign Relations (CFR), taking advantage of the disarray caused by the conflict, hatched its War and Peace Studies project.[17] Seeking to steer US Department of State foreign policy, CFR analysts advocated the creation of a State Department committee (to be supplied with research by the CFR, of course) that would guide US diplomatic strategy in the war's aftermath.

In 1942, the CFR got its wish: the Advisory Committee on Postwar Foreign Policy was born.[18] Populated by key Council members, the committee began laying the groundwork for a number of international institutions, including the World Bank, the International Monetary Fund, and of course the United Nations, all of which were established directly on the heels of the war. The committee also argued for the creation of a transatlantic body to foster dialogue—and, eventually, to forge a common foreign policy—between the US and Europe. This body would become one of the seeds of the Bilderberg Group weed.

The seed was planted in 1954 by a gaggle of globalists who came together to form the Bilderberg Group. Perhaps the best known of its founders was Prince Bernhard of the Netherlands. Bernhard was dogged by rumours of Nazi ties all his life, and not without reason. In 2010, a Dutch historian uncovered documents proving that the prince had, in fact, been a member of three Nazi organizations: the fraternity DSt (*Deutsche Studentschaft*, meaning German Student Union); the political party NSDAP (*Nationalsozialistische Deutsche Arbeiterpartei*, meaning National Socialist German Workers' Party, or *Nazi* for short); and the party's paramilitary wing, SA (*Sturmabteilung*, meaning Storm Detachment).[19] These revelations added to a scandal that erupted in 2007 when Dutch journalists came across documents demonstrating how Bernhard had used his position on the board of KLM to petition Switzerland to help Nazis escape to South America in 1948.[20]

But Prince Bernhard is far from the lone Nazi connection to the Bilderberg Group's inception. According to a US Senate Subcommittee hearing in the immediate wake of the Nazi defeat in World War II, top German industrialists held a secret meeting at Strasbourg's Maison Rouge Hotel in August 1944 to discuss their survival in postwar Europe.[21] The report, rediscovered in the 1990s and dubbed "The Red House Report" in honour of the hotel's name, details how top Nazi officials met with German industrialists, including representatives of IG Farben, to begin preparations for the eventual rise of a Fourth Reich, which was to be a pan-European financial empire.[22] As noted by British author Adam LeBor, the Nazis' answer to the question of how to maintain their power and influence in a post-war Europe was to cede their national sovereignty to a "supranational" body. This goal quickly became the driving force for European unification, and, ultimately, for the Bilderberg-inspired European Union.[23]

In this regard, it is hardly surprising to find Bilderbergers at the heart of the European Union project itself. Likewise, another Bilderberg founder, the otherwise obscure Polish diplomat Józef Retinger, was a key member of the European Movement, predecessor to the European Union. Retinger also helped recruit influential members of the European integration movement—among them European League for Economic Cooperation co-founder Paul van Zeeland—to join the Steering Committee of the Bilderberg Group.[24]

From its very first meeting, held in 1954 at the Hotel de Bilderberg in the sleepy Dutch village of Oosterbeek, there was no question as to why the Bilderberg Group was convening: it sought to merge the political, economic, and social institutions of the Atlantic nations in a fascistic corporate-governmental structure. Such a delicate topic was broached cautiously, with American representative Gardner Cowles politely complaining to the assembled elite that America and Europe had divergent foreign policy stances toward Asia.[25]

It didn't take long, however, for the Bilderbergers to begin raising this point in a more forceful manner and as part of an even more ambitious agenda. The next year's get-together chillingly harkened back to the Red House Report's call for a pan-European Fourth Reich. Attendees talked frankly about the "need to bring the German people, together with other peoples of Europe, into a common market."[26]

At that second conference, the Bilderbergers also discussed a plan to "arrive in the shortest possible time at the highest degree of integration, beginning with a common European market." Just two years later, the signing of the Treaty of Rome—which established the European Economic Community—signaled the official start of the European Union. Unsurprisingly, the official signers of the treaty included several confirmed Bilderberg attendees, among them Paul-Henri Spaak.

Fast forward forty-plus years. In the late 1990s, along came the euro, placed like a cherry atop the EU sundae. We don't have to go far to discover the Bilderberg hand in the creation of this currency. In fact, former EU Commissioner Étienne Davignon admitted it openly to the eu*observer* in 1999:

> When we were having debates on the euro, people [at the Bilderberg conference] could explain why it was worth taking risks and the others, for whom the policy was not to believe in it, were not obliged not to listen [sic] and had to stand up and come up with real arguments.[27]

Fast forward another two decades, and now the next logical step is being taken: the regional government that the Bilderbergers helped forge, the European Union, is being merged with its across-the-ocean partner, the United States.

Naturally, it is the Bilderbergers who are pushing for this ever-wider economic integration. One proposal to emerge from it was the now-abandoned Transatlantic Trade and Investment Partnership (TTIP), a trade agreement that would have formed, in the words of Bilderberg attendee David Cameron, "the biggest bilateral trade deal in history."[28] And, befitting a deal involving Bilderberg participants and their cronies, TTIP negotiations took place in secretive, closed-door sessions. The text of the deal itself was locked away in a secure "reading room" in Brussels that could be accessed only by authorized personnel.[29]

Now that we know something about the history and ambitions of this conclave, we are confronted with a question: why should we be opposed to Bilderberg? To that query we have two solid answers.

First, the agenda of the Bilderberg Group is aggressively and explicitly fascistic in nature. Consider the talk George Ball gave at the 1968 Bilderberg Conference in Canada. In it, Ball laid out a new world economic order based on the concept of a "world company."[30] Having been

Undersecretary of State for Economic and Agricultural Affairs under Kennedy and Johnson, a senior managing director for Lehman Brothers Kuhn Loeb Inc., and a member of the exclusive Bilderberg Steering Committee, Ball was in a position to understand this agenda from all sides. He stressed in no uncertain terms that the elimination of the nation-state and the creation of supranational entities were dual preconditions for the formation of this global fascist state. "Where," he asked rhetorically, "does one find a legitimate base for the power of corporate managements to make decisions that can profoundly affect the economic life of nations to whose governments they have only limited responsibility?" Of course, Ball left unasked the question of where the Bilderbergers find their legitimacy in making those decisions in their secret meetings.

Second, the Bilderberg conferences are aggressively and unashamedly conspiratorial in nature. As we've already observed, every year, one hundred and fifty of the world's most affluent and influential politicians, corporate magnates, financiers, and royals meet in seclusion, away from prying eyes and ears. As Ball notes, while sequestered away from the outside world, these conspirators collude on agreements that affect the economic life of entire nations. This concealment has been essential to the Bilderberg Group ever since its inaugural meeting, when Prince Bernhard spoke passionately about the importance of maintaining secrecy if the group were to accomplish its goals.[31]

And here is where we reach the real purpose of this treatise. We must not only ask *why* we must oppose Bilderberg, but more crucially, *how* we must oppose it. Thankfully, the answer to this question turns out to be remarkably simple: we can oppose Bilderberg most effectively by exploiting its Achilles heel.

And what is Bilderberg's Achilles heel? We have already established that Bilderberg's existence is predicated on secrecy, so it follows that its downfall hinges on exposure. Its greatest strength, we might say, can be turned into its greatest weakness.

We've already made great strides in uncovering Bilderberg's secrets, thanks in large part to the work of the pioneers who have been relentlessly investigating this once-hidden club for decades. A few journalists—notably the late Jim Tucker and the late Westbrook Pegler—not only revealed the cabal's existence but cultivated trustworthy sources at its conferences, and these insiders have provided juicy details of the clandestine proceedings over the years.

Now, the burden of exposing these conspirators falls to a new generation of activists. Leading the charge are topnotch sleuths like Charlie Skelton, Dan Dicks, and Luke Rudkowski. Skelton, a comedic writer, covered the 2009 conference in Greece for a mainstream British publication, expecting to get fodder he could use to poke fun at "delusional conspiracy theorists." Instead, he had the life-changing experience of being hounded by police merely for showing up in the vicinity of the meeting with the intention of reporting on it. As a result, Skelton now writes pieces fiercely opposing the Bilderberg Group and their hush-hush meetings.[32]

Dicks and Rudkowski, too, have had their share of run-ins with the gathering's goon squad. These two gumshoes invaded the Bilderbergers' treasured secrecy by infiltrating the Austrian mountaintop hotel where the 2015 meeting took place. Before being ordered to leave, they actually glimpsed the hallowed room where attendees would soon be conferring.[33] Just a year earlier, at the Copenhagen confab, the intrepid pair was arrested for daring to approach members of the Bilderberg Steering Committee in a public space. As film footage of the incident shows, Bilderberg members viciously prosecute anyone who tries to expose their existence and purpose.[34]

The good news is that we have a secret weapon on our side: You. Me. All of us.

Sure, the Bilderbergers may be able to arrest, obstruct, marginalize, and silence the occasional reporter who shows up at their conference sites and who, with hidden video cameras rolling, confronts them and broadcasts their conspiratorial doings. But they cannot stop all of us from working, each in our own way, to unveil their despotic agenda. Singly, we are divided and powerless. Together, we are stronger than they could ever be.

There are billions of us, one hundred and fifty of them. So, what do we have to fear? Nothing.

Won't you join us, then, in moving beyond the question of *why* we must oppose Bilderberg, and toward an understanding of *how* best to expose the group and derail its agenda?

Consider this an open-ended invitation to do just that.

NOTES

1. "About Bilderberg Meetings." Bilderberg Meetings. archive.fo/ORXTo

2. "Bilderbergers bepalen wel degelijk het beleid voor het komende jaar (2): Ex-Secretaris-Generaal van de NAVO bekent." Zonnewind. June 4, 2010. archive.md/ImL6Y

3. Tucker, James P., Jr. "Secretive Bilderberg Meeting Begins Near DC." Rense.com. June 1, 2002. archive.fo/Vr4W9

4. "Intelligence Sources Say Bilderberg Targeting Patriots." Prison Planet. May 28, 2005. archive.fo/XU89G

5. "Innovation Agenda | Barack Obama | Talks at Google." YouTube, uploaded by Talks at Google, November 14, 2007. youtu.be/m4yVlPqeZwo

6. Clinton, Hillary Rodham. "Remarks at the Transparency International-USA's Annual Integrity Award Dinner." U.S. State Department. March 22, 2012. archive.is/j71a0

7. "Transparency." YouTube, uploaded by 10 Downing Street, November 18, 2010. youtu.be/0stXV_fWWtU

8. "Cameron to attend 'secretive' Bilderberg meeting." BBC News. June 7, 2013. archive.is/LHl4K

9. "PM speech at Open Government Partnership 2013." GOV.UK. November 6, 2013. archive.is/GD5U1

10. "Behind the Scenes: Obama press 'hijacked' during Clinton meeting." CNN Politics. June 6, 2008. archive.is/XSuaP

11. MacAskill, Ewan and Suzanne Goldberg. "Clinton and Obama 'laughing' after secret late-night meeting." The Guardian. June 7, 2008. archive.is/tUlfH

12. Zeleny, Jeff. "Two Rivals Sneak Away to Meet, and the Hunt Is On." The New York Times. June 7, 2008. archive.is/gudUj

13. "Sunday Update – 2011/06/05." The Corbett Report. June 5, 2011. corbettreport.com/?p=2213

14. Clinton, Bill. My Life. Volume I: The Early Years. (New York: Vintage, 2005). Page 482.

15. 1993 Bilderberg Meeting Participant List. Public Intelligence. February 14, 2010. archive.is/5LLaK

16. 2003 Bilderberg Meeting Participant List. Public Intelligence. February 18, 2010. archive.is/ZgLT3

17. The War and Peace Studies of the Council on Foreign Relations, 1939–1945. (New York: The Harold Pratt House, 1946.)

18. Schlesinger, Stephen C. Act of Creation. The Founding of the United Nations: A Story of Superpowers, Secret Agents, Wartime Allies and Enemies, and Their Quest for a Peaceful World. (Boulder, CO: Westview Press, 2003.) Page 38.

19. Waterfield, Bruno. "Dutch Prince Bernhard 'was member of Nazi Party.'" The Telegraph. March 5, 2010. archive.is/uY5Ak

20. "KLM Accused of Helping Nazis Flee." BBC News. May 8, 2007. archive.is/RD4jh

21. "Elimination of German Resources for War. Part 2: Testimony of the State Department." (Washington, D.C.: United States Government Printing Office, 1945.) Pages 30–32.

22. Jeffreys, Daniel. "Fourth Reich Plot Revealed." The Independent. September 7, 1996. archive.fo/Ewbs7

23. LeBor, Adam. "Revealed: The secret report that shows how the Nazis planned a Fourth Reich . . . in the EU." The Daily Mail. May 9, 2009. archive.fo/BPcz1

24. "Józef Retinger." Bilderberg Meetings. archive.fo/wcw21

25. "Bilderberg Meetings 1954 Conference Report Osterbeek, Netherlands." Public Intelligence. June 11, 2016. archive.is/LGPmw

26. "Bilderberg Meetings 1955 Conference Report Garmisch-Partenkirchen, Germany." Public Intelligence. June 12, 2016. archive.fo/srko8

27. Rettman, Andrew. "'Jury's out' on future of Europe, EU doyen says." euobserver. March 16, 2009. archive.fo/W0R8N

28. "Remarks by President Obama, U.K. Prime Minister Cameron, European Commission President Barroso, and European Council President Van Rompuy on the Transatlantic Trade and Investment Partnership." The White House. June 17, 2013. archive.fo/5iLp3

29. Boren, Zachary Davies. "TTIP controversy: Secret trade deal can only be read in secure 'reading room' in Brussels." The Independent. August 14, 2015. archive.fo/eAkGJ

30. "Bilderberg Discussion Paper: Some Implications of the World Company." Public Intelligence. May 29, 2017. archive.fo/rtCfS

31. See endnote 25.

32. Skelton, Charlie. "Our man at Bilderberg: Six days to lost innocence." The Guardian. May 18, 2009. archive.fo/3JA75

33. "The Only Journalists To Ever Be Inside Bilderberg During Lockdown." YouTube, uploaded by WeAreChange, June 9, 2015. youtu.be/nkxu_O7m-II

34. "Dan Dicks and Luke Rudkowski Describe Their Bilderberg Arrest." The Corbett Report. May 29, 2014. corbettreport.com/?p=9322

A Brief Introduction to Spontaneous Order

Quick. What do you think of when you hear the word "order"?

If you're like most people, the first thing that comes to mind is "law and order"—the old adage connoting justice and safety in a well-regulated society. That's no surprise. After all, the pressing need to restore "law and order" is invoked by any number of politicians in any number of countries around the world every single day. And, if nothing else, that phrase has been drilled into the minds of the television viewing public since the launch of the legal drama series *Law & Order* in 1990.

Politically savvy folks—this book's readers among them, no doubt—will likely think of "New World Order," a phrase popularized by President George H. W. Bush in his now-infamous September 11th (1990) speech.[1] Known by its acronym, NWO, the New World Order actually boasts a colourful past that dates back to the post-WWI era of Wilsonian diplomacy[2] and to H. G. Wells' 1940 book of the same name.[3]

Researchers of the esoteric may even connect the word "order" to the Latin *Ordo Ab Chao*, or "order from chaos," which is, not coincidentally, a motto of the 33rd Degree of the Scottish Rite of Freemasonry.[4] Also not coincidentally, "order out of chaos" perfectly describes false flag terrorism and other methods of manipulating public opinion carried out by a handful of influential individuals who are in a position to wreak havoc for the purpose of imposing their pre-ordained "order."

But whether we're discussing "law and order" or the "New World Order" or "order out of chaos," we're ultimately talking about the same thing: an "order" based on a hierarchical view of society, in which the lawmakers and their corporate cronies seek to regulate, proscribe, manipulate, inhibit, and control the actions of the masses.

So, what if I were to tell you that there's an entirely different concept of societal order—one that not only rejects hierarchical "order" but actually *refutes* the concept of top-down control? Well, there is, and it's called "spontaneous order."

The hierarchical model of control orders society in a pyramidal structure where rules and regulations dictated by the "elite" at the top are forced on the masses at the bottom by a bureaucratic class in the middle. Spontaneous order, on the other hand, posits that society best functions as a decentralized network of free individuals participating in voluntary interactions.

The principle of spontaneous order has arguably been around since the 4th century BC, when Chinese philosopher Zhuang Zhou conceived the idea that "Good order results spontaneously when things are let alone."[5] It was further developed in the 18th century by Scottish Enlightenment intellectuals[6] and in the 19th century by thinkers like Frédéric Bastiat.[7] Not until the 20th century, however, was the theory of spontaneous order named, codified, and popularized by Austrian-born philosopher and economist F. A. Hayek.

In his 1966 article on "The Principles of a Liberal Social

Order," Hayek described spontaneous order this way:

> The central concept of liberalism is that under the enforcement of universal rules of just conduct, protecting a recognizable private domain of the individuals, a spontaneous order of human activities of much greater complexity will form itself than could ever be produced by deliberate arrangement.[8]

When put into ordinary English, Hayek's observation is at once embarrassingly simple and surprisingly profound: the social order that arises from the free choice of individuals acting to protect their own interests will always be more secure and more complex than any rationally ordered, centrally controlled system could ever be.

To see why this is so, let's turn to Leonard Read's ingenious 1958 essay, "I, Pencil," in which an ordinary pencil narrates the unexpectedly complex process by which it is assembled and manufactured from its constituent ingredients:

> I, Pencil, simple though I appear to be, merit your wonder and awe, a claim I shall attempt to prove. In fact, if you can understand me—no, that's too much to ask of anyone—if you can become aware of the miraculousness which I symbolize, you can help save the freedom mankind is so unhappily losing. I have a profound lesson to teach. And I can teach this lesson better than can an automobile or an airplane or a mechanical dishwasher because—well, because I am seemingly so simple.[9]

The central idea of the essay is that, as simple as the pencil appears to be, "not a single person on the face of this earth knows how to make me."

Why not? Because the creation of a pencil is not a one- or two-step process of assembling a few locally obtained materials in a factory, but a globe-spanning operation involving the harvesting of cedar in Oregon, the mining of graphite in Ceylon, the collection of clay from Mississippi, the reaping of rapeseed in Indonesia, and the gathering of dozens of other natural resources from similarly far-flung locations.

Then, each of these products has to be prepared in its own way. The cedar logs are shipped hundreds of miles from their forest of origin to be cut, kiln-dried, tinted, waxed, and kiln-dried again. The clay is refined with ammonium hydroxide, mixed with graphite and sulfonated tallow, and baked at 1,000 degrees Celsius before being treated with a hot substance comprised of candelilla wax from Mexico, paraffin wax, and hydrogenated natural fats. The oil from the rapeseed is reacted with sulfur chloride and mixed with various binding, vulcanizing, and accelerating agents.

As confusing as this pencil recipe is threatening to become, it is but a partial list of constituents, and it only scratches the surface of what is really involved in coordinating the assembly of these ingredients. Just think of all the people involved in the mining and transportation of the graphite for the pencil's core. They include not only the miners of the graphite in Ceylon, but also those who make their mining tools ... and those who make the paper sacks the graphite is transported in ... and those who make the string for tying the paper sacks ... and those who load the sacks onto ships for transport ... and those who make the ships themselves.

Then there are the ship's captain and crew, the harbour masters and lighthouse keepers who guide the ships to their destination, the truck drivers and train conductors and airplane pilots who transport the materials the rest of the way to the factory, not to mention the employees in the service industries supplying all these workers with food and clothes and other necessities. And that's just the graphite.

In the end, it's truly mind-boggling to contemplate the complexity of the pencil's production. Surely no one person could itemize and keep track of all this activity, let alone direct it all. And yet it goes off without a hitch, creating millions of new pencils each year to be used by people in every walk of life in every corner of the globe. The "simple" little pencil sitting on your desk is proof of that.

The lesson of Read's essay is that, counterintuitive as it may seem, extremely complex operations require no organizing body to order them. In fact, given the limits of our knowledge, no such body could even exist. What *does* exist, as evidenced by these complex operations, is spontaneous order.

Intriguing as Read's insight into complexity is, it may still be unclear how far this insight can be extended beyond the production of pencils. So, let's look at a different example of something we use every day: automobiles. Statistics show that driving a car is one of the most dangerous activities we undertake each day.[10] To many of us—steeped as we are in the mindset of top-down control through laws and regulations—the idea of removing traffic lights, speed limits, lane markings, and other devices for demarcating the "rules of the road" sounds insane. Surely the rules of the road are what keep traffic flowing smoothly, aren't they? Surely the withdrawal of these injunctions would lead to a rise in accidents, wouldn't it?

Would you believe that just the opposite is the case? It's

true. Every time traffic restrictions have been removed in towns and cities across the world, the result has been safer streets—not to mention the added perks of reduced commute times and more courteous, less-stressed drivers and pedestrians.

If you're incredulous at this claim, consider what happened in the English town of Portishead, whose experiment in removing traffic lights from a key junction was so successful that the townsfolk decided to make it permanent.[11] Far from a fluke, Portishead is just one data point in a growing body of evidence that the road design ideology known as "Shared Space" actually works to the benefit of all.[12]

Relying on the principles of spontaneous order, Shared Space advocates postulate that making the road "riskier" in fact makes them safer. Rather than forcing drivers to negotiate with the impersonal and inflexible rules of the road (signs, lights, and markings), roads without such regulations require them to negotiate with the other drivers directly. Thus, instead of seeing other road users as mere obstacles between themselves and the next green light, drivers are now compelled to see and interact with their fellow road users as actual humans.

Hans Monderman, a Dutch traffic designer who was one of the pioneers of this approach to rethinking the roads, developed over 100 Shared Space plans in the provinces of Friesland, Groningen, and Drenthe. He observed of the current system, in which wide roads are plastered with plenty of signs presuming to regulate and manage every action that the driver takes: "All those signs are saying to cars, 'this is your space, and we have organized your behavior so that as long as you behave this way, nothing can happen to you.' That is the wrong story."

Monderman also believed the existing system degrades and dehumanizes drivers and at the same time deceives them into a false sense of security. "When you treat people like idiots, they'll behave like idiots," he reasoned.[13] And vice versa: when we treat adults as capable, independent human beings, they will, more often than not, rise to the challenge and act accordingly.

Shared Space is no mere pipe dream; it has already been implemented in numerous towns across Europe, from Ipswich in England to Ejby in Denmark to Ostende in Belgium and Makkinga in the Netherlands.[14] The result has been a dramatic decline in accidents across the board even as commute times have been significantly reduced. It seems that drivers, when left to negotiate with others for space on unrestricted roads, *do* act like the adults they are, and a type of order emerges from their civility.

But can spontaneous order govern us in other settings, even ones where criminality is the norm? After all, it's one thing to bring about spontaneous order on the roads, but quite another to implement it in institutions designed to catch, convict, sentence, and lock up robbers, rapists, and murderers. Is it possible, then, to deal with felons differently from the way our current system does? Can we replace legislators and law enforcers, attorneys and judges, prison wardens and guards with a decentralized, non-hierarchical, non-authoritarian system of justice? What would such a system look like and how would it operate?

Here again, the notion of giving free rein to spontaneous order may seem absurd, but only because we've been conditioned to believe that the current setup of legislatures, courts, police departments, and penitentiaries is the sole form of justice that is effective. Under the established system, we have decided that "law" is whatever is voted into existence by legislators, gaveled down by judges, or attested to by police. We have also decided that ordering offenders to pay fines to the state or locking them in cages for prescribed periods of time or compelling them to work "community service" hours are the only possible ways to exact justice for their crimes.

Flying in the face of our customary system of retributive justice, however, is an altogether different conception of jurisprudence—one built on what is called "restorative justice." In restorative justice, victims and members of the community are invited to come together and decide how they want to deal with the criminal who has harmed them individually and has thus harmed society.

As opposed to the restrictive system of retributive justice, in which the end point of any successful prosecution is a proscribed fine or prison sentence, the restorative justice model opens the possibility for a wide range of outcomes. What if, say, the victims of a robbery, in tandem with a jury of peers selected from the community, decide that everyone would benefit more from confronting and dialoguing with the offender than they would from locking him up in a prison cell for x number of years? In other words, why not give victims of crimes a say in what happens to their transgressors?

Just as with our previous examples, letting spontaneous order operate in the penal system might seem counterintuitive. Yet the restorative justice process has been shown to leave victims with less post-traumatic stress and less longing for revenge than does retributive justice. What's more, the restorative method renders violent offenders less likely to re-offend than those who undergo traditional court trials.[15] The process has been used to great effect literally all over the world, from the dangerous slums of urban Brazil[16] to Hawaiian prisoner rehabilitation programs[17] to a growing number of schools.[18]

We've touched on ways the economic system, the road system, and the justice system can benefit from spontaneous order. In each case, we've proved that central planners and glorified "lawgivers" are not needed to maintain "order."

This is not to say that we can transition from a highly centralized society to a completely decentralized one overnight. We have been programmed our whole lives to interact with others through the laws, rules, and procedures constructed by our top-down, federalized system of government. It will take much deprogramming for us to discover how to negotiate with our fellow human beings without such institutions of top-down control. *But it can be done.*

In effect, we are on the cusp of a transition from *dependence*—dependence on "Mommy" government to wipe our bottoms and "Daddy" government to mete out punishment and "Big Brother" government to watch our every interaction—to *independence* as we learn how to order and govern ourselves. Completing the transition will not be easy, nor will the final outcome be utopian; there will always be lawbreakers and those who reject the social order. But we must understand that the false belief that disorderly elements can be dealt with only by ceding more of our power to centralized authorities is exactly what has led us to the brink of economic and societal collapse.

History is replete with great thinkers who have gestured toward this simple truth: "That government is best which governs least." You may recognize this phrase by Henry David Thoreau,[19] but do you know the context in which he wrote it?

> I heartily accept the motto, "That government is best which governs least"; and I should like to see it acted up to more rapidly and systematically. Carried out, it finally amounts to this, which also I believe—"That government is best which governs not at all"; and when men are prepared for it, that will be the kind of government which they will have.[20]

There, in a nutshell, is our lesson on spontaneous order. As our civilization has matured, we have been gradually learning how to govern ourselves. Someday, when we have outgrown our adolescence, we will no longer need the ineffective "order" promised by governments and would-be rulers.

This concept of spontaneous order and self-governance, radical as it may appear to our 21st-century selves, is timeless wisdom that has been passed down through the generations for thousands of years. The Chinese philosopher Lao Tzu put it this way in Chapter 57 of the *Tao Te Ching* more than two millennia ago:

> *Do not control the people with laws,*
> *Nor violence nor espionage,*
> *But conquer them with inaction.*
>
> *For: the more morals and taboos there are,*
> *The more cruelty afflicts people;*
> *The more guns and knives there are,*
> *The more factions divide people;*
> *The more arts and skills there are,*
> *The more change obsoletes people;*
> *The more laws and taxes there are,*
> *The more theft corrupts people.*

Yet take no action,
*　　and the people nurture each other;*
Make no laws,
*　　and the people deal fairly with each other;*
Own no interest,
*　　and the people cooperate with each other;*
Express no desire,
*　　and the people harmonize with each other.*[21]

NOTES

1. Bush, George H. W. "Address Before a Joint Session of the Congress on the Persian Gulf Crisis and the Federal Budget Deficit." George H.W. Bush Presidential Library & Museum. archive.is/nR8DF

2. Conway-Lanz, Sarh. "World War I: A New World Order—Woodrow Wilson's First Draft of the League of Nations Covenant." Library of Congress. April 5, 2017. archive.fo/plzEp

3. Wells, H. G. *The New World Order*. (London: Secker and Warburg, 1940).

4. "Ordo Ab Chao." The Masonic Dictionary Project. archive.fo/P3DXH

5. Rothbard, Murray N. "The Ancient Chinese Libertarian Tradition." Mises Institute. archive.fo/EYjb0

6. Barry, Norman. "The Tradition of Spontaneous Order: A Bibliographical Essay by Norman Barry." Online Library of Liberty. archive.fo/w2svl

7. Bastiat, Frédéric. "Natural and Artificial Social Order." The Library of Economics and Liberty. archive.fo/4IlVT

8. Hayek, F. A. "The Principles of a Liberal Social Order." Il Politico, vol. 31, no. 4. 1966. Page 603.

9. Read, Leonard E. "I, Pencil: My Family Tree as told to Leonard E. Read." The Library of Economics and Liberty. archive.fo/IkG4X

10. McMillin, Zach. "The most dangerous activity: driving." The Seattle Times. January 5, 2010. archive.fo/HvsJk

11. McKone, Jonna. "'Naked Streets' Without Traffic Lights Improve Flow and Safety." TheCityFix. October 18, 2010. archive.is/7PUoS

12. Toth, Gary. "Where the Sidewalk Doesn't End: What Shared Space has to Share." Smart Growth Online. October 26, 2016. archive.fo/6B1CK

13. "Hans Monderman." Project for Public Spaces. December 31, 2008. archive.fo/x15Aw

14. Schulz, Matthias. "Controlled Chaos: European Cities Do Away with Traffic Signs." Spiegel Online International. November 16, 2006. archive.fo/nMyDD

15. Wachtel, Joshua. "Restorative Justice: The Evidence — Report Draws Attention to RJ in the UK." International Institute for Restorative Practices. May 16, 2007. archive.fo/IiEBu

16. Wachtel, Joshua. "Toward Peace and Justice in Brazil: Dominic Barter and Restorative Circles." International Institute for Restorative Practices. March 20, 2009. archive.fo/gwtey

17. Walker, Lorenn and Rebecca Greening. "Huikahi Restorative Circles: A Public Health Approach for Reentry Planning." Federal Probation Journal, vol. 74, no. 1. June 2010. archive.fo/o5cKS

18. Moss, Vanessa. "Healthier Delray Beach helps bring Restorative Justice Practices to a local school." Palm Health Foundation. October 30, 2017. archive.fo/IuPMf

19. Volokh, Eugene. "Who Said 'The Best Government Is That Which Governs Least'?" Foundation for Economic Education. September 16, 2017. archive.fo/8eSv8

20. Thoreau, Henry David. "On the Duty of Civil Disobedience." Project Gutenberg Australia. archive.fo/Usjji

21. Tzu, Lao. *Tao Te Ching*. "Chapter 57. Conquer with Inaction." Zenguide. archive.fo/AmYlL

Who Controls the Environmental Movement?

IF you were asked to name an environmentalist, who would you choose?

Would it be John Muir, the turn-of-the-twentieth-century preservationist who co-founded the Sierra Club and is celebrated for his role as "Father of the National Parks" in the United States?

Or would it be Rachel Carson, the famed marine biologist whose 1962 book on the dangers of pesticide use, *Silent Spring*, is often credited with the birth of the modern environmental movement?

Perhaps you would name David Suzuki or David Attenborough or some other broadcaster whose presentations have molded the environmental consciousness of generations of television viewers.

Whatever names spring to mind when you think of famous environmentalists, though, it's safe to say that Madison Grant is not one of them. Yet, as *The New Yorker* noted in a 2015 article, Grant sports the credentials to be recognized as a pioneer of the American conservationist movement. In addition to describing him as a "credible wildlife zoologist," the piece notes that Grant "was instrumental in creating the Bronx Zoo, and founded the first organizations dedicated to preserving American bison and the California redwoods." It then highlights his association with Teddy Roosevelt and the other Manhattan socialites who spearheaded the early efforts to preserve America's natural resources.

> Grant spent his career at the center of the same energetic conservationist circle as Roosevelt. This band of reformers did much to create the country's national parks, forests, game refuges, and other public lands—the system of environmental stewardship and public access that has been called "America's best idea." They developed the conviction that a country's treatment of its land and wildlife is a measure of its character.[1]

Given his social status and impressive career, it's not immediately clear why Grant is not remembered as a founding father of the modern environmental movement. The answer becomes apparent, though, when one learns that Grant's other major "achievement" was *The Passing of the Great Race: Or, The Racial Basis of European History*, his 1916 screed warning of the "resurgence of inferior races and classes throughout not merely Europe but the world."[2] Adolf Hitler, for one, was so impressed by Grant's theory of Nordic superiority that *der Führer* penned a personal letter to the author in which he referred to the book as "my Bible."[3]

These days, Grant is remembered for his white supremacism while his work in the conservation space has been largely forgotten. If informed of Grant's environmental contributions, many would doubtless be taken aback. After all, how could someone who was so forward-thinking on the environment hold such retrograde beliefs about race? Upon further examination, however, this seemingly strange juxtaposition of interests is not so strange after all.

As it turns out, Grant's obsession with race didn't make

him an outcast from the conservationist movement of his day. If anything, he was simply giving voice to the views that were fashionable among his high-society friends. President Teddy Roosevelt praised *The Passing of the Great Race* in a personal letter that was used as a blurb in subsequent editions. To Roosevelt, Grant's work was "a capital book, in purpose, in vision, in grasp of the facts our people most need to realize."[4]

Other leading lights of the early conservationist movement who extolled Grant's work included Henry Fairfield Osborn, trustee of the American Museum of Natural History, head of the New York Zoological Society, and member of the United States Geological Survey. In the book's foreword, Osborn opined that the "conservation of that race which has given us the true spirit of Americanism is not a matter either of racial pride or of racial prejudice; it is a matter of love of country."[5]

The link between "conservation of the Northern European race" and "conservation of the environment," although not obvious to us today, was well understood by Grant and his contemporaries. Clues to this connection can be found in the fact that Grant himself was interested only in the "majestic" elements of nature—the moose, the mountain goat, the ancient redwoods. (In a similar vein, his conservationist cohort Roosevelt celebrated the "noble" elk and buffalo, two species he both preserved and hunted.) Yet when it came to the "smaller forms of animal or bird life"—the kind supposedly undeserving of titles like "lordly" and "noble" and "majestic"—Grant, his obituary informs us, was completely uninterested in their plight.[6]

The common thread between all these men and their notions about nature is the old obsession of would-be aristocrats everywhere: eugenics. According to this narrative, just as the noble and lordly genes of the rich and successful families of Grant's milieu were under threat from the wild and savage genes of the lower races, so, too, were the noble, lordly, and majestic beasts under constant threat, requiring careful preservation.

This important point is not shied away from by the environmental eugenicists themselves. For instance, we find John Glad, a retired professor and former director of the Woodrow Wilson International Center for Scholars, observing in the Executive Summary of his book, *Future Human Evolution: Eugenics in the Twenty-First Century*:

> Eugenics views itself as the fourth leg of the chair of civilization, the other three being a) a thrifty expenditure of natural resources, b) mitigation of environmental pollution, and c) maintenance of a human population not exceeding the planet's carrying capacity. Eugenics, which can be thought of as human ecology, is thus part and parcel of the environmental movement.[7]

Indeed, everywhere you look in the upper ranks of the environmental movement, you find the same eugenical urge for "race purification" and eradication of the lower classes of men and women, who these elitists believe to be polluting the gene pool in much the same way as they believe them to be polluting the environment.

Teddy Roosevelt, a leading member of the conservationist movement, was himself an avowed eugenicist. He chastised white women who didn't want to have children as participants in "race suicide." And in his personal letters to the academic leader of the American eugenicist movement, Charles Davenport, Roosevelt ventured that "society has no business to permit degenerates to reproduce their kind."[8]

Henry Fairfield Osborn—the aforementioned geologist who authored the foreword to Grant's book and who founded The Conservation Fund—was not only a confirmed eugenicist, he was also the uncle of Frederick Osborn, founding member of the American Eugenics Society and founding president of John D. Rockefeller III's Population Council. The latter organization was dedicated to solving the "problem" of the growing population of undesirable races in the Third World.[9]

Julian Huxley—grandson of Thomas Henry Huxley, known as "Darwin's bulldog" for his ferocious defense of Darwin's work on human evolution, and brother of *Brave New World* author Aldous Huxley—was himself a devotee of the eugenics religion. A Life Fellow of the British Eugenics Society who served as president of that organization from 1959 to 1962, Julian also helped establish the United Nations Educational, Scientific and Cultural Organization (UNESCO), becoming its founding director in 1946. He used the body's founding document, "UNESCO: its purpose and its philosophy," to promote a specifically eugenics-driven agenda:

> At the moment, it is probable that the indirect effect of civilisation is dysgenic instead of eugenic; and in any case it seems likely that the dead weight of genetic stupidity, physical weakness, mental instability, and disease-proneness, which already exist in the human species, will prove too great a burden for real progress to be achieved. Thus even though it is quite true that any radical eugenic policy will be for many years politically and psychologically impossible, it will be important for

UNESCO to see that the eugenic problem is examined with the greatest care, and that the public mind is informed of the issues at stake so that much that now is unthinkable may at least become thinkable.[10]

Precisely what was meant by this eugenics-by-stealth creed became apparent in 1961, when Huxley and fifteen of the world's so-called "leading conservationists"[11] signed the Morges Manifesto, a declaration calling for the formation of a registered charity in Switzerland to act as a trust for a new wildlife conservation organization.[12] That trust, subsequently formed in September of the same year, was the World Wildlife Fund. Joining Huxley in establishing the WWF were:

- Prince Bernhard of the Netherlands, its founding president, who also founded the Bilderberg Group in 1954;

- Prince Philip of England, founding president of the WWF's first national organization, the British National Appeal, who once declared, "In the event that I am reincarnated, I would like to return as a deadly virus, to contribute something to solving overpopulation"[13]; and

- Godfrey A. Rockefeller, a member of the infamous Rockefeller dynasty and grandson of the Standard Oil co-founder.

The Rockefellers, in particular, have long had close ties to the eugenics movement. They funded the Eugenics Record Office in the US and the Kaiser Wilhelm Institute in Germany, both of which were essential in spreading the message and mission of eugenics around the world.[14]

In addition, the Rockefeller clan has had an outsized influence on the global environmental movement, both directly through the Rockefeller Foundation and indirectly through David Rockefeller protégé and fellow oil baron Maurice Strong.

Strong, who was "discovered" by David Rockefeller when he was working as a junior security officer at the UN in 1947, went on to become the most influential man in the twentieth-century environmental movement. He served as the first director of the United Nations Environment Programme; organized the 1992 Rio "Earth Summit"; spearheaded the creation of the Earth Charter (along with Steven C. Rockefeller); and served on the board of a bewildering array of environmental and development organizations in between his time as president of Canada's national oil company, Petro-Canada, and as chairman of Ontario Hydro, North America's largest electric power utility. Strong also helped organize the Fourth World Wilderness Congress in Colorado in 1987. (For more information on Strong and his activities, see "The Strange Life of Maurice Strong" elsewhere in this book.)

At that 1987 Congress, Edmund de Rothschild, who belongs to the notorious Rothschild banking dynasty, proposed creating a world conservation bank, which today is known as the multibillion-dollar Global Environmental Facility.

Indeed, in recent years the Rothschilds have begun catching up to the Rockefellers in their involvement with the environmental movement. Young David Mayer de Rothschild—dubbed "Plastics Jesus" for sailing across the Pacific Ocean in a sixty-foot catamaran built out of reclaimed plastic bottles—proselytizes on the pressing danger of climate change.[15] Bizarrely, the audiences to whom this "Plastics Jesus" delivers his sermons on sustainable living have a combined net worth and "carbon footprint" several orders of magnitude smaller than his own.

There are many more tales of unlikely environmental crusaders to be found in the annals of the modern environmental movement. Al "Inconvenient Truth" Gore, whose family's fortune was made through his father's work for Occidental Petroleum and whose personal wealth was greatly expanded through a business deal with oil-rich Qatar, is one ready-to-hand example of this phenomenon.[16] Sir James Goldsmith, a member of the Goldsmith family banking dynasty and founder of *The Ecologist* magazine, is another.[17] And, of course, there are the Rockefellers, whose own family charities have been funding the attacks on Exxon Mobil—itself the progeny of the Standard Oil monopoly from which the Rockefeller fortune springs.[18]

But perhaps the strangest aspect of this story about the plutocrats, polluters, and population control freaks who mastermind environmental organizations is that no one ever asks *why* these rich, ruthless royals and "oiligarchs" are so passionate about conservation.

One answer is historical: The environmental movement has *always* been steered by racists, eugenicists, and elitists. The links in this "great chain of being" remain unbroken—from the infancy of the conservation movement, when rabid racists and eugenicists like Madison Grant organized the first conservancy organizations, right up to the present day, when the scions of the Rockefeller and Rothschild families fund the research institutes, advocacy organizations, and publications that lead the environmental charge.

The other answer is obvious: elitist, racist eugenicists are selfish. They aim to own the planet. Their conservation agenda is a convenient excuse for these imperialists to monopolize ever more of the earth's resources for themselves and their progeny.

Yet it is all too evident that the opulent monopolists who head up the environmental cause care about *more* than controlling the planet and its resources. At base, what they desire is to eradicate the "lower" forms of life that threaten to sully the "royal" bloodlines of the "noble" species. In short, their environmental impulse is identical to their eugenical urge.

In 1909, Grant wrote that natural selection had given way to humanity's "complete mastery of the globe," meaning that his generation had been given "the responsibility of saying what forms of life shall be preserved."[19] Decoded: The duty to determine whether a being—human or animal—deserves to live or die resides with the inbred royals, billionaire oilmen, and financial oligarchs who bankroll the most influential environmental and conservancy organizations. By their snobbish standards, it would appear very few of us are fit for preservation.

NOTES

1. Purdy, Jedediah. "Environmentalism's Racist History." The New Yorker. August 13, 2015. archive.fo/Oe7kW

2. Grant, Madison. *The Passing of the Great Race: Or, The Racial Basis of European History by Madison Grant*. Fourth Revised Edition. (New York: Charles Scribner's Sons, 1923.) Page xxxi.

3. Ryback, Timothy W. "A Disquieting Book From Hitler's Library." The New York Times. December 7, 2011. archive.fo/HURVH

4. See endnote 1.

5. See endnote 2. Page ix.

6. "MADISON GRANT, 71, ZOOLOGIST, IS DEAD; Head of New York Zoological Society Since 1925 Sponsored the Bronx River Parkway." The New York Times. May 31, 1937. archive.fo/JoCNl

7. Glad, John. "Executive Summary" of Future Human Evolution: Eugenics in the Twenty-First Century. WhatWeMayBe.org. archive.fo/UraI

8. Roosevelt, Theodore. Letter to Charles Davenport, January 3, 1913. The Eugenics Archive. archive.fo/6rTm8

9. Why Big Oil Conquered the World. The Corbett Report. October 6, 2017. corbettreport.com/bigoil

10. Huxley, Julian. UNESCO: its purpose and its philosophy. UNESDOC. 1946. bit.ly/2ZTgxZN

11. "Our Story." WWF. archive.is/14MEQ

12. Baer, J.G. et al. "We Must Save the World's Wild Life: An International Declaration." WWF. April 29, 1961. bit.ly/2FzMlve

13. Goldhill, Olivia. "'I am rude but it's fun': Prince Philip in his own words." The Telegraph. May 4, 2017. archive.fo/v8aX7

14. See endnote 9.

15. Roberts, Michael. "Plastics Jesus: David de Rothschild." Outside. December 1, 2009. archive.is/QpGuz

16. Henneberger, Melinda. "Al Gore's petrodollars once again make him a chip off the old block." The Washington Post. January 8, 2013. archive.fo/4394q

17. Smith, Sally Bedell. "Billionaire with a Cause." Vanity Fair. May 1997. archive.fo/33P4S

18. Schwartz, John. "Exxon Mobil Accuses the Rockefellers of a Climate Conspiracy." The New York Times. November 21, 2016. archive.is/bD6r7

19. See endnote 1.

Escaping The Grand Chessboard

WE ALL KNOW how to play chess, right?

OK, perhaps not everyone knows how to play chess (much less how to play it well), but at least we all know what chess *is*, don't we?

If not, here's an overly simplified single-paragraph crash course in the game, courtesy of the good ol' *Encyclopedia Britannica*:

> Chess, one of the oldest and most popular board games, [is] played by two opponents on a checkered board with specially designed pieces of contrasting colours, commonly white and black. White moves first, after which the players alternate turns in accordance with fixed rules, each player attempting to force the opponent's principal piece, the King, into checkmate—a position where it is unable to avoid capture.[1]

Yes, *that* game of chess. The "royal game," as it's come to be known through the centuries due to its popularity among the nobility.

It isn't difficult to see why the game of chess has captured the imagination of tyrants, despots, and dictators throughout history: it's a metaphor for the grand geopolitical struggle between nations.

This is not a novel observation. In fact, the identification of chess with war and conquest is almost as old as the game itself.

It's been nearly 1,500 years since Khosrow II, the ancient Sasanian king, asked: "If a ruler does not understand chess, how can he rule over a kingdom?"[2]

It's been 250 years since Johann Hellwig, a mathematics instructor at the military academy of Brauncschweig, used a repurposed, 1,617-square chessboard as the basis for the first modern wargame.[3]

And it's been 150 years since Leo Tolstoy reflected on the similarities between war and chess in *War and Peace*.[4]

Of course, as students of modern political history will know all too well, the appeal of the "royal game" to those seeking control of the global chessboard is not a relic of the past. Sadly, the struggle for geopolitical dominance continues to preoccupy schemers and strategists of world empire to this very day.

Take Zbigniew Brzezinski. He was US President Jimmy Carter's National Security Advisor and an infamous Machiavellian schemer at the heart of America's foreign policy establishment from the late-twentieth century until his death in 2017. In his 1997 opus, *The Grand Chessboard*, Brzezinski not only wrestled with the problem of how the US could continue to project its global dominance into the twenty-first century, he also explicitly identified the Eurasian landmass as "the chessboard on which the struggle for global primacy continues to be played."[5]

Brzezinski's choice of metaphors was no accident. Instead, it reflects the fact that empire builders, both ancient and modern, really do imagine themselves to be grandmasters of this international game. And, by extension, these geopolitical strategists—maneuvering their pieces around the global board in their quest for world control—regard the commoners at the bottom of the power pyramid as mere pawns to be sacrificed as needed.

Yes, New World Order lackeys like Brzezinski really do treat the globe as a chessboard. But that raises a few questions:

How does this game of global empire compare to the game of chess with which we are all familiar?

What strategies do these would-be world rulers employ to take control of the global chessboard?

And, most important of all, how can we "pawns" escape the clutches of these scheming strategists and end this game of conquest altogether?

PAWNS ON THE CHESSBOARD

WE'D BE HARD-PRESSED to find a better example of chessboard politics playing out in the real world than in the history of Afghanistan.

Conveniently situated on the main land route between Iran, Central Asia, and India, Afghanistan has been in the crosshairs of conquerors for millennia. From the Macedonians to the Mongols, the Seleucids to the Sikhs, the Achaemenids to the Americans, imperialists through the ages have been preoccupied with devising stratagems to seize the Afghan square of the global chessboard.

In the nineteenth century, for example, the struggle for control over this crucial chessboard square took the form of "The Great Game," a proxy battle between the British Empire and the Russian Empire. The conflict was not even about Afghanistan itself. The military strategists in Britain's foreign office viewed Afghanistan as a convenient buffer between their Russian rivals and the crown jewel of the British Empire, India. The Russians, meanwhile, saw control of Afghanistan as a key to stopping Britain's expansion into Central Asia. Over the course of numerous skirmishes, battles, campaigns, and full-blown wars throughout the century, the people of Afghanistan ended up paying for their convenient chessboard location with their lives.

In the late-twentieth century, Afghanistan once again became a key battleground on the grand chessboard. This time, the fighting erupted when the country's Soviet-backed government tried to implement a series of land and social reforms, provoking a reaction from Afghanistan's anti-communist Islamic hardliners and their supporters in the wider Muslim world.

But this was no spontaneous people's uprising. As it turns out, the unrest that led to the decade-long Soviet-Afghan War (1979-1989) was the result of a cunning stratagem devised by that grand geopolitical chess master himself, Zbigniew Brzezinski. Calculating that he could use the internal tensions in Afghanistan as a ploy to lure the Soviets into a protracted guerrilla war in the country and thus bleed the Red Army dry, he launched a secret operation (dubbed "Operation Cyclone") to fund and arm the Afghan rebels.

Archival footage of the operation shows Brzezinski helicoptering to a spot on the Afghanistan-Pakistan border to address the Islamic militants taking up arms against their Soviet enemy. Standing before these Afghan soldiers like a king motivating his pawns to sacrifice themselves for the team, Brzezinski dramatically raised his finger in the air and proclaimed his allegiance to these soldiers' "holy" cause.

> That land over there is yours. You'll go back to it one day, because your fight will prevail. And you'll have your homes and your mosques back again because your cause is right and God is on your side.[6]

Of course, this was manipulative hogwash. Neither Brzezinski nor the empire he represented cared about the fate of these fighters or the holiness of their struggle. Instead, they were interested in using these fighters as pawns in the grand struggle against the Soviets.

Brzezinski even boasted of his deceitful gambit in a 1998 print interview. When asked if he regretted his role in fostering the rise of Islamic terror in Afghanistan, he replied:

> Regret what? That secret operation was an excellent idea. It had the effect of drawing the Russians into the Afghan trap and you want me to regret it? The day that the Soviets officially crossed the border, I wrote to President Carter, essentially: "We now have the opportunity of giving to the USSR its Vietnam war." Indeed, for almost 10 years, Moscow had to carry on a war that was unsustainable for the regime, a conflict that brought about the demoralization and finally the breakup of the Soviet empire.[7]

These are not the words of a man whose heart ached for the plight of the poor, put-upon Afghan Muslims. No, these are the words of a man who literally wrote the book on *The Grand Chessboard*—a self-proclaimed geopolitical grandmaster strategizing several moves ahead as he maneuvers his pawns around the board in an effort to checkmate his opponent.

Sadly, the people of Afghanistan have enjoyed no peace after serving their role as sacrificial pawns in this game of empire. Instead, their "reward" has been a front-row seat as their country devolves into chaos, poverty, and civil war.

The withdrawal of the Soviets led to internal fighting for control of Afghanistan. The Taliban's assumption of political power in the 1990s led to the rise of Al Qaeda—yet another convenient pawn in the US Empire's quest for world domination. Then, in the wake of September 11, 2001, the US led a NATO invasion and occupation of the country. Twenty years later, the abrupt and chaotic withdrawal of American forces resulted in the re-establishment of Taliban rule.[8]

Amid the turmoil, the land of Afghanistan has been reduced to rubble. Its people, still without true independence, are scarred by decades of fighting and undermined by the destruction of much of the country's infrastructure.

Even the Afghan collaborators in the twisted US stratagem—those who volunteered themselves as pawns in the game of conquest on behalf of their occupiers—were duly sacrificed when the grandmasters of that game deemed it convenient.

Consider the case of Zemari Ahmadi, an Afghan who worked for an American NGO delivering food to his malnourished countrymen in the final years of the USA's occupation. In the manic days preceding America's rushed withdrawal from the country in the summer of 2021, an American MQ-9 Reaper drone mistook Ahmadi's Toyota Corolla—loaded with water bottles to be distributed around his neighbourhood—for a terrorist vehicle loaded with explosives. The order was given to destroy his truck. The missile strike killed the innocent Ahmadi and nine of his relatives, including seven children.[9] After reporting the act as a successful counterterrorism operation, the Pentagon was forced to issue a retraction and confess the "tragic mistake."[10] Yet, after a months-long investigation, it was ultimately determined that neither the drone pilots nor their superiors would receive any punishment for the "mistake."[11]

Such is the logic of chessboard politics. "Freedom fighters" who are wooed, tricked, bribed, or cajoled into joining one team or another on the grand chessboard eventually realize they have been betrayed and abandoned by their newly adopted king. They discover they were merely pawns in a game they weren't even aware they were playing.

Far from an isolated example, the story of the Afghans is but one demonstration among many of how the chessboard strategists recruit and sacrifice pawns to achieve their geopolitical aims.

For another illustration of how this grand game of deception and betrayal works, we turn to the story of the Kurds.

Members of a distinct Iranian ethnic group with their own language and culture, the Kurdish people inhabit the geographical region of Kurdistan. Unfortunately for them, Kurdistan is not a country. Instead, their traditional homeland straddles southeastern Turkey, northern Iraq, northwestern Iran, and northern Syria—nation-states in which they remain a sizeable but politically marginalized minority. Although some aborted attempts at Kurdish kingdoms, republics, and Soviet administrative units were made in the chaotic post-WWI period, the Kurds have remained stateless for centuries.

Yearning for autonomy, the Kurds have seldom had comfortable relations with the various governments ruling over their diaspora. The Turks, for example, refused to even acknowledge the existence of Kurds as a distinct ethnicity until the 1980s. When it was finally admitted that there *were*, in fact, Kurds living in Turkey, that recognition served merely as an excuse for the Turkish military to more thoroughly repress any expression of Kurdishness, from the speaking of the Kurdish language to the playing of Kurdish music.[12]

Meanwhile, in Iraq, the Kurds' fight for self-rule intensified in the 1960s and continued escalating—with only brief periods of respite—throughout the Iran-Iraq War (1980-1988). It culminated in a genocidal anti-Kurdish campaign[13] in which Saddam Hussein's Ba'athist government employed ground offensives, aerial bombing, systematic destruction of settlements, mass deportations, firing squads, and attacks with chemical weapons.[14] (These chemical weapons were not Iraqi in origin, of course; they were generously provided to Saddam's forces by the governments of the US, the UK, Germany, and France.[15]) Saddam's campaign resulted in the death of 182,000 Kurds.[16]

Given the Kurds' tumultuous history, it is no surprise that they heeded then-US President George H. W. Bush's infamous call in the final days of the Gulf War for "the Iraqi people to take matters into their own hands and force Saddam Hussein, the dictator, to step aside."[17] Taking this pronouncement as an implicit guarantee that the US military—already routing Saddam's forces in the waning days of the Gulf War—would back them up, the Kurdish pawns painted themselves in the American team colours and dutifully assumed their place on the chessboard.

But the uprising in Iraq was yet another cynical chessboard stratagem on the part of the grandmasters of the American empire. Bush's stirring pledge of support for the Kurdish cause proved to be every bit as manipulative and deceitful as was Brzezinski's promise to the Afghans. As soon as the Kurds took up arms against Saddam Hussein's government, they were brutally slaughtered by Iraqi helicopters, long-range artillery, and armoured ground forces. President Bush merely watched the slaughter take place, refusing to aid the very insurgency he himself had encouraged.[18]

Nor would this be the last time that the Kurdish pawns were cavalierly sacrificed for the benefit of the American Empire. In a 2019 article on the subject, researcher Jon Schwarz identified no less than eight separate times the US government has betrayed the Kurds.[19] The lowlights of this history include a secret 1970s agreement between Henry Kissinger and the Shah of Iran to arm the Iraqi Kurds *just enough* for them to help bleed Saddam's government but not enough for them to actually win independence.[20]

That history of American treachery also includes the neocons' use of the Kurds as a convenient excuse for the illegal invasion of Iraq in 2003. In fact, of all the many despicable acts in the annals of US exploitation of the Kurds, this one was perhaps the most galling.

In 2002, as the neocons started making their case that their newly launched "War on Terror" now involved regime change in Baghdad, American media outlets once again took up the Kurdish cause. They argued that Saddam Hussein's crimes against the Kurds provided a humanitarian justification for the invasion of Iraq.[21] The Kurds, however—by this time rightfully wary of the American foreign policy establishment—demanded an assurance that they would not be abandoned once again if they took up arms against Saddam. That assurance came in a dramatic 2003 C-SPAN debate in which arch-neocon Bill Kristol (aided by unlikely bedfellow Christopher Hitchens) assured viewers that the US would not betray its Kurdish allies *this* time ("We will not. We will *not!*").[22]

Unsurprisingly, that assurance, too, was a bald-faced lie. A mere four years after his impassioned speech on C-SPAN, that same Bill Kristol published an article in his magazine, *The Weekly Standard*, explaining why it was absolutely necessary to betray the Kurds *this* time.[23]

Time and again, the Kurds trusted in the lies of the American foreign policy strategists and were rewarded with dirty tricks and betrayal. In this way, they serve as yet another stark warning to never trust a chessboard king's promises. He will happily sacrifice his loyal pawns whenever it suits his broader geopolitical objectives.

There are many more pawns on the chessboard whose stories deserve to be told. Ukraine is a prime example of the grand geopolitical chess match in the twenty-first century. Caught between American and Russian grandmasters, the Ukrainians have found themselves—like the Kurds, the Afghans, and countless others throughout history—in the crosshairs of empire simply because they have the ill-fortune of occupying a much-coveted square of the grand chessboard. And, like all such pawns in this imperial game, the people of Ukraine are learning that promises of support from their would-be kings are not guarantees of security or independence. Instead, they are death pacts in which ordinary Ukrainians must sacrifice themselves on the proverbial chessboard for the benefit of a foreign power.

As bleak as this picture is, however, it at least presents us with a comfortingly straightforward explanation for the geopolitical machinations taking place around us. In a nutshell, this chessboard politics analogy assures us that empires are simply trying to win the grand chess game and reminds us that they war with each other in order to secure control over this or that square of the board.

But students of suppressed, conspiratorial history understand that this isn't an accurate representation of reality. After all, how can a simple, two-dimensional chessboard really represent the intricacies of the struggle for global control among the many actors vying for that control?

Of course, it can't.

But a three-dimensional chessboard *can*.

HOW TO PLAY 3D CHESS

Presumably by now we're all up to speed on regular old chess, both the literal game and the global geopolitical contest that we have just identified. But if we are to *really* flesh out this metaphor, we're going to have to consider a variant of the game: three-dimensional chess.

If you're like me, you might associate 3D chess with the sci-fi TV series, *Star Trek*. In 1966, its second pilot episode, "Where No Man Has Gone Before," introduced Trekkies to a futuristic-looking, multi-tiered, 3D chessboard.[24]

But you probably haven't heard that an actual, functioning three-dimensional chessboard was first constructed more than a century earlier—in 1851. That's when the Baltic German grandmaster Lionel Kieseritzky introduced his own eight-by-eight-by-eight cubic version of the game to German grandmaster Adolf Anderssen at the first international chess tournament in London. This version of the game, dubbed *Kubikschack*, took the form of "a large glass case separated into small cube-shaped boxes in which chess pieces were hanging on strings." During his demonstration, Kieseritzky is said to have excitedly exclaimed, "I shall mate the black king from above with the white knight!"—before doing exactly that.[25]

A number of chess afficionados have developed their own 3D chess variants in the century-and-a-half since Kieseritzky's dramatic demonstration, but all of these variants generally follow the same basic principles. Like the two-dimensional game we're all familiar with, 3D players move their pieces around the board (or should that be "cube"?), attempting to checkmate the opponent's king. Unlike the 2D game, however, 3D chess allows players to move their pieces through the third dimension; they can "jump" up to or "fall" down on their opponent's pieces. These moves create an added level of excitement for the players, who now have to be aware not only of the pieces threatening them from the sides, but also of pieces above or below them—pieces not visible to players thinking on a two-dimensional plane.

Imagine being one of the pieces in the three-dimensional game—a pawn, say, or a rook—while *thinking* you were playing a regular game of 2D chess. Unable to see the pieces above or below you, you would of course be shocked and confused by the events taking place on your two-dimensional board "Where did that piece come from? Who's controlling it? Why did it appear there?" But once you're made aware of the third dimension of the playing area, imagine how differently you would perceive the game.

This is no mere thought experiment. As it turns out, making an analogy to 3D chess is actually the best way to understand the modern version of the age-old geopolitical chess game.

Here's why: Hitherto, we've considered how the machinations of the strategists of empire resemble (by their own reckoning) a series of chess moves on a grand chessboard. But anyone who studies the true nature of global politics has learned that the grand chessboard is not a two-dimensional playing surface on which nation-state struggles against nation-state for supremacy. Rather, it's a three-dimensional game where hidden actors and shadowy forces manipulate events in ways that are incomprehensible and even invisible to those observing the game on the 2D level.

This view of politics can be called the conspiracy realist view. It used to be relegated to the fringes of mainstream discourse. Acknowledging the role of the Bilderberg Group in the creation of the European Union, for instance—though perfectly documentable and undoubtedly accurate (see "Why We Must Oppose Bilderberg" elsewhere in this book)—was derided as "conspiracy theorizing" and excluded from serious discussions about history and politics.

But in recent years we have seen a dramatic shift in the discussion. Numerous authors have raised the specter of the "deep state" in books published by major publishing houses. Mainstream interviewers have hosted conversations about the deep state on PBS. Even the World Bank has posted blogs about how the deep state is preparing itself to confront "the accountability revolution." Far from denying the deep state's existence, op-ed writers in leading newspapers even point out that "The Establishment" of the country now *openly embraces rule by a deep state*.[26]

So, now that the deep state's puppeteering of events from behind the scenes is an openly acknowledged reality, it seems obvious that our previous, two-dimensional understanding of politics—in which "Team America" is battling "Team Russia" for this or that square of the chessboard—needs updating.

After all, the very term "deep state" suggests there is an

extra dimension to this political entity. It isn't something operating on the regular 2D plane of politics, but something "deeper"—something underlying the superficial, simplistic, left/right, red/blue, NATO/BRICS dichotomies that the establishment media reifies.

Consider the Cold War. From the 2D perspective, the narrative, as told by the West, is straightforward enough. The USA controlled the white pieces, the Soviets controlled the black pieces, and these two well-matched opponents battled for decades—mostly in Afghanistan and in Vietnam and in other "peripheral" areas of the board—before the game became too expensive and the Soviet team resigned. Game over.

But this two-dimensional take comes up short in describing the actual events of the twentieth century, raising a host of seemingly insoluble questions:

- If Western governments really were engaged in an existential struggle against the Soviets, why did they prop up the Soviets with technology transfers, not just in the early stages of the Bolshevik Revolution,[27] but right through the heart of the Cold War?[28]

- Why did the US government continue to supply and equip its erstwhile rivals via a lend-lease program throughout this supposed war—a program that transferred both atomic information and uranium to Soviet Russia?[29]

- Why did American corporations provide the means for the creation of the Soviet war machine?[30]

- Why was the Ford Motor Company allowed to sign a deal with the Soviet Union in 1929 to provide technical assistance in setting up automobile production lines at the Gorki Automotive Plant?[31] After all, as historian Antony Sutton documents in his study *Western Technology and Soviet Economic Development*, the Soviet press touted the plant's military production capabilities, and, in fact, "Gorki military vehicles were later used to help kill Americans in Korea and Vietnam."[32]

- Why did the industrial architecture firm of Albert Kahn, Henry Ford's architect, design the Volgograd Tractor Plant,[33] a major tank production facility that was built from steel manufactured in New York by the McClintic-Marshall Company in a construction process overseen by American engineers?[34]

- And why did the Johnson administration waive its own export control laws to allow multiple US companies to work alongside Fiat in the construction of the Volgograd Automobile Plant in the late 1960s? As Sutton once again documents, not only did essential components of the plant's highly specialized equipment—from foundry machines and heat-treating equipment to transfer lines for engine parts to machines for body parts—come from US suppliers, but the Volgograd plant possessed well-known military potential. It had been constructed at the height of the Vietnam War, during which "the North Vietnamese received 80 percent of their supplies from the Soviet Union."[35]

There *are* answers to these questions. But we won't find them by scrutinizing the 2D chessboard. What seems baffling from a two-dimensional perspective becomes quite obvious if we take into account the third dimension of the game.

Thus, in the case of the Cold War, that third dimension was occupied by a clique of powerful oligarchs who wielded enormous wealth and political influence over the world to their advantage. They dropped chess pieces on the board at strategic points to prolong a conflict here or to end a conflict there. These 3D players, unseen by anyone studying the pieces on the 2D chessboard, could secretly manipulate the game at will. They used the term "conspiracy theorist"—a CIA-crafted epithet designed originally to dissuade researchers from examining the deep state's role in the JFK assassination[36]—to deride anyone who dared look beyond the second dimension to explain the moves being made in the game.

To be sure, this 3D analysis doesn't merely apply to the Cold War. Let's use this newly acquired understanding of the third political dimension to examine the phenomenon of false flag terrorism.

Viewed from a 2D perspective, the official story of the rise of the Al Qaeda terrorist organization and the subsequent September 11, 2001, attack on the United States leaves us with more questions than answers:

- How could Osama bin Laden (and, by extension, the Al Qaeda organization he would go on to create) switch from being an American ally during the Soviet-Afghan war—note that the BBC,[37] British journalist Simon Reeve,[38] and British Foreign Secretary Robin Cook[39] all allege American funding and support for bin Laden in

the 1980s—to America's mortal enemy in 2001
then back to an ally in the 2010s?[40]

- How did a ragtag band of outcasts in Afghanistan coordinate a sophisticated penetration of the air defences of the world's largest superpower, not once or twice but *four times* in a single day?

- And why did America's defences seemingly stand down on 9/11 despite numerous indicators that an attack was being prepared?[41]

Once again, what seems perplexing from the 2D point of view makes sense when we think in three-dimensional terms, recognizing that hidden forces (the "deep state") were able to control elements of both the American government *and* the Al Qaeda threat.

In fact, once we learn that all of the incidents of false flag terrorism throughout history involve covert forces attacking members of their own chessboard team—from the staged attack on Finnish border posts that kicked off the Russo-Swedish War in 1788, to the Mukden incident justifying Japanese occupation of Manchuria in 1931, to the apartment bombings that rallied Russian domestic support for Putin's war in Chechnya in 1999[42] —it becomes obvious that the 3d analysis is the only way to explain this phenomenon.

We could also use our 3D understanding to answer the many questions that arise from the neo-Cold War that is shaping up between China and the US.

- Why did *Yale News* openly brag in 1972 that "Without Yale's support Mao Tse Tung may have never risen from obscurity to command China"?[43]

- Why did David Rockefeller's political operative, Henry Kissinger, engage in a secret diplomatic trip to China in July 1971 to prepare the normalization of US-China relations[44] at the very same time that Chinese forces were aiding the Vietcong in their battles against American forces in Vietnam?[45]

- Why was this move praised by grand chessboard master Zbigniew Brzezinski, who was supposedly Kissinger's rival from the "other side of the aisle" of the foreign policy establishment?[46]

- Why did Brzezinski continue to push forward this normalization of relations when he took over as President Jimmy Carter's National Security Advisor in 1977?[47]

- Why did David Rockefeller assemble "senior executives of close to 300 major US corporations" in the penthouse of the Chase Manhattan Bank Building in June 1980 for a meeting with Rong Yiren, chairman of the state-owned China International Trust Investment Corporation?[48]

- Why did Rockefeller use that meeting to formalize an agreement between the Chinese government, the Bank of China, and Chase Manhattan Bank to "identify and define those areas of the Chinese economy most susceptible to American technology and capital infusion"? And why did Chase commit "to recruit specific American firms to provide both the know-how and the money" for that infusion?[49]

- Why did DuPont, Ford, General Electric, General Motors, IBM, Intel, Lucent Technologies, Microsoft, Motorola, Rohm and Haas, and other Western technological and industrial powerhouses all open up research and development facilities in China in the 1980s and 1990s?[50]

- Why did American companies actively break the law in the 1990s by assisting the Chinese government with its ballistic missile program?[51]

- Why do so many of the high-tech, cutting-edge gadgets in the Chinese military arsenal—from the Shenyang J-31 fifth-generation stealth fighter to the Sunward SVU-200 Flying Tiger unmanned helo to the Donqfeng EQ2050 (known as the "Chinese Humvee")—just happen to closely resemble American military technology?[52]

- And why does that "Chinese" technology hew to US military specifications so strictly that it even displays information to its Chinese operators in English—an oddity that prompted even the staunchly anti-conspiratorial *Popular Mechanics* to ponder "whether or not software and other technology originally from the United States and other Western countries is flying on Chinese military aircraft"?[53]

Once again, answers to our questions are not forthcoming if we accept the grand chess match as a straightforward struggle on a two-dimensional chessboard. However, when we posit a 3D alternative—namely, the idea that there are hidden powers employing financial, economic, and military resources not visible from the

2D perspective—a light bulb switches on. It all suddenly makes sense.

Who are these 3D players? They are people in positions of power and influence whose allegiance lies neither with "Team West" nor "Team East." They are not "Team America" or "Team China" or "Team Russia." They do not identify with "Team NATO" or "Team BRICS" or any other nation-state or military alliance or regional grouping. Instead, their allegiance is to their fellow international oligarchs.

These oligarchs, after all, are of a like mindset. Their aim is not to control this or that square of the chessboard, but to control the *minds of the masses*. And, by bamboozling the public with patriotic propaganda and employing other divide-and-conquer tactics, they hope to consolidate their position of ultimate power.

Lest the role of these deep state actors in manipulating the 3D chessboard be dismissed as conspiracy theory, it is worth noting that the existence of this clique is not a matter of speculation. In fact, over the decades various insiders and confidantes have openly written about being a member of its ranks.

In 1928, Edward Bernays—Sigmund Freud's American nephew and the man credited by *The New York Times* as the "father of public relations"[54]—wrote not only of the existence of this group but also of its hidden influence over society:

> The conscious and intelligent manipulation of the organized habits and opinions of the masses is an important element in democratic society. Those who manipulate this unseen mechanism of society constitute an invisible government which is the true ruling power of our country.[55]

Four decades later, Carroll Quigley—a renowned professor of history whom Bill Clinton regarded as a mentor during his undergrad days at Georgetown University[56]—fleshed out Bernays' claim. In his 1966 opus, *Tragedy and Hope: A History of the World in Our Time*, Quigley confirmed that such an "invisible government" does indeed exist. He further asserted that this "network," as Quigley called the coterie of power brokers, had granted him access to its secret archives, where he found evidence confirming some of the "conspiratorial" claims of rightwing partisans.

> There does exist, and has existed for a generation, an international Anglophile network which operates, to some extent, in the way the Radical right believes the Communists act. In fact, this network, which we may identify as the Round Table Groups, has no aversion to cooperating with the Communists, or any other group, and frequently does so. I know of the operation of this network because I have studied it for twenty years and was permitted for two years, in the early 1960s, to examine its papers and secret records. I have no aversion to it or to most of its aims and have, for much of my life, been close to it and to many of its instruments. I have objected, both in the past and recently, to a few of its policies [...] but in general my chief difference of opinion is that it wishes to remain unknown, and I believe its role in history is significant enough to be known.[57]

Winding the clock forward another four decades, we find a *third* insider's corroboration—this one from David Rothkopf, a Clinton administration official who served as a managing director of Henry Kissinger's advisory firm, Kissinger Associates, after leaving government service. In his 2008 book, *Superclass: The Global Power Elite and the World They Are Making*, Rothkopf revealed the existence of an elite group of six thousand people capable of implementing financial and political plans across international boundaries:

> A global elite has emerged over the past several decades that has vastly more power than any other group on the planet. Each of the members of this superclass has the ability to influence the lives of millions of people in multiple countries worldwide. Each actively exercises this power, and they often amplify it through the development of relationships with others in this class.[58]

Mind you, these are just a few of the many on-the-record statements that these deep state insiders and 3D chess players are willing to put on paper or reveal in interviews. We can only wonder what they discuss at Trilateral Commission, Bohemian Grove, or Bilderberg gatherings or at any of their other globalist conclaves. Some rare snippets of their private conversations have been leaked from behind closed doors, one of which is (surprise, surprise!) a chess analogy. In 1976, investigative journalists Bob Woodward and Carl Bernstein reported that Kissinger had "referred pointedly to US military personnel as 'dumb, stupid animals to be used' as pawns for foreign policy."[59]

Virtually all knowledgeable commentators now concede that the deep state exists. And, as Rothkopf and Bernays and Quigley have correctly pointed out, these deep state players are manipulating the grand chessboard largely out of the general public's sight.

This leads us to the most important question of all:

Now that we are aware of the 3D chess game, how do we reject our assigned role of pawn and stop playing their deep state game altogether?

REVOLT OF THE PAWNS

IN JANUARY 2009, Zbigniew Brzezinski—self-proclaimed grandmaster of the global chessboard—penned a journal article in which he outlined a significant new sociopolitical phenomenon: "the global political awakening." Observing the worldwide growth in political awareness and activism around "issues such as climate, environment, starvation, health and social inequality," he wrote:

> These issues are becoming more contentious because they have come to the fore in the context of what I have described in my writings as "the global political awakening", itself a truly transformative event on the global scene. For the first time in human history almost all of humanity is politically activated, politically conscious and politically interactive. There are only a few pockets of humanity left in the remotest corners of the world that are not politically alert and engaged with the political turmoil and stirrings that are so widespread today around the world. The resulting global political activism is generating a surge in the quest for personal dignity, cultural respect and economic opportunity in a world painfully scarred by memories of centuries-long alien colonial or imperial domination.[60]

In fact, this "global political awakening" became something of a fixation of Brzezinski's around this time. He mentioned it in a series of op-eds[61] and interviews[62] and in secret, off-the-record speeches[63] he delivered in 2008 and 2009.

It's not difficult to understand why such a giant revolution in political consciousness would occupy the attention of Brzezinski. As this master manipulator rightly points out, for the first time in history, average people have access not only to vast sums of knowledge but to the technology that allows them to share that knowledge online with everyone in the world instantaneously and simultaneously. What's more, the technology is relatively affordable and can comfortably fit in a pocket. Such ubiquitous access to information and opinion has understandably led to a flowering of political awareness and a corresponding blossoming of political activism (see "Reportage: Adventures in the New Media" elsewhere in this book).

But while most of us would consider this phenomenon to be a net good, Brzezinski saw it as a problem. In a moment of candor as remarkable for its honesty as for its blood-curdling implications, he revealed what this "global political awakening" *really* represents to the Machiavellian schemers on the grand chessboard.

> But these major world powers, new and old, also face a novel reality: while the lethality of their military might is greater than ever, their capacity to impose control over the politically awakened masses of the world is at a historic low. To put it bluntly: in earlier times, it was easier to control one million people than to physically kill one million people; today, it is infinitely easier to kill one million people than to control one million people.[64]

Here we have, in all its brazen candor, the bottom-line

calculation of the grandmasters of the global chessboard: is it easier to control the masses or to kill them? And, if it *is* easier to kill a million people than to control them, why not do just that?

There is no doubt that Brzezinski's analysis is essentially correct: humanity's continued existence depends on the whim of a cool calculation by the would-be world rulers. When it becomes easier to kill the pawns than to control them, the despotic kings of the 3D chessboard will choose to do precisely that.

The gravity of the situation also leaves no doubt that something must be done about this predicament. And, given everything we've learned so far, it's tempting to frame our response to this threat in chessboard terms: How can we win this game? Can we pawns form our own team? Can we attack the deep state kings and queens who are attempting to control us? Can we reclaim any squares on the grand 3D chessboard?

But to ask such questions is to fall into a trap. By accepting the fundamental premise of the chessboard analogy, we thereby accept the implications of that analogy. After all, if the world itself really is a chessboard, then it follows that we really are engaged in a grand game for control of that board. And, once we become engaged in such a contest, it follows that wealth and land and resources and even people themselves really *are* just chess pieces to be manipulated by this or that player in pursuit of geopolitical dominance.

If we *were* to play this game of empire, however, we would not only end up adopting the twisted mentality of the Brzezinskis and Kissingers of the world—treating our fellow human beings as pawns to be controlled and sacrificed as needed—but we would also find ourselves in a no-win situation. Every strategy afforded us in the grand chess game would simply lead us back to the same spot.

So, should we attempt to regain control of the chessboard by "voting harder" and electing better representatives into office?

Upon a moment's reflection, we would conclude that this strategy is ineffective at best and delusional at worst. As we've already seen, the 2D chessboard and the surface political institutions that are visible to the public are, in fact, largely powerless. The elected politicians are controlled by the deep state through bribery, blackmail, extortion and, if need be, assassination. Voting between deep state puppets hardly offers a real solution to our problem. Worse, our participation in the phoney, rigged political system would only signal our support for the status quo and its outcomes.

Should we engage in violent revolution, then? Take up arms against the deep state and try to win back the chessboard by force?

That path, too, would lead to certain disaster. As Brzezinski correctly observed, given the advances in the technology of warfare, it is now "infinitely easier to kill one million people than to control one million people." We know the ruling psychopaths would not hesitate to unleash the apocalypse if they ever felt genuinely threatened by a mass uprising. Given that they are sitting on the nuclear stockpiles and the bioweapons labs and the increasingly automated armed forces, and given that they have spent decades building up the machinery of technological tyranny under the "homeland security" pretense, is there any doubt who would win such a contest?

Might we form alliances with so-called "resistance bloc" countries and use their muscle to overpower the 3D deep state grandmasters of the West? Couldn't we ally ourselves with, say, the Chinese and the Russians to take back control of the board?

Alas, that strategy, too, is doomed to fail. It starts from the false premise that the Chinese and Russians and the other perceived enemies of the West represent a true threat to the power structure. But Russia and China, despite being supposed rivals of the NATO bloc, continue to signal their full-throated support of the technocratic globalist agenda, from their commitment to the supremacy of the United Nations to their adherence to the Sustainable Development Goals to their assent to the creation of an international biosecurity grid.[65]

What's worse, even if this strategy were successful—if the governments of China and Russia and other countries could somehow "defeat" the US and its NATO allies on the global chessboard—we would still be mere pawns on the board, beholden to other wannabe kings and queens. Whether those would-be rulers are based in China or Russia or America or Madagascar makes no difference. Our situation would stay the same.

No, none of these strategies suffice. The only winning move in this game of empire is to reject the game entirely.

So, let us reject it. Starting now.

Our planet *is not* a chessboard. It *does not* consist of squares to be divvied up and occupied by competing teams. It *is not* populated by chess pieces to be manipulated by this or that player in service of some grand geopolitical agenda.

Instead, it is a world filled with sovereign human beings, each of us born with the natural right to make our own individual choices about how we live our lives.

It is a world in which each of us is free to transact and

interact with others as we see fit. Free to speak our mind. Free to move from place to place and free to pursue our own interests and free to make our own decisions about our bodies and our health and our food and our medicine. In short, free from all outside compulsion or control.

It is a world in which we and our fellow human beings are recognized as autonomous individuals deserving of dignity, not chess pieces to be manipulated by others.

Life is *not* a zero-sum, win-lose competition for a slice of a fixed pie. No. Life is a win-win quest for cooperation and exploration and adventure on a beautiful, flourishing, abundant, ever-expanding pie.

Our world *does not* require a top-down order imposed by elite members of an exclusive "superclass" who, by virtue of some magical political ritual, are able to impose their will on the common man without his consent. On the contrary. A thriving society requires the spontaneous order that develops when everyone is free to form voluntary relationships based on mutual consent.

We *are not* pawns on a chessboard to be exploited in a battle for political dominance, and we *do not* need to win any grand chess game in order to take control of our own lives. Instead, we are simply human beings who are finding ways to live side by side with other human beings and a multitude of nonhuman beings on a fertile, living planet.

It is not until we completely reject the mindset of the Brzezinskis and the Kissingers and the other self-styled grandmasters of the so-called grand chessboard that we can truly begin to take back our rightful power.

We don't need to take over their chessboard. We don't even need to flip it over. Instead, we need to simply walk away from the "game" entirely.

After all, the would-be grandmasters can't play chess with our lives if we refuse to be their pawns.

The "royal game" of global geopolitical chess, it turns out, is a strange game. The only winning move is not to play.

NOTES

1. Soltis, Andrew E. "Chess (game)." Britannica. Updated December 23, 2023. archive.is/VEA5F

2. Bituin, Gregorio V., Jr. "Chess and Leadership." Writing Red, Blue and Green. January 26, 2009. archive.is/DLtUP

3. Peterson, Jon. *Playing at The World: A History of Simulating Wars, People and Fantastic Adventures, from Chess to Role-Playing Games.* (San Diego: Unreason Press, 2012.) Pages 212-221.

4. Tolstoy, Leo. *War and Peace.* (London: Penguin Books, 1997.) Page 855.

5. Brzezinski, Zbigniew. *The Grand Chessboard: American Primacy and its Geostrategic Imperatives.* (New York: Basic Books, 1997.) Page 31.

6. "Soldiers of God." Cold War, season 1, episode 20, CNN, 1998.

7. Gibbs, David N. "Afghanistan: The Soviet Invasion in Retrospect." International Politics, Vol. 37, No. 2, 2000. Page 242.

8. Corbett, James. *False Flags: The Secret History of Al Qaeda.* The Corbett Report. corbettreport.com/alqaeda

9. Aikins, Matthieu, et al. "Times Investigation: In U.S. Drone Strike, Evidence Suggests No ISIS Bomb." The New York Times. Updated November 3, 2021. archive.md/BUVW9

10. Schmitt, Eric and Helene Cooper. "Pentagon acknowledges Aug. 29 drone strike in Afghanistan was a tragic mistake that killed 10 civilians." The New York Times. Updated November 3, 2021. archive.md/usYIx

11. Schmitt, Eric. "No U.S. Troops Will Be Punished for Deadly Kabul Strike, Pentagon Chief Decides." The New York Times. December 13, 2021. archive.md/2BA6W

12. Aslan, Selem. *Nation-Building in Turkey and Morocco: Governing Kurdish and Berber Dissent*. (New York: Cambridge University Press, 2015.) Page 131.

13. "Genocide in Iraq: The Anfal Campaign Against the Kurds." Human Rights Watch. July 1993. archive.is/liHLX

14. *Human Rights in Iraq*. (New Haven: Yale University Press, 1990.) Pages 75-85.

15. Paterson, Tony. "Leaked report says German and US firms supplied arms to Saddam." Independent. December 18, 2002. archive.is/XlHPs

16. See endnote 13.

17. "War in the Gulf: Bush Statement; Excerpts From 2 Statements by Bush on Iraq's Proposal for Ending Conflict." The New York Times. February 16, 1991. archive.is/IOE0M

18. Zenko, Micah. "Who Is to Blame for the Doomed Iraqi Uprisings of 1991?" The National Interest. March 7, 2016. archive.is/C01BE

19. Schwarz, Jon. "The US is Now Betraying the Kurds for the Eighth Time." The Intercept. October 7, 2019. archive.is/gYFaK

20. Diamond, Gregory Andrade, editor. *The Unexpurgated Pike Report: Report of the House Select Committee on Intelligence, 1976*. (New York: McGraw-Hill, Inc., 1992.) Page 139.

21. Goldberg, Jeffrey. "The Great Terror." The New Yorker. March 17, 2002. archive.is/xmnWn

22. "War with Iraq." C-SPAN. March 28, 2003. bit.ly/3tHJQmW

23. Rubin, Michael. "Enabling Kurdish Illusions." AEI. March 19, 2007. archive.is/zEgCF

24. "Three-dimensional chess." Memory Alpha. archive.is/7L0HL

25. Pritchard, D. B. *The Encyclopedia of Chess Variants*. 2nd ed. (Harpenden: John Beasley, 2007.) Page 230.

26. Corbett, James. "Deep State Rising: The Mainstreaming of the Shadow Government." The Corbett Report. January 5, 2016. corbettreport.com/?p=17362

27. Sutton, Antony C. *Western Technology and Soviet Economic Development: 1917 to 1930*. (Stanford: Hoover Institution Press, 1968.)

28. Sutton, Antony C. *Western Technology and Soviet Economic Development: 1945 to 1965*. (Stanford: Hoover Institution Press, 1973.)

29. "Hearings Regarding Shipment of Atomic Material to the Soviet Union During World War II." Hearings Before the Committee on Un-American Activities. House of Representatives, Eighty-First Congress, First and Second Sessions. (Washington: United States Government Printing Office, 1950.)

30. Sutton, Antony C. *The Best Enemy Money Can Buy*. Internet Archive. bit.ly/4bvIJHX

31. "Assembly Line at Ford Motor Company Moscow Plant, 1930." The Henry Ford. archive.is/nUPse

32. See endnote 29. Page 34.

33. Crawford, Christina E. "Soviet Planning Praxis: From Tractors to Territory." Centerpiece, Spring 2015, Volume 29 Number 2. Weatherhead Center for International Affairs at Harvard University. archive.is/gG0wL

34. "Volgograd Tractor Plant." Wikipedia. Archived April 14, 2022. archive.is/H0tiG

35. See endnote 29. Page 33.

36. "Countering Criticism of the Warren Report." Mary Ferrell Foundation. January 4, 1967. bit.ly/4af0XMV

37. "Al-Qaeda's origins and links." BBC News. July 20, 2004. archive.is/wbeYn

38. Reeve, Simon. *The New Jackals: Ramzi Yousef, Osama bin Laden and the future of terrorism*. (London: Carlton Books, 1999.) Page 168.

39. Cook, Robin. "The struggle against terrorism cannot be won by military means." The Guardian. July 8, 2005. archive.is/p1tqB

40. Freeman, Elliot. "From 2012: Senior CFR official: Free Syrian Army needs al-Qaeda support." Syria Resources Archive. August 27, 2012. archive.is/qb1vo

41. Corbett, James. "9/11 War Games." The Corbett Report. September 11, 2018. corbettreport.com/911wargames

42. Corbett, James. "A Brief History of False Flag Terror." The Corbett Report. September 11, 2013. corbettreport.com/a-brief-history-of-false-flag-terror

43. "Yale Group Spurs Mao's Emergence." Yale Daily News. February 29, 1972. archive.is/w9LwH

44. William Burr, editor. "The Beijing-Washington Back-Channel and Henry Kissinger's Secret Trip to China." National Security Archive Electronic Briefing Book No. 66. February 27, 2002. archive.is/5uATt

45. "China Contributed Substantially to Vietnam War Victory, Claims Scholar." Wilson Center. January 1, 2001. archive.is/mmWP0

46. "Negotiations for U.S and China diplomatic relations." YouTube, uploaded by CGTN America, January 3, 2014. youtu.be/L4qHN0clNfE

47. Wang, Chi. "How Zbigniew Brzezinski Shaped US-China Relations." The Diplomat. July 1, 2017. archive.is/RvlMu

48. Chossudovsky, Michel. *Towards Capitalist Restoration? Chinese Socialism after Mao.* (New York: St Martin's Press, 1986.) Page 140.

49. See endnote 48.

50. Moris, Francisco. "U.S.-China R&D Linkages: Direct Investment and Industrial Alliances in the 1990s." InfoBrief. NSF 04-306. February 2004. bit.ly/49Iub5U

51. "U.S. National Security and Military/Commercial Concerns with the People's Republic of China." GovInfo. archive.is/KYArv

52. Corbett, James. "China's Suspiciously American Arsenal: A Closer Look." The Corbett Report. corbettreport.com/arsenal

53. Mizokami, Kyle. "China's CH-4B Drone Looks Awfully Familiar to a U.S. Drone." Popular Mechanics. July 29, 2016. archive.is/afEQj

54. "Edward Bernays, 'Father of Public Relations' And Leader in Opinion Making, Dies at 103." The New York Times. March 10, 1995. archive.is/KLFpf

55. Bernays, Edward L. *Propaganda*. (New York: Liveright Publishing Corporation, 1928.) Page 9.

56. Clinton, Bill. "Address Accepting the Presidential Nomination at the Democratic National Convention in New York." The American Presidency Project. July 16, 1992. archive.is/b6Ldt

57. Quigley, Carroll. *Tragedy and Hope: A History of the World in Our Time*. (San Pedro, California: GSG & Associates, 2004.) Page 950.

58. Rothkopf, David. *Superclass: The Global Power Elite and the World They Are Making*. (New York: Farrar, Strauss and Giroux, 2009.) Pages xix-xx.

59. Woodward, Bob and Carl Bernstein. *The Final Days*. (New York: Simon and Schuster, 1976.) Page 194.

60. Brzezinski, Zbigniew. "Major foreign policy challenges for the next US President." International Affairs, vol. 85, no. 1, 2009. Page 53.

61. Brzezinski, Zbigniew. "The global political awakening." The New York Times. December 16, 2008. archive.is/lV30h

62. Scowcroft, Brent. *America and the World: Conversations on the Future of American Foreign Policy*. (New York: Basic Books, 2008.) Pages 229-230.

63. Gerczak, Deborah. "Obama Adviser Brzezinski's Off the Record Speech to British Elites: The Whitehead Lecture — Major Foreign Policy Challenges For The New US Presidency." Biblioteca Pleyades. archive.is/81ZMc

64. See endnote 60. Page 54.

65. Corbett, James. "Episode 416 - SHOCKING Document Reveals Trudeau's REAL Plan!" The Corbett Report. March 19, 2022. corbettreport.com/putin

And Now For Something Completely Different...

BACK IN 2006, the BBC published an online article about a lone hiker in western Japan who tripped, fell, and was knocked unconscious.[1] He survived in the cold autumn weather for twenty-four days without food or shelter by lapsing into a state of hibernation. When he was found, his pulse was almost non-existent, his organs had "shut down," and his body temperature was 22°C. He had no brain function, multiple organ failure, blood loss, and severe hypothermia. Yet he was released from the hospital only six weeks later, having completely recovered. Even physicians were amazed that he hadn't died. A British Dietetic Association representative, Dr. Frankie Phillips, noted, "I find it quite incredible that he had no fluid at all [during the twenty-four-day ordeal]. Physiologically that isn't possible."

I remember the story vividly because it was so bizarre, so miraculous, that it seemed to deserve special treatment—beyond merely committing it to memory as a factoid. So, I saved it to my hard drive. Though that was a first for me, saving important articles to my hard drive eventually became my standard operating procedure. From a very strange event, a useful habit was born.

I was similarly intrigued by a story that played itself out in 2014—this time at 38,000 feet above sea level. A teenager managed to stow himself away in the wheel well of Hawaiian Airlines Flight 45 from San Jose to Maui and survived the full five-and-a-half-hour journey. Scrunched into a space not designed for humans, he had to deal with oxygen deprivation and frigid temperatures. But he made it. According to Dr. Armand Dorian, a physician who had experience with such cases, sometimes "the planets align," protecting the stowaway from dying of either hypoxia (lack of oxygen) or hypothermia (lack of warmth). In rare cases, the effects cancel each other out: "the need for oxygen declines as the body cools. It's exactly like the concept of cryogenic freezing . . . . The boy's body went into a frozen state."[2]

But why am I talking about hikers and stowaways in a book about the New World Order?

To answer this question, we need to look at the wildcard phenomenon, the "unknown unknowns" that come along and completely upend our understanding of the world. Sometimes these wildcards are medical phenomena like human hibernation, which may prove to be nothing more than interesting anecdotes. But other times they are much bigger discoveries or out-of-the-blue events that entirely alter the course of history.

Penicillin was famously discovered when Alexander Fleming took an August vacation from his work researching bacteria and allowed some of his dirty bacteriological samples to pile up. When he returned to the lab in September, he noticed that mold had started growing on one of the dishes. Lo and behold, the mold killed off the colonies of *Staphylococcus* that Fleming was studying. A great deal of research later, penicillin was born.[3]

Willhelm Röntgen discovered the X-ray by accident while experimenting with cathode rays; a screen nine feet away from the device glowed green when the rays were activated. One week of trial and error later, Röntgen had taken the first X-ray photograph—a haunting image of his wife's left hand, complete with wedding ring.[4]

The microwave oven came about when Percy Spencer, an engineer at Raytheon, found that the peanut cluster bar in his pocket melted when he walked in front of a magnetron (a vacuum tube used to generate microwaves). After some experimentation, he invented the first microwave oven in 1946. It would be more than twenty years before the technology had been sufficiently miniaturized to be offered for use in homes and another twenty years before sales took off.[5]

These wildcard events are not limited to scientific discovery, however.

In 1768, the Genoese agreed to cede their claim to the island of Corsica after centuries of struggling against local independence movements, invading Turks, and other inconveniences. The French, suffering from losses in the Seven Years' War and eagerly eying the island, took up the Republic of Genoa on its offer to retreat and began their conquest of Corsica, which they completed one year later, in 1769.[6]

That same year, Napoleon Bonaparte was born in Ajaccio, the capital of Corsica. Only through the random happenstance of world events had Corsica become part of France, and that's how this native-Italian-speaking son of Genoese nobles who practiced Italian customs was able to join the French Army and go on to become the Emperor of France. Even at the end of his life, Napoleon spoke French with a heavy Corsican accent that was often mocked by the people of the French nation he commanded.

Wildcard happenings are also responsible for drastic

changes to the world economy every generation or so. In 1857, lawyer George Bissell and banker James Townsend of the Pennsylvania Rock Oil Company hired Edwin Drake, an unemployed railroad conductor, to travel to Titusville, Pennsylvania, on the shores of Oil Creek, to drill for crude oil. Drake and his assistant met with such little success and so many setbacks that the company withdrew its support. Undeterred, Drake took out a personal line of credit so he could continue drilling with an old steam engine he had rigged up for the purpose. On August 27, 1859, just days away from having used up all his credit, Drake struck oil at 69 feet below ground.

This was a transformative event not just for western Pennsylvania—it set off the first US oil boom in the area—but for the world in general. For it was the first example of a large-scale commercial oil drilling operation, and as such it led to the oil boom that changed the face of the world economy. Unfortunately for Drake, though, the oil industry was soon dominated by the likes of John D. Rockefeller, Sr. and his monopolistic clan. Meanwhile Drake, not having had the foresight to buy up the land around his drilling site or patent his own drilling technique, ended up dying in poverty years later.[7]

Similarly, the transformative event of our own era, the advent of personal computing and global networking, had its origins in an unlikely wildcard. On June 5, 1943, a construction contract was signed between the US Army and the University of Pennsylvania to develop an electronic device that could be used for calculating artillery firing tables for the Army's Ballistic Research Laboratory. The product of that contract, the Electronic Numerical Integrator and Computer—or ENIAC, as it was called—was revealed to the public in February 1946.[8] Described as a "Giant Brain," it was a modular, programmable, general-purpose computer that was capable of addition and subtraction and could hold a ten-digit decimal number in its memory. It accepted input from an IBM card reader and used an IBM card punch for output.

However impressive ENIAC must have seemed to the tech nerds of the day, no one back then could have possibly envisioned the current age of ubiquitous computing. Today, microprocessors and other engineering marvels have progressed to the point where the average person has more computing power on their wrist or in their pocket than would have been imaginable when ENIAC was born more than 70 years ago.

At this point, you might expect me to launch into a lecture on how changes can come out of nowhere and how we have to be prepared, financially and emotionally, to roll with the punches. This is of course true, and there are some good points to be made in that regard. But that's not my purpose today.

No, I am penning this piece with the hope of re-instilling in my readers a sense of wonder and a sense of humility—feelings that seem to have been sucked out of this age of know-it-alls who have seen everything and are surprised by nothing. Contrary to what cynics believe, the universe is far more wondrous than we could ever imagine.

It is the height of hubris to insist that the next major discovery—the find that will totally transform our understanding of the world—*will not* be a flat-out surprise. It's equally arrogant to assume that the next momentous occasion—something that will redirect the course of human history—*will not* be an accident, *will not* be some unexpected, unplanned event that will knock us from our horse, reminding us that we don't know everything.

How easy it would be for us to scoff at the "futurists" of yore who looked at one technological feat of their time, say, the invention of the blimp, and predicted the creation of a vast fleet of blimps for ferrying people across the oceans. How much harder it is to realize that our vision of the future will appear equally ridiculous to succeeding generations.

Reigniting our wonder and humility will allow us to separate what we deem truly significant about us—who we are on the inside and what we do as a reflection of our "who-ness"—from the random happenstance of discoveries and events.

Consider this: everything we think we know about the world is wrong—or at least significantly incomplete. Our conception of medicine, physics, math, history will be turned on its head by upcoming technological breakthroughs and intellectual advances. Our textbooks will be obsolete in the eyes of our children's children. In all likelihood, none of the geopolitical hotspots that preoccupy us today will be the spot where the next major conflict actually touches off. The wisdom of today's markets will be the ridicule of tomorrow.

In the end, *what is it about us that is essential?* Not our supposed knowledge of the world, our flawed—if not backward—conceptions of the universe. Rather, our humanity. For it is our humanity that forms the cultural legacy we leave in our wake. It shapes the morals, values, principles, ethics, and ideals—in a word, the character—of this generation, and it will guide the character of the next generation.

Our humanity is the only thing that matters when all is said and done. And, in order to rediscover how to access that human element, what we really need is to regain our sense of wonder.

NOTES

1. "Japanese man in mystery survival." BBC News. December 21, 2006. archive.is/vtkU

2. Mather, Kate and Joseph Serna. "Teen stowaway survives, but how? 'Boy's body went into a frozen state.'" Los Angeles Times. April 22, 2014. archive.is/RSwQn

3. Ligon, B. Lee. "Penicillin: its discovery and early development." Seminars in Pediatric Infectious Diseases, Volume 15, Issue 1. 2004. Pages 52–57.

4. "Roentgen's discovery of the x-ray." British Library. archive.is/w2hGw

5. Blitz, Matt. "The Amazing True Story of How the Microwave Was Invented by Accident." Popular Mechanics. February 24, 2016. archive.is/bxPQQ

6. "Corsica." Encyclopædia Britannica. September 26, 2017. archive.is/cqfAO

7. Yergin, Daniel. *The Prize: The Epic Quest for Oil, Money & Power.* (New York: Free Press, 2008.) Pages 10–13.

8. Kanellos, Michael. "ENIAC: A computer is born." CNET News. February 13, 2006. archive.is/Hdl7r

A Letter to the Future

"The lamps are going out all over Europe;
we shall not see them lit again in our life-time."
EDWARD GREY

April 11, 2020

I DO NOT write these words for my contemporaries. We are the damned. It is our lot now to watch as the lamp of liberty is extinguished. It is our burden to bear witness to the final flickering of the flame of freedom.

No, I don't write these words for my peers. I write them for those yet to come. For the inhabitants of that future dystopia whose birth pangs we are experiencing. For the remnant of once-free humanity who might—through some miracle I can't even imagine—come across this electronic message in a bottle.

I know it's almost hopeless. The chance of these words surviving the coming internet purge is slim at best. Even if—against all odds—this message does wash up on your digital shores, the chance of these words being understood by you is even slimmer. Not because you don't understand English, but because these words are no longer in your dictionary: Freedom. Humanity. Individual.

Still, I am here to record the end of an era. So, I will press on in the hope against hope that someone, somewhere in that future Digital Dark Age, will have eyes to see and ears to hear.

The darkness is descending.

Let there be no mistake: We all know this.

We know what it means when 17 million Americans—a full 10 percent of the workforce—are added to the unemployment rolls in a mere three weeks.[1] When they are joined by millions more newly unemployed ex-workers all around the globe.[2] When modern-day bread lines stretch for miles in the heart of America's once-proud cities.[3] When the phoney fiat money debt rises to over $24 trillion[4] and the Fed's Sovietization of the US economy is complete.[5]

We know what it means when enforcers of the newly minted biosecurity state start shooting people dead for not wearing a mask.[6] When drones police quarantines from the sky[7] and robots police lockdowns on the ground.[8] When governments admit to tracking every movement of every citizen[9] and install internal checkpoints where digital immunity passports determine who may pass and who must stay in their home.[10]

We know what it means when billionaires start telling us that only their new, experimental mRNA vaccines will be able to save us from this nightmare.[11] When they threaten to mark us with invisible ink tattoos that ID the vaccinated.[12] When they warn us that we will not be able to buy or sell or participate in the economy until we can prove our "immunity."[13]

It means that the Corona World Order has arrived.

Oh, sure, some still deny this reality. But they are only fooling themselves. They're afraid to admit it's true. Many are still under the old conditioning that told them to bleat "conspiracy theorist" at anyone who dares question authority.

We have a name for that kind: sheeple. The trusting masses in our day are kept in their pens by the jackbooted sheepdogs of the police state and are led along by their political shepherds. Occasionally, a wise old ram in the flock cottons on to the game. But the shepherd has only ever fleeced the flock, never hurt them, so the enlightened elder bites his tongue and resigns himself to his fate. Why struggle? The fleecing is mostly painless.

Never did the sheeple suspect that someday the shepherds would lead them to the slaughter.

It is a term of derision, of course. "Sheeple." But I like to think that it doesn't just speak to our stupidity. It also speaks to a naivety, an innocence. We are trusting and gentle creatures by nature. Peaceable. Cooperative. That is nothing to be scorned. In fact, if it weren't for the predators in our midst, this failing would be counted as a virtue.

But I am not here to say that. I am here to say this: Resist! Struggle! Fight!

You are *not* cogs in a machine. You are free and beautiful human beings. You are *not* born under the authority of another. You choose how you live your life, not some bureaucrat, not some police robot, not some "immunity checkpoint" algorithm or QR code.

You do *not* need permission to buy or to sell or to assemble or to speak your mind or to leave your house. You are *not* an "asymptomatic carrier" of whatever virus your misleaders are instructing you to be afraid of. You do *not* have to shelter in place because someone in a white lab coat ordered you to do so.

I want you to understand that, once upon a time, the government didn't have the right to know where you were, who you were meeting with, what you were purchasing, and what you were doing 24/7. Hell, the government didn't even have the ability to do that.

I need you to know that there was a time when you could leave your house when you wanted. Travel where you wanted. Transact as you saw fit. Meet freely with your neighbours. Rally. Protest. Party.

I say to you: LIVE! Live as free human beings are meant to live!

Oh, what am I writing? These words. This language. It makes no sense to you, does it? These concepts don't exist in your time, do they?

I can't blame you, after all. You're trusting and naïve and peaceful. Like a sheep.

But oh, how I weep for what you have become. I tried to avert it. Please believe me. I really tried.

The lamp of liberty is being extinguished. And I am bearing witness.

I don't know if history is a subject you study anymore, but, in case it is not, let me bring you up to speed.

According to the mainstream history books of our age, British Foreign Secretary "Sir" Edward Grey made his observation about the lamps "going out all over Europe" at the end of the so-called Twelve Days.[14] That was the period during the summer of 1914 when, we are told, the British government was trying to avert a World War. We are asked to believe that this prescient remark proved Grey to be a sage diplomat who was wracked with grief over the pain and suffering he sensed was about to be unleashed upon the world.

But this is history-written-by-the-winners of the worst kind. In truth, Grey was one of the conspirators who were actively working to bring about the First World War, not avoid it.[15] What's more, the source of this quotation is in fact Grey himself; it was first recorded in his own postwar memoir.[16] Any tears he may have shed over the snuffing out of those lamps were crocodile tears, to be sure.

One can well imagine that the history books of your era will record some similarly portentous remark by Bill Gates at the onset of the corona crisis. His own post-covid memoir will no doubt tell us that, upon gazing out the window of his $127.5 million, 66,000-square foot "Xanadu 2.0" mansion in Washington State's King County[17]—coincidentally, the very county we were told was the epicenter of the US covid outbreak[18]—he remarked, "The lights are going out all across the globe; we shall not see them lit again in our lifetime."

But that memoir will also doubtless fail to inform us that Gates was smirking as he said it.

To my children, or my children's children, or whatever remnant of once-free humanity happens to unearth these words in the God-forsaken future into which we are goose-stepping: I'm sorry. I failed you. We all failed you.

But remember this: As long as the blood of your forebearers flows through your veins, the lamp of human freedom shall not be extinguished forever.

Let it shine, dear sheep. Let it shine.

NOTES

1. Richter, Wolf. "Week 3 of the Collapse of the US Labor Market." Wolf Street. April 9, 2020. archive.is/YPoAf

2. Linge, Mary Kay. "Global economy screeches to a halt as coronavirus job losses take toll." New York Post. April 4, 2020. archive.is/Iz1g8

3. Conley, Julia. "'Government Needs to Step In': Food Banks Across US Report Unprecedented Demand—and Shortages—as Coronavirus Pandemic Ravages." Common Dreams. April 2, 2020. archive.is/Z7MF0

4. Maharrey, Michael. "National Debt Tops $24 Trillion." SchiffGOLD. April 9, 2020. archive.is/PqGaX

5. "Wall Street Has Now Morphed Into A Full Blown Soviet Sausage Factory." Global Macro Monitor. April 9, 2020. archive.is/2fvB4

6. "Man shot dead in Philippines for flouting coronavirus rules." Al Jazeera. April 5, 2020. archive.is/og36J

7. Das, Shaswati and Neetu Chandra Sharma. "Drones come in handy for police in enforcing lockdown." Mint. April 6, 2020. archive.is/l34Pf

8. "'Show me your ID': Tunisia deploys 'robocop' to enforce coronavirus lockdown." The Guardian. April 3, 2020. archive.is/9L5vg

9. Hamilton, Isobel Asher. "Compulsory selfies and contact-tracing: Authorities everywhere are using smartphones to track the coronavirus, and it's part of a massive increase in global surveillance." Business Insider. April 14, 2020. archive.is/pL2ze

10. Harris, Margot. "The Chinese Government is using color-coded QR codes to track citizens amid the Coronavirus outbreak." INSIDER. February 18, 2020. archive.is/VuX3Y

11. Engdahl, F. William. "Coronavirus, Vaccines and the Gates Foundation." GlobalResearch. May 2, 2020. archive.is/DhsXZ

12. Tangermann, Victor. "Invisible Ink "Tattoos" Could Be Used to ID Vaccinated Kids." NEOSCOPE. December 19, 2019. archive.is/LGg2B

13. Gates, Bill. "I'm Bill Gates, co-chair of the Bill & Melinda Gates Foundation. AMA about COVID-19." reddit. March 18, 2020. archive.is/B9cRD

14. Headlam, J. W., M.A. *The History of Twelve Days: July 24th to August 4th, 1914*. (New York: Charles Scribner's Sons, 1915.)

15. Corbett, James. *The WWI Conspiracy*. The Corbett Report. November 19, 2018. corbettreport.com/wwi

16. Grey, Edward, Viscount of Fallodon, K.G. *Twenty-Five Years: 1892–1916*. (London: Hodder and Stoughton Limited, 1925). Page 20.

17. Fiorillo, Steve. "Bill Gates' House: A Look at Xanadu 2.0." TheStreet. September 17, 2018. bit.ly/48cqWn2

18. Holcombe, Madeline et al. "This nursing home has become the US epicenter of the coronavirus outbreak, but patients' family members say they're left in the dark." CNN. March 9, 2020. archive.is/71D00

Why I Write

"From a very early age, perhaps the age of five or six, I knew that when I grew up I should be a writer. Between the ages of about seventeen and twenty-four I tried to abandon the idea, but I did so with the consciousness that I was outraging my true nature and that sooner or later I should have to settle down and write books."

GEORGE ORWELL,
"WHY I WRITE"[1] (1946)

WHEN I WAS SEVEN years old, I resolved to write a screenplay for a comedy/action television show (or was it a movie?) involving ninjas and talking cars. I only ever got a few sentences down on paper before my attention wandered, but I remember being particularly pleased with an idea for a scene involving two ninjas engaged in a frenzied sword fight next to a brick wall. I pictured the camera cutting from a tight close-up of the battling warriors to a wide shot revealing that all of their frantic sword-clanging had resulted in the word "NINJA" being inadvertently slashed into the wall.

Although I can no longer explain why, I remember being convinced that this fight scene was an incredibly funny idea. I proudly showed my script-in-progress to my mother, who, though apparently less convinced of the scene's inherent humour, was nonetheless encouraging and supportive in the way mothers are.

When I was eleven years old, I responded to a class writing assignment with a page about an axe-wielding fantasy hero returning from a battle and falling asleep in his bed. The scene was, I imagined, the opening passage of an epic novel detailing the exploits of a brave hero in his quest to rid the world of some great evil.

The friend to whom I showed the paper didn't seem to share my vision of a larger, novel-length tale. After scanning it and quickly handing it back to me, he merely asked why I'd written an entire page about someone coming home and falling asleep.

When I was thirteen, my class read George Orwell's *Animal Farm*, after which our Language Arts teacher asked us to write a sequel to the story. The best idea in my version of *Animal Farm 2* (and the only one I remember) was to portray the space race as a literal foot race between two of the farmyard animals, one representing the Soviets and the other the Americans. Truth be told, the idea wasn't even mine. The teacher had suggested it to me.

Nonetheless, she was evidently impressed enough with my literary prowess to share the story with her colleagues in the break room. The very next week, our Social Studies teacher made the rest of the class read my story and answer a quiz about it. I recall sitting there with my head down on my desk, doing my level best not to die of embarrassment. I especially remember the moment my crush rolled her eyes at her friend over the sheer tediousness of the exercise. Needless to say, we never dated.

When I first arrived in Japan, fresh off the boat (so to speak) and looking to start a new chapter in my life, I decided to break the bad habit of writing only when inspiration struck—my modus operandi up to that point—and instead start writing regularly. Every morning, rain or shine, I would head to the local café and spend an hour with a cup of coffee in one hand and my pen in the other, working on a short story, a manuscript, a diary entry, a dream journal—anything at all, so long as I was writing.

Two years into this routine, I had amassed an impressive-looking batch of documents, including a completed manuscript of one novel and a half-completed manuscript of another.

I guess I don't need to explain that from a very early age I knew I was going to be a writer. A novelist, to be precise, writing fiction in the style of Joyce and Faulkner and Proust and Conrad and Orwell and my other favourite authors. It was what I did. It was who I was. There was no escaping it. That was okay. Far from attempting to flee from that fate, I embraced it.

But then something strange happened: *I didn't become a writer.* At least, not in the sense I was expecting. Instead, I became a . . . podcaster? Talking about . . . conspiracies? On . . . the internet?

And, just like that, the life path I had been absolutely certain I would tread disappeared from under my feet.

I can even pinpoint the precise date on which I realized my life was about to go in a very different direction than I had imagined: March 21, 2007. It's right there in my journal, where I found myself musing on the "conspiracy" information that was fast eclipsing my interest in literature.

> And after all, how far will this new philosophy take me? It's funny how quickly this new way of seeing the world gave the lie to my old aspirations, self-involved, of being some jet-setting millionaire literary savant with a nifty pen name. Mere wankery and delusion, playing their own game as if winning is actually desirable. I say they can keep them, these holdover remnants of

adolescent pinings, a child's view of the way the world works. The question then becomes how best to dedicate myself to that which really matters, the glamourless work to which our forefathers set themselves, the work of defending freedom and liberty? It is as a scribe, no doubt, that I will have the most utility. Now time to rise with anger, to sound the alarm, to rouse those around me from their slumbers. A Jonathan Swift against the New World Order? If it be so deemed. All I know is that if he lived in the present day, he'd have a website. And, perhaps, so must I. And to those running the game, I say: "Beware! You never know what'll happen when we start leaving the table."

And so, the act of falling down the rabbit hole—the one that began in my new apartment in the fall of 2006 (see "Reportage: Adventures in the New Media")—ended with me suddenly renouncing my long-held literary aspirations in my own journal. Although the entire process that led me to discover this new path was bewildering and disorienting, it needn't have been surprising. It was all laid out half-a-century before by the author whom I now reference more than any other, the one who caused me such embarrassment in junior high: George Orwell.

In 1946, Eric Arthur Blair (better known by his pen name, George Orwell), wrote an essay entitled "Why I Write." Although just forty-three years old when the essay was published in the pages of the short-lived literary journal *Gangrel*, Orwell—who by this point had already gained international renown for *Animal Farm* and had just begun work on *Nineteen Eighty-Four*—had earned the right to reflect upon his life in letters.

Wrestling with the question of what compels him to

put pen to paper, Orwell runs through what he identifies as the four great motives for writing, namely:

(i) Sheer egoism. Desire to seem clever, to be talked about, to be remembered after death, to get your own back on grown-ups who snubbed you in childhood, etc., etc. It is humbug to pretend this is not a motive, and a strong one. [...]

(ii) Aesthetic enthusiasm. Perception of beauty in the external world, or, on the other hand, in words and their right arrangement. [...]

(iii) Historical impulse. Desire to see things as they are, to find out true facts and store them up for the use of posterity.

(iv) Political purpose — using the word 'political' in the widest possible sense. Desire to push the world in a certain direction, to alter other people's idea of the kind of society that they should strive after. [...]

These four motives, Orwell insists, "exist in different degrees in every writer, and in any one writer the proportions will vary from time to time, according to the atmosphere in which he is living."

If you were to read only the first half of a biography of Blair and tried to extrapolate the rest, it would be easy to wrongly imagine the type of writer he was going to become. As the great-grandson of a wealthy country gentleman whose parents were desperately clinging on to what was left of the family fortune and (perhaps more importantly) social status, Blair grew up even more class-conscious than the average Englishman. When he decided to enter the Indian Imperial Police in Burma after graduating from the prestigious Eton College—an almost unthinkable move from a comfortable position in the inner sanctum of the upper class to a lowly position in the farthest-flung corner of a fading empire—it marked merely the first instance of a lifelong habit of eschewing privilege and comfort in favour of developing keener insight into how the world really works.

This pattern continued when, having resigned his post in Burma and vowing to become a writer, Blair once again renounced the comfort of his home life to become a tramp. Adopting the name "P.S. Burton," Blair began living and working among the lowliest members of society in the East End of London and in the working-class district of Paris. These experiences gave rise to essays like "The Spike"[2] and "How the Poor Die,"[3] which provide his readers with an unflinching look at the squalor that the downtrodden labourers of the era endured and which led to his first book, *Down and Out in Paris and London*, published under the name "George Orwell" because he wanted to spare his class-conscious family the embarrassment of having their name associated with someone who had spent time as a vagrant.

Anyone armed with knowledge of Blair's formative experiences and the contents of Orwell's next books—*Burmese Days*, *A Clergyman's Daughter*, *Keep the Aspidistra Flying*, and *The Road to Wigan Pier*, all published in short order between 1934 and 1936—might be tempted to guess the trajectory of this young writer's fledgling literary career. Here, after all, is the prodigal son of a family of declining fortune rejecting his own comfortable position in society to become a (doubtless middling) writer of (ultimately forgettable) socialist literature.

But thankfully for us, this was not the end of Orwell's story.

As important as his early writing may have been in terms of the development of his no-nonsense, straightforward style of writing, Orwell was, by 1936, still a relatively unknown and largely unheralded author who, had he continued down that path, would hardly be remembered today. It was not until the series of world events culminating in WWII began to crescendo in the late 1930s that we see Orwell take the first steps down another path—one that would lead to him becoming the world-renowned and still-remembered author of *Animal Farm* and *Nineteen Eighty-Four*.

Horrified by the rise of fascism and—out of step with many of his English contemporaries—taking the threat of Hitler and the totalitarian ideology he represented very seriously, Orwell was quick to understand that the overthrow of the Second Spanish Republic by the Nazi-backed Francisco Franco faction was a pivotal historical moment. In late December of 1936, just six months after his marriage to Eileen O'Shaughnessy, Orwell was in Barcelona, telling John McNair—the man coordinating British volunteers for the Republican militia in Spain on behalf of the Independent Labour Party—that "I've come to fight fascism."[4]

His experiences in the Spanish Civil War culminated in the May Days of 1937, when the various factions on the Republican side of the conflict began engaging each other in a series of street battles in Catalonia. Orwell, fighting for the anti-Stalinist "Workers Party of Marxist Unification" (POUM), found himself and many of his fellow soldiers targeted by the Soviet-backed communist press as "fascist collaborators." Narrowly escaping the subsequent purge of POUM members—which claimed the lives of many of his friends—left an indelible mark on Orwell.

As he noted in his "Why I Write" essay:

> The Spanish war and other events in 1936-37 turned the scale and thereafter I knew where I stood. Every line of serious work that I have written since 1936 has been written, directly or indirectly, against totalitarianism and for democratic socialism, as I understand it. It seems to me nonsense, in a period like our own, to think that one can avoid writing of such subjects. Everyone writes of them in one guise or another. It is simply a question of which side one takes and what approach one follows. And the more one is conscious of one's political bias, the more chance one has of acting politically without sacrificing one's aesthetic and intellectual integrity.

Having narrowly escaped a Soviet-backed purge, Orwell was uniquely situated among English socialists to understand the threat of totalitarianism, not just from fascism but from communism as well. It was this sense of the real horrors of totalitarianism, garnered not from philosophical study but from actual lived experience, that set Orwell apart from so many of his contemporaries. And it was in the soil of this realization that the flower of Orwell's artistic expression was able to fully bloom.

> What I have most wanted to do throughout the past ten years is to make political writing into art. My starting point is always a feeling of partisanship, a sense of injustice. When I sit down to write a book,

I do not say to myself, "I am going to produce a work of art."

I write it because there is some lie that I want to expose, some fact to which I want to draw attention, and my initial concern is to get a hearing.

The fruits of his efforts "to make political writing into an art"—*Animal Farm* and *Nineteen Eighty-Four*—are by now celebrated around the world. But there can be little doubt that they would have never flowered at all had Orwell not lived through the tumultuous events of the 1930s.

And, just as Orwell observed that it is "nonsense" to think any author of his era could avoid writing of the totalitarian threat then menacing the world, so, too, do I think it is nonsense to believe that any writer of our era could avoid addressing the totalitarian threat of our own age: the move toward a global technocratic biosecurity state predicated on complete control of every human down to the genomic level. Although arguably a mere extension of the age-old quest for world domination that has motivated every would-be tyrant throughout history, this latest iteration of the totalitarian threat—fueled as it is by technologies that even Orwell could never have dreamed of—represents the greatest peril that the human species has ever faced.

So, why do I write? That is the question even Orwell himself had to concede he could never fully answer:

> Looking back through the last page or two, I see that I have made it appear as though my motives in writing were wholly public-spirited. I don't want to leave that as the final impression. All writers are vain, self-

ish, and lazy, and at the very bottom of their motives there lies a mystery. Writing a book is a horrible, exhausting struggle, like a long bout of some painful illness. One would never undertake such a thing if one were not driven on by some demon whom one can neither resist or understand.

I certainly wouldn't disagree with that.

But why has my writing not taken the form of literary fiction, as the younger incarnation of myself was so convinced would be my career trajectory? Because, knowing what I know about the world as it is, I could not conceive of using my facility with language in any other way than in ringing the alarm bell as loudly as I can about the existential threat facing humanity.

Dear reader, please don't misunderstand my intentions. I am not in any way attempting to compare myself to Orwell or to put my amateur literary scribblings on the same pedestal as his monumental work. I merely offer this by way of explaining—as much for my own sake as for yours—how I came to be here, a podcaster dedicating his life to sounding the alarm about the New World Order rather than a (likely unpublished) author of (doubtless middling) works of fiction.

But still, for whatever it is worth, I find some sort of comfort in the irony that my non-literary literary career has come full circle back to the man who inspired my earliest literary "success," *Animal Farm 2*. Far from waning in influence over me or over the world at large, Orwell's stature only grows with each passing year. He has, after all, provided the very vocabulary—from *doublethink* and *thoughtcrime* to *memory hole* and *Big Brother*—with which we describe the events taking place around us today. In fact, as I am constantly at pains to note, it is nearly impossible to encounter yet another example of the encroaching technocratic police state without identifying it as "Orwellian."

Sadly, I think Orwell, in his grave, takes little solace in that fact. But perhaps he can appreciate that, as long as there are those among us still heeding his warnings, we have not lost the war.

NOTES

1. Orwell, George. "Why I Write." The Orwell Foundation. 1946. archive.is/TwFpv

2. Orwell, George. "The Spike." The Orwell Foundation. 1931. archive.is/uBBnQ

3. Orwell, George. "How the Poor Die" in Fifty Orwell Essays. Project Gutenberg Australia. Posted August 2003. Updated April 2019. archive.is/hMlgX

4. Syeda, Seema. "War Reporters: George Orwell." Military History Matters. July 22, 2019. archive.is/yk2yD

Index

9/11

Commission (The National Commission on Terrorist Attacks Upon the United States) 16, 20-21, 95, 97, 227-229
money trail 13-21, 91-92, 97, 224-225, 227
Truth Movement iv, 3-4, 47
US government response vii, 50, 113, 215
and Bin Laden (see "Bin Laden, Osama")
and FAA (see "Federal Aviation Administration")
and NORAD (see "North American Aerospace Defense Command")

A

Abbey, Edward 134
Afghanistan 14, 185, 275-78, 286, 289
Africa 113, 119, 198, 200
African-American Institute 202
American Airlines 13
American Independence Day 211
Americanism 263
American Scholars Symposium 4
anarchism 128, 134
Animal Farm 324, 326, 329, 331-32

Annan, Kofi 193-94
Argentina 160
Arizona State University 118

B

Baca Ranch 203-4
Bank for International Settlements (BIS) 33-34, 46
Bank of America 14
Bank of Canada 109
Bank of England 109
Barroso, José 39
Beijing 193, 196
Belgium 14, 255
Bernhard, Prince 72, 239-40, 243, 266
Bilderberg 34-37, 118, 233-36, 238, 241-45, 266, 285, 294
Bin Laden, Osama 18, 185, 223, 288
Black, Edwin 78
Boston 9/11 Truth Tea Party 47
Brave New World 182-83, 265
Britain, 72-73, 275
Brzezinski, Zbigniew 54-56, 274-77, 280, 290, 295-98, 300
Buck, Carrie 76-77
Buckingham Palace 66
Burma 328

335

Bush
    family 17, 66, 77,
    George H. W. 18, 155, 238, 249, 280-81
    George W. 17, 228, 237
Business Council of Canada 115, 117

C

Cameron, David 236-37, 242
Canada 26, 73, 109, 114-15, 117, 195-98, 201, 206-7, 213-14, 238, 242
Canada Smart Border Declaration 115
Canadian Council 115, 117
Canadian Food Inspection Agency 153
Canadian International Development Agency 195, 197-98
Carlyle Group 18
Carter, Jimmy 54, 274, 290
Center for North American Studies 118
Central Intelligence Agency (CIA) 4, 18-19
China 46, 119, 196, 207, 289-91, 299
Citigroup 14
Clarke, Richard 93
Climate Change 195, 202, 268
Clinton
    Bill 32, 238, 293
    Hillary 35, 236-37
Cold War 286, 288
Common Core State Standards Initiative 126
Copley, Marion 145-46
Corbett Report 7, 115, 118
Corsica 309

CropLife International 147
Crop Trust 62-65
Crusaders 106-7

D

Darwin, Charles 66, 69, 71-72
Davos 194-95
democracy 8-9, 28, 42
Department of Homeland Security (DHS) 114-15
Dicks, Dan 244
Drake, Edwin 310
Dubos, René 200

E

Earth Charter 202, 204-5, 267
Earth Council Institute 204
Earth Summit 201-2, 267
England 31, 33, 65, 109, 213, 237, 255, 266
English feudal system 213
environmental movement 200, 261-62, 268
Eugenics
    eugenicists 72, 81-82, 163-65, 264-65, 268
    Eugenics Record Office (ERO) 75, 266
    Eugenics Review 71
    in America 74-77, 81, 163, 264, 265
    in Britain 71, 73, 80-81, 265
    in Germany 77-80
Europe 31, 62, 109, 113, 119, 140, 234, 239, 241, 255, 262
European Central Bank (ECB) 34, 109

European Food Safety Authority (EFSA) 147-48

F

Federal Aviation Administration (FAA) 91-92, 94-95
Federal Bureau of Investigation (FBI) 15, 52, 91-92, 95-98, 227
Federal Reserve 6, 34, 45, 109
fiat money 108-9
Fichte, Johann Gottlieb 121-23
Food and Agricultural Organization (FAO) 153, 162, 165
Food and Drug Administration (FDA), US 143, 147, 153, 155, 166
Forbes 151
Fourth World Wilderness Congress 201, 267
France 14, 26, 121, 238, 280, 309
Freedom of Information Act (FOIA) 20

G

G20 meeting 46
Galton, Francis 67-68, 70, 81
gene revolution 155, 157, 164, 169
Genetic Literacy Project 144, 147
Germany 14-15, 26, 77-79, 121, 123, 238, 266, 280
globalism 49, 127, 135
God 61, 64, 82, 122, 276
Goldman Sachs 49, 120

government
    central 109
    federal 93
    foreign 15
    supranational 38
    tyrannical 130
green revolution 156-60
Grove, Richard Andrew 224-25
Gulf War 280

H

Hamilton, Lee 91, 228-29
Harper, Stephen 116, 238
Hayek, F. A. 250-51
Hayes, A. Wallace 148, 151
Hussein, Saddam 280-81
Huxley
    Aldous 182-85
    family 70
    Julian 71-72, 265-66

I

IBM 91-92, 291
India 119, 160, 275
Intergovernmental Panel on Climate Change (IPCC) 195, 202
International Agency for Research on Cancer (IARC) 141-42, 144
International Basic Economy Corporation (IBEC) 158
International Development Research Centre (IDRC) 198-99
Iraq 160-61, 235, 280-81

J

Japan 1, 14, 34, 109, 324
Jefferson, Thomas 124, 127
Jennings, Barry 222-23
Jerusalem 106-7

K

Kaiser Wilhelm Institutes 78-79
Kean, Thomas 228-29
Kerrey, Bob 228-29
Kieseritzky, Lionel 283-84
Kissinger, Henry 200, 228, 281, 290, 293-94, 297, 300
Kurdistan 279-81
Kurds 279-82

L

Lasko, Gary 224
Linnean Society 72
London 33, 62, 213, 283, 328

M

Manitoba 195, 213
Manley, John 116-17
Mexican American Development Corp 157
Mexico 114-15, 117, 156-57, 252
Monderman, Hans 254-55
Monod, Noah 197
Monsanto 141, 144-46, 148-53, 155, 160, 166-67
Multilateral System 162

N

Nairobi 198, 200
National Institute of Standards and Technology (NIST) 223, 226
nationalism 121, 124, 126-27, 135
Netflix 184
New World Order 36, 46, 204, 215, 249-50, 275, 308, 326, 332
New York 3, 33-34, 50, 94, 98, 197, 287
New York Times 54, 140, 151, 183, 228, 237, 292
New York Zoological Society 263
North America 35, 115-16, 118-20, 140, 233-34, 267
North American Aerospace Defense Command (NORAD) 94-95
North American Center for Transborder Studies 118
North American Competitiveness Council (NACC) 115
North American integration 118-19
North Atlantic Treaty Organization (NATO) 36, 49, 91, 215

O

Obama, Barack 35, 62, 117, 235-38
Orwell, George 181, 183, 323-33

P

Paris 328
Paul, Ron 47
Pennsylvania 310
Petro-Canada 195, 200, 267
Posilac 166
Postman, Neil 182

Q

Qaim, Martin 140
Quigley, Carroll 31-33, 36, 43, 46, 293-94

R

Rockefeller
    David 197, 200-1, 204, 267, 290
    John D. 81, 157, 265, 310
    Laurance 203-4
    Nelson 157-58, 205
    Steven C. 205, 267
Rockefeller Archive Center 158
Rockefeller Brothers Fund 158
Rockefeller Foundation 78, 80, 156-57, 159, 162, 199, 267
Rome 38, 194, 241
Roosevelt, Teddy 262-64
Rothschild
    David Mayer de 267-68
    Edmund de 201-2, 207, 267
    family 66, 207, 268
Round Table Groups 31-33, 293
Russia 49, 119, 299
Ryan, Kevin 17-18, 225-27

S

Saudi Arabia 90, 223
Schwab, Klaus 194
Science Media Centre 147
Security and Prosperity Partnership (SPP) 115-16
Séralini, Gilles-Éric 146-152
Shared Space 254-55
Skelton, Charlie 244
Small Business Administration (SBA), US 98
Smart Border Declaration 116
Social Biology 81
Soviets 180, 276-77, 279, 286, 324
Soviet Union 180, 195, 286-87
S&P 500 Index 17
Spartacus 212
Spooner, Lysander 130
Stengel, Richard 7-9
Stratesec 17-18
Strong, Maurice 193-97, 201, 207, 267
Strong, Anna Louise 195-96
Supreme Court 75-77
Sutton, Antony 287
Suzuki, David 261
Sweden 200

T

Tea Party (see "Boston 9/11 Truth Tea Party")
Third Reich 79-80
Third World 159, 199, 201, 265
totalitarianism 330
Treaty of Rome 38, 241
Trudeau, Justin 194
Trump, Donald 48-49, 62
Tyler, Wat 213

U

Ukraine 282
UNESCO 126, 265-66
United Nations (UN) 29, 42, 72, 120, 140, 194-95, 205, 239, 299
    Conference on Environment and Development (Rio Earth Summit) 201-2, 206, 267
United States Attorney 98
United States Geological Survey 263

V

Vietnam 286-87, 290

W

Wedgwood, Josiah 70
Wells, H. G. 72, 249
White House 20, 66, 91-92
Wikipedia 196-97
Wilson, Woodrow 125
Wolfensohn, James 193-94, 198
Woodward, Bob 294
World Bank 29, 34, 36, 120, 160, 193, 198, 201-2, 239, 285
World Conservation Bank 201, 267
World Conservation Union (IUNC) 202
World Core Curriculum 126
World Customs Organization 120
World Economic Forum (WEF) 194-95, 202
World Health Organization (WHO) 29, 120, 141, 153
World Resources Institute 202
World Trade Center 4, 17, 95, 222-23, 225-27
    Building 7 190-191
World Trade Organization 29, 120, 165
World War 80, 240, 318
World Wildlife Fund (WWF) 72, 202, 266

Y

Yom Kippur War 200
YouTube 3-4

ABOUT THE AUTHOR

JAMES CORBETT was born in Calgary, Alberta, Canada, in 1979, the youngest of three sons. His father was an architectural draughtsman, his mother a housewife, the young married couple having moved from Gateshead, in the north of England, to Canada in 1972.

James attended the University of Calgary, where in 2001 he was awarded a Bachelors degree with First Class Honours in English Literature, and Trinity College in Dublin, Ireland, where he received a Masters degree (M. Phil.) in Anglo-Irish Literature in 2003.

He moved to Japan in 2004, where he is now married and the father of two young children.